Redesigning the Stock Market

Redesigning the Stock Market

A Fractal Approach

Pravir Malik

SAGE | Response Business Books

www.sagepublications.com

Los Angeles • London • New Delhi • Singapore • Washington DC

First published in 2011 by

SAGE | Response Business Books

SAGE Response
B1/I-1 Mohan Cooperative Industrial Area
Mathura Road, New Delhi 110 044, India

SAGE Publications Inc
2455 Teller Road
Thousand Oaks, California 91320, USA

SAGE Publications Ltd
1 Oliver's Yard, 55 City Road
London EC1Y 1SP, United Kingdom

SAGE Publications Asia-Pacific Pte Ltd
33 Pekin Street
#02-01 Far East Square
Singapore 048763

Published by Vivek Mehra for SAGE Publications India Pvt Ltd, typeset in 10/13pt Berkeley by Star Compugraphics Private Limited, Delhi and printed at Chaman Enterprises, New Delhi.

Library of Congress Cataloging-in-Publication Data Available

ISBN: 978-81-321-0718-7 (HB)

The SAGE Team: Rekha Natarajan, Anupam Choudhury, and Nand Kumar Jha

This book is dedicated

to the Earth Mother,

and

to all who love Her.

Thank you for choosing a SAGE product! If you have any comment, observation or feedback, I would like to personally hear from you. Please write to me at contactceo@sagepub.in

—Vivek Mehra, Managing Director and CEO,
SAGE Publications India Pvt Ltd, New Delhi

Bulk Sales

SAGE India offers special discounts for purchase of books in bulk. We also make available special imprints and excerpts from our books on demand.

For orders and enquiries, write to us at

Marketing Department
SAGE Publications India Pvt Ltd
B1/I-1, Mohan Cooperative Industrial Area
Mathura Road, Post Bag 7
New Delhi 110044, India
E-mail us at marketing@sagepub.in

Get to know more about SAGE, be invited to SAGE events, get on our mailing list. Write today to marketing@sagepub.in

This book is also available as an e-book.

Contents

Part V: Redesigning the Stock Market

List of Figures

Acknowledgments

About one year ago I was wondering what project I should take on next in the writing sphere. *Connecting Inner Power with Global Change: The Fractal Ladder* (Malik, 2009b) had just been published, and I thought it would be good to use some of the key principles and insights obtained from writing that book and apply them to a global problem of some magnitude. I was mulling over this in an inspirational area in Sri Aurobindo Ashram, Pondicherry, India, and then, I had the distinct idea that it would be good to apply what I had learned to the global financial crisis, in particular, to the stock market, which, to me, has always been at the very center of global financial dysfunction.

I quickly jotted down my thoughts, which came to a couple of pages, and that evening contacted Dr Sugata Ghosh of SAGE Publications to set up a meeting for the following week in New Delhi. We met, and he stated that he had done a search on books about stock market redesign and had not found anything in the area. I presented my initial four-page outline to him, and a couple of months later, after further elaborating it, and going back and forth a few times, we had entered into an agreement for a new book: *Redesigning the Stock Market*. To Dr Ghosh and to SAGE Publications: my gratitude for their trust in me.

This book has taken close to a year to write. The reason is that there is so much going on in the financial space that to distill and make sense of it is non-trivial. I had to go through a rapid education and there are some resources that were instrumental in providing this. To understand the broad financial space, I began to read the *Financial Times* daily. I am grateful for the width and depth of coverage it provides. I am also grateful to Wikipedia, which I literally perused daily to both understand more about the financial space, and subsequently leverage it in my research efforts in writing this book. I am grateful to numerous authors who had just written books about the financial crisis and about systemic problems in the financial space in general. These include Thomas Greco for his book

The End of Money and the Future of Civilization (2009), Niall Ferguson for his book *The Ascent of Money* (2008), John Authers for his book *The Fearful Rise of Markets* (2010), and Nouriel Roubini and Stephen Mihm for their timely analyses in *Crisis Economics* (2010).

As compared to *Connecting Inner Power with Global Change*, this book was research-intensive. I spent a lot of time on Yahoo! Finance and a fair amount of time on the website of World Federation of Stock Exchanges, and subsequently leveraged data and graphs from both sources. My gratitude to both for providing the permission to do so.

I am grateful to my family, Chitvan, Chaitanya, and Aditya, for putting up with me as I spent most weekends this year working on this book.

I am also grateful to the many members of SAGE Publications who have worked to make this book a reality. These include Rekha Natarajan, Executive Editor, Sachin Sharma, Associate Commisioning Editor, and Anupam Choudhury, Production Editor, who have managed the editing and production of the book. In addition, there are other members who have worked behind the scenes. To all, my gratitude for making this book a reality.

Introduction

We live in unprecedented times. Business has become synonymous with the meaning of life, and to grow economies and exercise one's prowess in business realms are considered the epitome of possible aims. Yet this bearing has come with a high cost. We are destroying the very bases all life depends on. Ecosystems and the invaluable and life-giving services they provide are being severely damaged or simply wiped out. The underlying business-asset mentality has warped all perception and we have come to equate value by a surface and short-sighted mathematics. Formidable problems such as Climate Change have arisen as a result.

Our global reward systems continue to reinforce short-sighted action. This book, *Redesigning the Stock Market: A Fractal Approach*, aims to alter the very heart of the global business machinery through integrating more long-sighted heuristics into trading mechanisms. The trading mechanisms encompass both the macro-environment as it relates to the stock market, and the micro-act of stock trading.

This book is divided into 5 parts. Part I, "Bases," starts with a Utopian dream in Chapter 1—Utopian Patterns, of what business can look like. Judgment is suspended and a possible reality 30 years from now envisioned. Chapter 2—The Power of Patterns, lays out the basis of analysis to be used through the rest of the book. This framework for analysis is based on a fractal model described in *Connecting Inner Power with Global Change: The Fractal Ladder* (Malik, 2009b), which connected the micro with the macro and highlighted a particularly powerful fractal—that of sustainable progress. Three fundamental states—the physical, the vital, and the mental—are used to gain insight into the nature of patterns and into the very behavior of global markets. Chapter 3—Pandorian Business, takes a macro-level view of business by looking at what industry has become today. This chapter starts with key vital-level patterns across business, and how these have played out at the macro level, industry by industry.

The industries considered are—food, beverage, and agriculture, pharmaceuticals, energy, water, and retail. Chapter 4—The Stock Market Role, looks at the current-day questionable environmental, and social and governance practices of leading corporations across key industries, which have received major impetus for their growth from the stock market. There is, hence, a huge apparent gap between the ideal envisioned in Chapter 1, and the current-day reality of big business as indicated in Chapters 3 and 4. The practical question through the rest of the book is: What can the stock market do to close the gap in both the short term and the longer term?

The stock market is in fact seen as a major singularity that has bent all financial space, and therefore, as central in sustainably solving the global financial crisis that exists today. In the last year, many books about the global financial crisis have appeared. These include such books as Authers' *The Fearful Rise of Markets* (2010) and Roubini and Mihm's *Crisis Economics* (2010) among others, which focus on the macro-level changes to be made to set the crisis aright, but make no mention of any redesign that must take place at the level of the stock market in order to ensure a sustainable solution to the crisis.

Part II, "The Vital-level Macro-environment," analyzes the overall financial landscape to conclude that key components of it are indeed at the vital level. Chapter 5—Evolution of the Macro-environment, looks at how this came to be. Specifically, what changes over the last 60 years have taken place to shift the macro-environment from the physical to the vital level. Such an analysis is critical because dynamics at the vital level are entirely different from dynamics at the physical or mental levels. Such an analysis also helps us understand what needs to be done to create a more sustainable financial environment. Chapter 6—Where in the Fractal Journey is the Stock Market?, similarly analyzes what level the stock market is at. It does this through considering the increase in number of indexes, the increase in stock market volume, the velocity of loss and gain in daily prices, and the increase in number of crashes over the last couple of decades. Chapter 7—Theories and Tools to Manage Trading at the Vital Level, takes a critical look at the current theories and tools that drive trading today. These theories and tools have been created assuming that we are at the mental level. They are therefore entirely inadequate in driving trading at the vital level and result in the increasing problems we are experiencing today in the financial world. The chapter further looks at corrections to the mental-level tools to make them more appropriate for the vital level and proposes some additional tools that would be more appropriate for the vital level.

Part III, "Lessons from the History of Stock Market Crashes," seeks to analyze crashes from the physical–vital–mental perspective. Chapter 8—Stock Market Seed, takes a look at the history of stock markets and how they were created. It analyzes the seed, placing it securely at the vital level, and suggests that unless the seed is changed, it is futile to expect that the nature of financial crises is going to change. Chapter 9—Lessons from the 20th Century Stock Market Crashes, looks at key crashes, starting from the Crash of 1929 and ending with the Asian Financial Crisis of 1998, to glean important lessons from them. Chapter 10—Lessons from the 21st Century Stock Market Crashes, looks at key crashes, starting from the Dot-Com Crash of 2000 to the Greek Financial Crisis of 2010, and similarly raises important questions and lessons to be considered in the redesign of the stock market.

Part IV, "External Changes Affecting the Stock Market," shifts gears to examine the imperative of stock market change coming in from the outside. In Chapter 11—Current External Changes Affecting Stock Markets, major developments such as SRI (Socially Responsible Investing), GRI (Global Reporting Initiative), DJSI (Dow Jones Sustainability Index), and PRI (Principles for Responsible Investing) are examined. These are like flashes from the future that indicate the very change that must take place in the way trading on stock markets takes place at its very core. Chapter 12—Principles of Sustainability, looks at some key sustainability frameworks that go where even SRI, GRI, DJSI, and PRI have not gone yet. These principles get to the heart of the changes that must take place in the business world, and therefore also must play a key part in considering how stock markets are to be redesigned.

Part V, "Redesigning the Stock Market," suggests what changes need to actually occur at several different levels to move stock market functioning from the vital to the mental level. Chapter 13—Current Sustainability in Stock Exchanges, examines the state of sustainability in many stock exchanges around the world. This is important to understand so that a meaningful path forward can finally be recommended. Chapter 14—Summary of Stock Market Redesign Suggestions, draws out the key redesign suggestions that surfaced through the course of the book. Chapter 15—From the Vital to the Mental Level, rearranges the suggestions into more meaningful categories of changes to the macro-environment, new tools to facilitate the emergence of the mental level, new structures to facilitate the emergence of the mental level, and stock market guidelines. Finally, Chapter 16—The Path Forward, suggests the immediate path forward, given the reality of sustainability in stock exchanges as pointed out in Chapter 13.

Part I

Bases

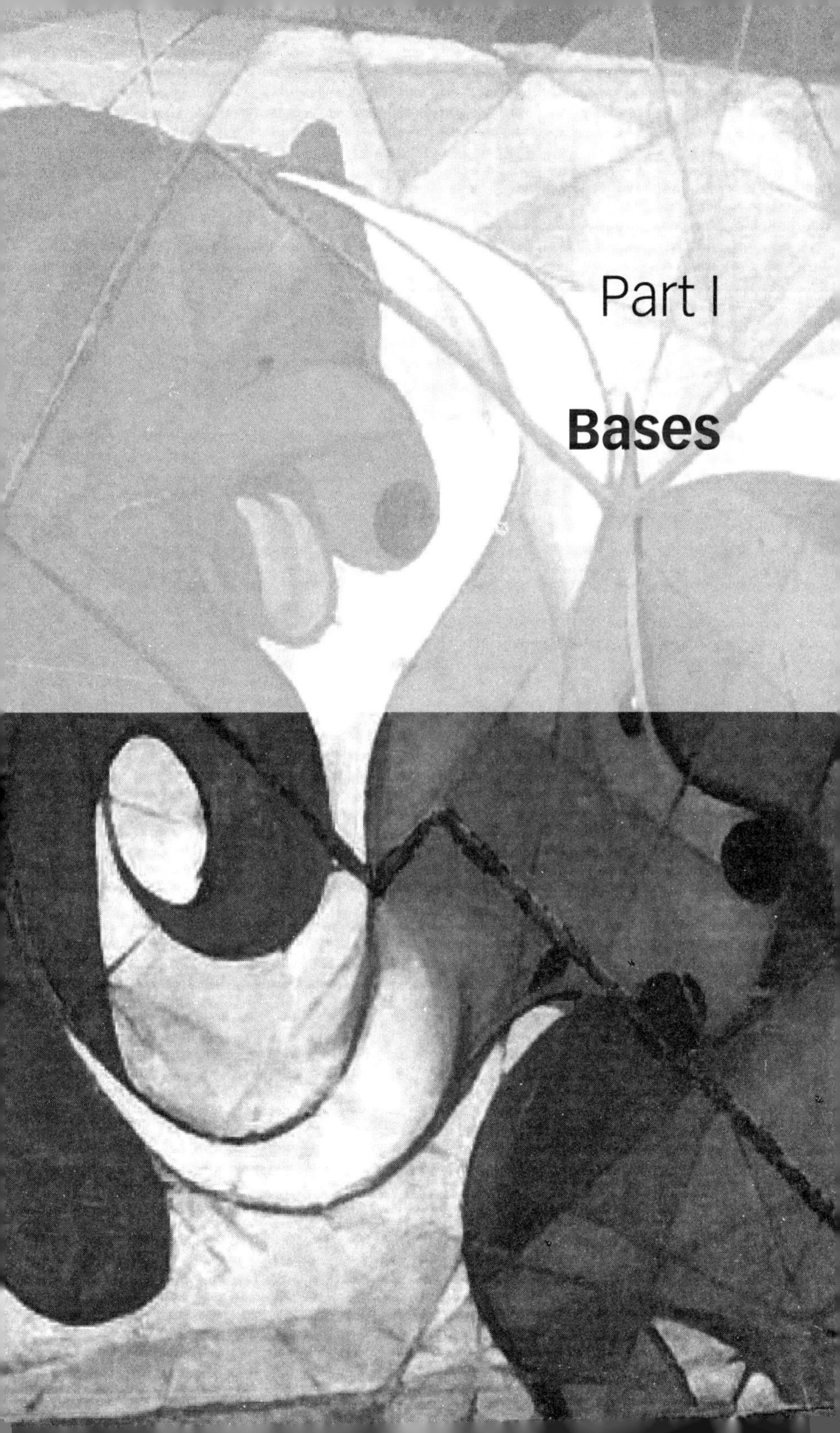

1

Utopian Patterns

There is a beauty in life which we catch sometimes in a silent hour. Our habitual tribulations cease and we are as if face-to-face with something that seems to be the fount of every positive energy we may ever wish to embody. Love, harmony, courage, self-forgetfulness, peace, wisdom, amongst many other possibilities, are aspects of it. In those moments, we seem to become other than our usual selves and are animated by a sacredness that makes every trial seem insignificant.

Or we may see this beauty in the way the wind tosses the leaves of a tree on a summer day, in the swaying of the branches, all dancing around the essential solidity of the central trunk. Or in the compelling color and shape of a small flower that seems to bring into being a corresponding response of joy from our hearts or in the way a flowing river freely pursues its course, all the while reflecting in diamond-like bursts the light from the noon-time sun high above.

There is such splendor in life. We breathe with ease in the presence of such grace and even become part of a harmony that far transcends our small view of things.

Everything around us, from the smallest to the largest—the worm, the bird, the tree, the person, the family, the village and town, the corporation, the economy, the country—is a construct of the underlying beauty and possibility spread luxuriantly around us. And these constructs being a creation of that possibility, ultimately bring unique faces, contours, details of that possibility to the surface. This is the purpose of the constructs, to bring the truth of their essential nature and of the infinity of essential possibility into dynamic expression.

The same must be true of business. Business too is a construct of nature but unlike many other constructs that have established their essential natures and already entered into a harmonious equilibrium with the fabric of life, it is still very much a work in progress. The established beauty we see around us and its implicit harmony with life has had millennium to work itself out. Business on the other hand is a recent construct and will require far more concentrated effort to find its own essential nature. There is dynamism, mutuality, harmony, and opportunity implicit in the nature of business. There is the chance that the sum of two and two will be greater than four; that the unique qualities of people will have a chance to flourish; that these qualities will not just be traded but will build circles of living possibility around them and alter the fabric of life in repeated and organic movements that will make life richer for all. There is the possibility that rather than being the tyrant and despot claiming all life as its servant, there will be a surrender so that the possibilities of life are served, in balance, by the institution of business.

Business must exist in harmony with its deeper nature to amplify and enrich life for all. Business must become a repository, an index, a dynamo, for the wisdom, the power, the sense of service, the harmony that lie embedded in the nature of possibility. This is its purpose and there is no other. To imagine that business exists to enrich the few to the detriment of the many, that business can freely exploit resources from the material to the intellectual in pursuit of a selfish smallness, that business is the be-all and end-all of existence and all other possibility submit to it in an act of unquestioning awe, is to buy in to the short-term dysfunction that is in process of working itself out. It is to unconsciously play out the very patterns that are calling for change. It is to forget the essential reason we are here for, that all constructs of nature are here for, that business and corporation are themselves here for—to bring into expression and progressive equilibrium that splendor that lies embedded in seed-form in the recesses, caves, and very substance of life.

A Utopian Glimpse

It is the year 2040.

You are in a huge metropolis—let us say New Delhi, India. There is no haze, there are no whiffs of diesel or other petroleum-based products in the air. In fact, quite the contrary, you smell the sweet smell of a variety of flowers and ripe fruit from the luxuriantly growing plants and trees in all the small community gardens and along every street of the city. You hear the beautiful chirping of birds producing unheard of ragas for the different times of the day, the different days of the week, and the different months of the year. The plumage is itself magnificent and competes with the colors and variety of flower and plant.

It is June, and you do not feel the hot loos and once oppressive heat of the summer. The numerous waterways running through the city and the variety of trees, including pine and fir, have forever altered the climate to make it much more temperate. You are struck too by the beauty of the architecture and the buildings. All melds into all, and the human-made structures could very well be an extension of Mother Nature. It is as though numerous micro-ecosystems have sprouted up where earlier there were jagged concrete structures. In fact, these almost self-contained micro-ecosystem communities have become the living and working quarters for people. Tall structures do exist—some very tall structures—that seem to touch the sky, and this is the preferred dwelling place of light eaters, those who get their direct sustenance from the light in the sun.

One does not see homeless people begging on the streets anymore. Poverty has been removed forever, and all people are part of communities that have become their real and extended families. You can see the glint in the eye and the confidence in bodies of health. There is a richness apparent in the walk and posture of all people. It is as though something gave them permission to be, and people are living a life that is attuned to their souls and more surely becoming the possibility resident deep within their breasts.

Highly efficient micro-solar panels, made with new technology, now provide power for all the communities and the entire city. Vehicles, on the roadways and the waterways, are solar-powered and silent. The roadways themselves are made from a material that seems to re-organize itself to maintain an essential solidity and harmony with the environment, based on the temperature, pressure, and demands of traffic. There is much less traffic and fewer larger vehicles of various kinds that carry more people. There is a variety of essentially mechanical mono-passenger vehicles designed to exercise different muscle-groups of the body. Such traveling has itself become a sophisticated means to continually develop the flexibility, durability, strength, endurance, resilience, lightness, and plasticity of the body, by also allowing an orchestrated flow of wind, light, and other electro-magnetic energy to pass over the appropriate meridians and even penetrate selected areas of the body. Such interactions have itself become an advanced means of healing and maintaining the body, and even reversing the cycle of degeneration. People now live much longer, healthier lives.

The practice of health care has completely altered. Community gardens now double as a natural, real-time, ever-available home pharmacy. The once rapidly growing pharmaceuticals industry is no more. Hospitals have been converted into health and expo-centers for the display and use of a variety of advanced natural healing devices.

There are no loud advertisements and signs along the roads, for there has been an essential shift from a push-the-consumer to a pulled-by-consumer model of business. Business itself has altered radically. More comprehensive, holistic, society- and community-aligned models for running business have come into being. The essential meaning of business has altered and now implies an organization or enterprise focused on providing goods and services to people. Business is run by stewards responsible to their communities and society to mobilize and convert resources to create goods and services that capture splendor in its various forms while increasing the overall wealth of those communities, society, planet earth, and every person involved. It is a noble profession that draws from inspired founts of creativity and those founts of creativity find their very bases in a redefined society.

In this redefined society there are multiple and independent sources of strength. No more do all exist for an unrefined business profit–motive. Business has discovered its true engine of being as have other great institutions—education, art, sport, service, research, engineering, amongst others. There was a time when all existed to prop up the unrefined engines of global business. This short-sighted global motive force has now been corrected and other institutions too have found their real reason for being. All is organically organized around unique personalities who breathe and live their truth into the organizations that are growing around them. Business is not a context in itself. It exists to further the broader context of progress for society, humanity, community, and person. But progress is not measured in narrow monetary and profit terms. It is measured in terms of deeper and authentic development.

Money moves, almost automatically, to support the development and creative expression of these unique personalities. There are no favored elite who control the issuance and flow of money. To build up personal wealth in terms of big bank balances or personal balance sheets of various asset-classes no more has meaning. If one is powerful, it is because they have begun to express the true power that defines who they uniquely are. If one has built up capital, it is because they have served community and society by exercising who they are. And that capital is not monetary capital. It is the capital of knowledge or the capital of courage or the capital of industry or the capital of service, amongst many different capitals. There is a place for all to be who they are.

No more does one need to learn a trade or learn to do business or learn to be an engineer because one is compelled, monetarily, to do so. There was a time when one had to earn money by doing something, even that was completely out-of-sync with who one was as a person and a possibility. But no more is this the case. Now if one pursues a field, it is because one's nature compels one to do so. And in the act of pursuing that which one's nature demands of him or her, the field of the act is enhanced in an extraordinary way. There is not the short-term reward that is the motive of the action. The motive is knowledge-fulfillment, service-fulfillment, amongst myriad other fulfillments, leading to self-fulfillment, community-fulfillment, and society-fulfillment.

Money is not the end. It is the means. To accumulate money means nothing. What really matters is the level of productivity of a person, and there are many, many currencies in which this is evaluated—the peace around a person, the joy, the harmony they create, the knowledge about a specific field, the perfection in art, the ability to diagnose a problem and suggest a meaningful solution, the care-free laugh, and so on. Each of these is the currency. They are not exchanged for money. They have value in and of themselves. Being who one is, is what defines richness. Money is mobilized to facilitate the emergence of this richness. It has no value in being stored.

Following the sustained global financial crises that continued for a decade, in spite of what seemed like several trends reversals and turnarounds, there was massive introspection on multiple levels. Many changes were made to the way money is issued, is distributed, and flows.

The essential monopolistic control of money, paradoxically upheld in the name of globalization and establishing fairness, was found to be the major cause of the financial crises. For it was always the few who wished to control its issuance, its flow, its valuation, at the expense of the many. As a result, unsubstantiated issuance and valuation of money, not backed by an equal foundation of potential industry and activity, continued to dilute its purchasing power and continued to sow the seeds of global inflation. It was also found that the de-monopolization of this critical symbol of energy needed to take place. Hence, the nature of its issuance has now changed. Communities create their own currencies that are managed and monitored locally by local leaders. At the same time, there are independent regional agencies that exist to monitor the value of community currencies and link them to each other in an equitable way to form an essentially regional network. There are similar national agencies that exist to monitor and link regional currencies together in a national network. There are similar international agencies that exist to monitor and link national currencies together in an international network.

Guidelines for the creation of such currencies involved representatives from all levels of society and all around the world on an essentially Internet-based collaborative platform. Such global communities for all interest groups have continued to flourish and have become technically savvier, integrating all senses in the interaction. Sophisticated nano-sized sensors see, touch, smell, and hear differently so that a variety of additional information becomes the norm. Keypads are things of the past, so that a whole new generation of mobile devices allows more detailed aspects of the world to be experienced by remote social platformers in far-parts of the globe. Such sensing also allows sophisticated analyses to understand the quality and make-up of all manner of remote communities. This further allows real-time, objective, and technical bases for guideline-aligned calibration and adjustment between the many currencies from around the world.

The need for business travel has obviously been reduced tremendously, given the embedding of more sophisticated information technology and telecommunications devices around the world. Aircrafts are light and strong and covered with a material whose properties can change in real-time to become unbreakable, unsinkable, bouncy, among other properties so that safety of passengers is never compromised, regardless of situation.

Focused R&D efforts that require major resources are now, based on estimated efforts, either allocated to the regional, national, or international efforts respectively. Often, breakthrough ideas are conceived by small communities. To make that real, they are allocated to the appropriate level of organization so that the appropriate level of effort and resources are automatically leveraged.

Short-sighted competition that was once the driver of innovation has been replaced by a sustainable multi-pillared foundation in which innovation flourishes organically. The pursuit of knowledge, now not tied up with the notion of rewards but existing to break the very barriers of knowledge, has engendered a whole other level of scientific discovery and engineering breakthrough. Further, it was found that where the pursuit of such knowledge is seamlessly supported by the similar pursuit of other deep and primal drivers, such as the pursuit of service, perfection, courage, harmony, art, adventure, amongst many other possibilities, it provides for a naturally progressive and sustainable foundation. Such rich human-systems aimed at the realization of the deepest human possibilities were found to be the magic key to unlocking a variety of wealth at every possible level imaginable—from the person, to the family, the community, to the ecosystem, to the region, to the nation, to the world. Such human-systems have become the basis of organizational building.

Terrorism and war have no need to be, since the basis of wealth has now been diversified and all are able to live a full life on the basis of who they are rather than what they have to do to support a once narrow and biased machinery of business. International relations have completely changed. Countries interact with countries, not based on exploitation or essential self-promotion, but because of the uniqueness that each country represents. There is something truer and deeper to be learned in the interchange in which all genuinely profit and the whole becomes greater than the parts. In that interchange, uniqueness is strengthened and so too is diversity. In that interchange, the bases of peace is further strengthened since each affirms the difference represented by the other.

There are far more Einsteins, Gandhis, Beethovens, and Tatas in the world than ever before. The world has become a rich place in which to encounter a person is to encounter a mystery of beauty.

All Is but Patterns

Here is the question: If life and business are to embody a possibility even close to that just elaborated, then what kinds of patterns will need to supplant our common patterns of today? For patterns are the stuffs of life. Mandelbrot's fractal geometry has shown that all of physical nature is comprised of fractals—patterns that repeat themselves on larger or smaller scale. Aristotle pointed out centuries ago, that we are what we repeatedly do—excellence, for example, is not an act but a habit. That is, who we are is also a pattern. We become brave by continuously acting brave. We become compassionate by myriad acts of compassion. This simple truth is extended to illustrate that the macro is determined by the micro (Malik, 2009b). Small patterns repeat themselves and become the very fabric of larger and larger realities. If markets and the institution of business is dysfunctional, then that is because there are micro patterns that have made this so. Conversely, if markets and business are to become highly functional in the utopian sense described above, then the very patterns that determine them too need to change. That is the point of this book.

When we talk about 'Stock Market Redesign', this cannot take place in a vacuum. We have to understand the contextual patterns we live in that we ourselves are continually reinforcing. What patterns are being played out by stock exchanges today? Are these permanent in nature? What will it take to supplant dysfunctional by more functional patterns? What will markets and business look like if these patterns are to completely change? How and at what pace may patterns change? What patterns exactly will need to change? What might it take to create something like the utopia we have just glimpsed? Before we address these fundamental questions, we have to look more deeply at the power of patterns. This is the focus of the next chapter.

2

The Power of Patterns

As referred to in Chapter 1, much of the physical or material world is constructed using fractals. Fractals are essentially patterns that repeat themselves on different scale. Different seed fractals when replicated at different scale will create entirely different shapes. A very common example of a fractal is that of broccoli. On close examination, it will be noticed that the broccolette or smallest distinct shape of the broccoli repeats itself in the shape of the stem, which repeats itself in the shape of the whole broccoli. Conversely, if one wanted to change the shape of the whole broccoli, if one could first isolate the seed fractal responsible for it, then the change would proceed far more effectively.

A Fractal for Sustainable Progress

Connecting Inner Power with Global Change (Malik, 2009b) illustrates a fractal-model for sustainable progress. Simply put, it illustrates how sustainable progress has a similar pattern regardless of the level of organizational complexity. That pattern is true at the level of the person, the business, the market, and the economy. These levels are like rungs in a ladder and for large, macro-level progress higher up in the ladder to take place, parallel or more precisely, seed progress needs to occur at the micro levels lower down in the ladder. To solve macro-level problems like climate change and the global financial crises, we of necessity must facilitate a change in patterns at the very level of the perceptions of a person.

This fractal for progress was the result of stringing together three fundamental organizational building-blocks referred to as the physical building-block, the vital building-block, and the mental building-block. Like DNA, these building blocks can combine together in different ways, and it was proposed that there is only one sequence, the physical strung to the vital strung to the mental in that sequence with the mental orientation leading, that creates the conditions for sustainable progress. Organizations that were the result of building blocks combined together in any other sequence were actually being animated by contrary-fractals that were counter to the notion of sustainable progress.

But what does it mean to be physical, or vital, or mental? Since it was supposed that our world and everything in it is fractal in nature, it was hypothesized that one should be able to find the building blocks and the fractal for progress regardless of where one looked. This was made abundantly evident through observation. Thus, the pattern was found in the way people progress, both in short and longer time-frames—how complex theoretical frameworks change, how practical constructions such as businesses and the economy changes, and how nature itself changes.

To quickly illustrate the essence of the pattern, imagine the journey of a seed becoming a flower. In the beginning, the seed is a distinct, dormant entity with precise boundaries observable with the eye. Let us refer to this stage as the *physical-stage* of the seed–flower journey. Once the seed is put in the earth, then germination begins to take place and through the exchange of forces, the seed-flower journey enters a *vital-stage* or stage of vitality. This stage is characterized by movement. Tendrils reach out. The play of energies accelerates. The tendrils move toward the sun, the roots from the seed move deeper into the earth. There is more give and take; gases, water, and nutrients enter into the seed. Tendril structure and other compounds are simultaneously released. At the culmination of this play, a flower emerges, and it is at this stage that the meaning of the seed becomes clear. This is the *mental-stage*. Its identity and what it had secretly stood for in the play of things becomes clear. Yet it required the journey through the physical, the vital, and the mental for this to happen.

Now imagine if this journey did not culminate in the reality of the flower, that is, the journey through the three states had been forestalled. Then the possibility inherent in that creation would not be fully realized. Certainly, something would have been created, for that appears to be the implicit characteristic of life but it would have been only a shadow of what was possible. Now imagine that the many movements of the earth are not necessarily unfolding along the *physical–vital–mental* path, and further, that there are many movements that are in fact headed in the opposite of in lateral directions. What kind of earth would this create? Likely one filled with many, many contradictions.

It is also useful to perceive this very pattern on a completely different scale—something older and vaster than life itself: older than history and vaster than geography—in the interaction between the earth and the sun itself. If it exists in these two very different scales, then we can see how it might exist on every level in between, to be a pattern that repeats itself on different scale—that is, a fractal.

To elaborate this much vaster pattern, the earth has spun around its own axis day after day for supposedly 4.5 billion years. In that motion, there are three phases of the day that have arisen and these have been repeated endlessly such that these phases have been embedded into the fabric of life. As the sun first breaks across the horizon, light is shed upon the constructs on the earth and in that light there is an awareness of the boundary that defines each construct. Having awoken from slumber, each form as it were, becomes aware of what it is—there is an awakening to the *physical* structure that defines it. As the sun rises, the form becomes active and in that activity what it is and what it stands for becomes clearer. The activity expresses its *vitality* and in that vitality there is interaction and experimentation and the vast play of one life form with another. As the sun descends, so as to speak, and countless stars emerge in the sky, it is as though the myopia that had bounded our focused actions through the day is removed and we begin to see the stage of our day from many more perspectives. The phase of vitality has yielded to a phase of *mentality* where a relative increase in introspection, reflection, and consideration of many more points of view comes into focus.

These three phases—physicality, vitality, and mentality—have repeated themselves day after day since the earth and the sun first began their mutual dance with each other. In this manner of seeing, just as the constant exposure to the sun has filled up life forms with solar energy, so too the play of the mutual earth–sun movement has embedded these three phases into the very fibers of life. Perhaps it is fair to say that the DNA of the earth, of circumstances on the earth, is imbued with the physical, vital, and mental phases.

Since these three phases or building blocks will be the bases of the stock market analyses in this book, it is worth understanding what they mean practically.

> But what really, does it mean to exist in a physical phase, in practical terms? The emphasis in this phase is on the structure, on what is made visible by the first play of light on things, by what the eye first sees, when it sees the object. It is not necessarily seeing what the object is doing or what the object is expressing, but it is seeing what the object is physically. The defining characteristic, the mantra of the phase can perhaps be thought of as "reality that is experienced by what one sees with the physical eye." The form is the focus, and the form tends to be synonymous with the established order of things. It exists. It has a high measure of stability or even rigidity to it. Once established it takes a substantial passage of time to alter it. In other words, change is marginal, and can only occur in bounds or limits established by the structure. The structure has to be the basis of the change, and even when change does occur, it is incremental.
>
> In the larger play of life, hence, the basis is seen as the physical form. It is the interaction of form with form that creates other possibilities. This is the basis of creativity. Bring two gases together, for instance, and they will react in a particular way because it is the nature of the form of one gas to react in that precise manner with the form of another. Bring two children together, and it is the nature of the form that will cause them to play with each other. Bring two animals together, and depending on what type they are, they will play with, threaten, or devour the other. The system is a function of physical form, and just as there are fixed forms, so too, there are fixed laws that accompany the individual behavior of each form, and the interaction when one form is brought into proximity with another. In this view, nothing can change, because what is, is already determined by the form and the laws that accompany that form and the law that accompanies the interaction of form. In this play of life, if there is creativity, it is confined to the boundaries of the myriad laws already in place. Hence, it is marginal.
>
> In the vital phase, the emphasis is on assertion of energy. In this phase the life-constructions are absorbed in dynamic activity. They are now exercising their faculties in the play of life. Life-constructions seek to assert themselves

and grow through experimentation. It is as though the energy of the sun is translated into an abundance of different kinds of energies. Each form, relatively dormant at the break of day, now finds its innate energies being released and exercised. This phase is about the interaction of energies. Some energies overpower others. Some express themselves in harmony with others. Some combine with others to create new forms of energies. The searching and humming of bees interacts with the attractiveness of flowers. People and markets seek to grow in whatever ways they can. All is alive with activity, and in this activity the character and characteristics of each gets expressed and in one way or another, refined. The mantra of this phase is more likely "reality as experienced by assertiveness and the myriad play of energies."

In the larger play of life, hence, it is assertiveness and energy that dominates. The energy of each seeks to assert itself at any cost. It seeks to gather more energy by any means, and to establish its rule over other forms, that it may have a base by which to continue to increase its energy and exercise its assertiveness. There is vast experimentation in this phase, but it is not driven by thought or by order. There is a devouring to devour, a conquering to conquer, and it is perhaps the strongest and longest-lasting energy that triumphs in the end. There is constant change of form in this configuration, but the essential drive remains self-assertion and conquest. Change will continue to occur so long as some forms' assertiveness is accomplished in the bargain.

The phase of mentality is characterized by an increase of introspection, reflection, and assimilation. It is as though with the dawning of the stars, the focus has shifted from the here and now, to the mysteries of the unknown. What does one stand for? What will happen tomorrow? Who is one in the play of life? Why did today unroll the way it did? Such questioning leads to the meaning and perhaps even the trajectory of one's activities becoming clearer, and that which one is, that which one is secretly or even overtly working towards, comes more to the surface. Such questioning leads to a progressive understanding of the meaning of not only oneself, but of others in the vast play of life. And that questioning, to a deeper recognition that all forms exist for a reason, and just as self exists for a purpose, so to do all other selves. In such thought the purpose of form and the purpose of energy can also become clearer. The mantra of this phase is perhaps best characterized as "life as experienced by thought and the idea." (Malik, 2009b: 6–9)

Some Common and Destructive Patterns

Operating at the physical-vital end of the spectrum of possibilities will tend to create difficult problems. This is because possibility and therefore action are defined in narrow, short-sighted terms usually geared toward selfish fulfillment of a small notion of self. In the larger scheme of things, such thought, perception, and action always create unconsidered costs in its wake. These costs accrue to the people, communities, environments, and societies that are the field within which such action takes place, and when the accumulation of these costs becomes unbearable, it causes larger pressure for the seed–action or way of being to be controlled or altered. Climate change is a good example of this where for centuries greenhouse gases have been thoughtlessly spewed out by all manner of organization without regard to the accumulating costs to people, communities, environments, societies, and planet earth. It is only now, when the results of those actions have been more comprehensively understood in terms of their disastrous effect on climate, ecosystem degeneration, species extinction, food-chain destabilization, that the root actions are being monitored and even altered at their basis.

The global economy is at the transition between the vital and mental phases (Malik, 2009b: 149–53), and as is natural during any transition, all that represents the old way of being must rise vehemently to the surface to attempt to prolong its rule. Transition into the mental phase of the global economy fractal means that the very foundation and bases of business will be shaken to its core since the essential modus operandi will shift away from a primarily self-seeking to a primarily idea-enhancing and uniqueness-driven way of being.

In fact, as we objectively consider what is necessary for the long-term health of the economy, and our world in general, we see that such a transition and in fact anchoring in a mental way of being is nothing short of an imperative. The vital way of being is all about exercising energy, often irrational, in the pursuit of short-term and narrowly defined gains, that as discussed, often creates huge externalities in its wake. We will discuss this in more detail in the next chapter. The mental way of being, on the other hand, is about allowing true uniqueness and diversity to come to the surface. History has shown us time and time again that such diversity is the cornerstone of sustainability and true progress. The mental way of being promotes a deeper questioning, and therefore, also a genuine look at old operating assumptions that have outlived their utility.

To shed just such a light on the problem-ridden world we are the stewards of, is the necessity of today. We must penetrate into the heart of the irrationalities and short-sightedness we see all around us. We must be able to penetrate and forever alter the obstinacy in the notion that all are business assets for this perception is very often at the root of all our other stupidities. Often, there is a filter on all experience in which the experience becomes equivalent to a perceived monetary value. In fact, the experience, resource, circumstance, and fount of wealth are then shed aside and what is perceived to be more important is the monetary value of it. This is the outcome of a vital way of being.

Thus, Nature in its stupendous diversity is shortsightedly believed to be everlasting and a monetary value placed on every element in this bank of everlasting value. There is a monetary value prescribed to a tree, for example. This value does not capture the fact that a tree is in itself an awesome ecosystem with a vast number of life forms in and around it. It does not capture the fact that it has taken decades for that tree to come into being and in so doing has become an intricate part of an even vaster living ecosystem whose balance can be upset with its removal. What the value is equated to, however, is the value of the firewood or wood that a maker of some other product for which wood in a raw material would pay for it. The tree, hence, has become an easily replaceable, commodity-type business asset. The same is true of every other element in nature—air, water, earth, light, the countless animal and plant species, and so on. All have been replaced by a monetary value and become commoditized business assets. But this business asset mentality, the outcome of a vital way of being, does not stop there. Human beings are categorized as business assets as well. The executive who runs a business may be given a higher monetary value with more perks and better treatment in this strange mathematics while the front-line worker is ascribed less value and treated less well. The helpless woman and child may be ascribed the least value and even traded as cheap commodities in the marketplaces of lust and labor.

In the vital way of being, there are a few self-prescribed fountainheads of value, mountains that are more important than everything else and all else whirl insanely around them or artificially prop them up to maintain their short-sighted use and abuse of energy and perceptions of self-importance.

The uniqueness, the possibilities, and the souls of individuals are forgotten and all become cogs in a heartless machine that exists for no great reason but simply to proceed along its tortuous path toward an ultimate and inevitable self-destruction.

Progressive Patterns

When the mental way of being becomes active, the accompanying sincere questioning becomes a force to penetrate into the physical-vital facades that stand up as truth to thereby begin to uncover all the possibility behind the surface. This is incredibly significant because all along we have abandoned deeper possibility to live an interpretation of life that has been meted out by a vitally-anchored elite whose loud voices and insistences have continually stunted any other possibility that would minutely compromise their established sources of power. With this force of questioning, be it at the individual level, the community or corporate level, or the level of society, the facades come falling down and another way of being begins to surface instead. This way of being is in contrast to the monolithism of the physical-vital way of being, in that many diversified sources of power come into being.

Sincere questioning must disrupt at its very roots the notion that all exists for business. We are unique constructs projected to the surface by an underlying splendor and in the scheme of things it is in the interest of all to allow that uniqueness to flourish and create a foundation for all rich in its diversity. Business is one stream of development but other streams are equally important, and as in the physical-vital way of life, do not exist to prop up the most important business stream. Where questioning, reason, imagination are alive, there individuality is given wings and can take flight to prescribe a unique orbit that expresses the truth of what it is. Each orbit is as important as the next, and the combination of many, many orbits creates a world that is more expressive, alive, and complete with possibility.

In such a world the bases of power will be altered. It will be a truly multipolar world which will have completely moved away from the brutalities and harshness of a monopolar world and the sensitivities and instabilities of a bipolar world. World powers are not just the USA or the

USA and China, but the USA, China, Turkey, India, Malaysia, Kenya, amongst many, many other countries. It is not just Google, Apple, Intel, Cisco, Microsoft, Shell, Merck, and Honda that set trends and yield power but now there are many leaders in many industries driven by different ways and expressions of being. It is not just the US Dollar and the Euro that are the currencies to be accumulated and compared against but thousands of local, regional, and national currencies that express the creative power of life. Monopolies of any and every kind will shatter, simply because the force of questioning will not allow a substandard way of being to flood out the surfacing of deeper and varied possibility.

And why is such a world important? Because the one we live in now, in which all seeks to aggrandize itself, rather than the world, is an inadequate means for long-term sustainability. Why should a single corporation be single-mindedly revered or thoughtlessly emulated when the founts of creativity and innovation and the spell of infinity exist in every single person? Why should an outdated mode of development pursued by one country be pushed by institutions from that country and become the pattern by which all countries need to develop? Why should the standards that have defined the narrow boundaries of yesterday's global success continue to define tomorrow's global success? Why should a way of living in one part of the world be promoted as the true way of living for all parts of the world?

Continued thoughtless standardization in the face of increasing contrary signs is the sign of a physical-vital orientation. Physical, because it is the status quo and established "right" way of doing things that has to be upheld at any cost. Vital, because as already suggested, all energy must be used in the pursuit of promoting the one strong energy regardless of the result on any other energy. If such standardization is to be pursued, even though it is garbed in the appearances of seeming liberty and freedom and the way to development, we are perpetrating a crime against humanity by killing all other possibilities. What we want instead is numerous creative organizations and individuals to flourish. Different ways of being, different lines of development, and complete self-determination must come to the surface. This means that the mental way of being has to become active. Right now where is the self-determination when the greed of distant investment banks or traders reduces a country's wealth by half, sending that country into a state of disarray and austerity?

Where is the freedom when honest, hard-working individuals and the families are now thrown on the street because the corporations they worked for have become bankrupt overnight and they have to take to the streets and beg for their next meal? Where is the freedom when one's house is taken away from one because unlike the banks that have been bailed out by the government, you or the working person next to you has not? Where is the freedom when your livelihood was taken away through no fault of yours? Where is the freedom when one is dependent on one's next meal on a global trading system that is at the mercy of irresponsible individuals who care not on the *reason* on which trade is taking place but just care for making the quick buck for themselves in the bargain? And that is the point. It is the reason, the dream, the intention behind the practical system that has to become active. We have to make the shift from a physical-vital to a more mental way of being. This is an imperative at every level of living. It is a pattern that must become active at every level. A fractal that becomes alive in the affairs of our lives.

In the mental orientation, deeper questioning means that the assumptions of yesterday, be they in the way markets function, the motive corporations are really driven by, or the desires that propelled one to say and be a certain way, are sincerely questioned. In this sincere questioning, something other than the blind habits that drove the continued dysfunction becomes active. That is what it means to operate at the mental level. The forces of reason, of thought, of imagination, even inspiration, become more active in redefining who one is or what one stands for.

Why should money be the arbiter of life when clearly there are so many other dimensions of wealth? Why should one's success be solely determined by money and why should others look up to one who happens to have more of it? Why should the buyer of goods, because he happens to have the money, believe himself to be a god even though he has no god-like qualities in his breast? Why when one is out of money should they be looked down on and cast aside and thrown on the street? Why should worth and value be equated to one's bank account? And why should we give up all other dimensions of personal, communal, societal power to a fleeting energy that is not an end in itself but really only a means to facilitate more holistic development?

When reason becomes alive, we see how we have so easily surrendered our source of power to a facade that has no meaning in itself. Who is the banker or the lender of money or the investor or the trader or the dispenser of money in determining the wealth or poverty of a person, a community, or a society? Is it not that because we have allowed him to be falsely powerful that he is so? Our life, our way of being belongs to no one but ourselves. If current norms and society have made us poor because we lack money then clearly there is something wrong with that norm and it must be shattered once and for all. How can anything that has arisen from the underlying splendor and is a construct of infinite possibility ever lose that fount of power because they do not currently have money in their hands?

The mental way of being must become alive to get us closer to that state of truer freedom. All that has locked us into these chains of wealth-and-worth-defined-as-money must be removed forever. But that is no trivial task. The established physical-vital orientation runs deep and has infiltrated and defined our very view of ourselves and our view of life. Education, sport, art, and great institutions that exist to discover and express freedom have in a Faustian bargain become the ultimate means to enslave us to a life of triviality by themselves, existing now to further bind us in the chains of wealth-and-worth-defined-as-money.

Further, there is an inherent randomness to the vital view. Energies and flows, when self-referenced, manifest as emotion such as greed and fear. Living at the physical-vital level means that emotions such as greed and fear often dictate decision-making. These emotions have been said to be responsible for the great stock market crashes we have witnessed over the last century. We will have more to say about this later. Were we in the mental orientation, truly, then such irrationality would not find a place and the livelihood of many would not be wiped out in an instant.

Vaster Implication of Such Operation

That is why the mental orientation must become active. We want freedom to light freedom. One man's freedom inspires another's. Flame lights flame. All becomes aglow with a fire that burns up the pettiness of the past. We are essentially and innately creative beings. How can we be any other when we have arisen from the splendor that is the foundation of all creation? Our creativity, however, bound up in narrowly defined physical-vital chains has continued to reinforce the physical-vital past of yesterday. We have continued to live out the patterns of facades, reinforcing them with every small thought and act of ours.

It is only when the force of questioning becomes alive that the absurdity of our outdated thoughts and actions and the resultant energy that occupied us can be released and we create something different that will be noticed because it is now something new. In our perpetual creativity, we have continued to create the patterns of the past. Because these patterns already existed, we did not necessarily notice our innate creativity but when the old patterns are stopped, then the new patterns will immediately be noticed because they have not existed before.

And every pattern, being essentially creative, will seek to replicate itself on larger and larger scales and to reorient the dynamics of life around these new ways of being. Moving, therefore, to a mental way of being is going to radically alter the life we experience around us now. When we realize that we are each individually a fount of creativity and power and have innate self-worth not determined by the money we may or may not have, then that confidence is going to imprint life by becoming a sun around which other dynamics will have to orbit. That is the nature of creativity. A whole new multipolar world with many, many centers of unique power will have to result.

And in that fresh seeing, where we are not weighed down by the heavy chains of the past, even new dynamics of relationship and collective being will emerge. No longer will we give lip service to the great terms brotherhood, fraternity, and equality but actually mean them in our orientation and stance with one another. We will live and let live. And further, under the aegis of such a mental orientation, realize that we each truly need who the other is and stands for in the fulfillment of our own life and lives.

It will be impossible for money to become a binding chain since it will be seen as a great lubricator and enzyme of productive activity. The real focus will have to be that activity that each individual or collections of individuals, in their innate creativity, are compelled to work out because that is the reason for their being. That is the self-chosen task that unique projections of splendor feel compelled to work out. And as suggested before that activity could be of many different natures. It could be the pursuit of adventure and courage, or the articulation and pursuit of rare strains of knowledge, or engineering or artistic perfection, or service to herb and plant or animal or people for the sake of such service, or arranging greater and greater interchanges between unique expressions of creativity through ever-fulfilling live and Internet-based social platforms, and so on.

The constraints imposed by wealth-and-worth-defined-as-money will be removed. Even the sources of money will not be constrained by the methods of the past. Who after all is the Bank—national or international, or the global corporation, or a coterie of self-seeking industrialists, bankers, and politicians—to determine the way, means, and worth of productive activity of a splendor-projected uniquenesses of creativity? In the mental orientation more and more will money flow to where it is needed. This is inevitable.

The real question is how do we get there. That is the point of this book. Today stock markets are primary vehicles by which corporations, by many estimates the most respected institution of the day, receive their cash impetus to continue to develop or not. Stock markets have captured the imagination of common folk and set alight dreams of making the quick buck and retiring to a life of freedom. Stock markets provide the common man the sense that they can benefit from the fortunes of a company. Stock markets, through the design of rapid rewards or punishment, continue to reinforce the world of yesterday for both investor and company. Further, stock markets are now synchronized across the world and even strongly linked with many other financial vehicles that used to be considered different and unrelated. In a strange kind of way, an incredible monolithic structure has been created and if one part of this begins to sink it pulls down the rest of the structure with it.

A massive delinking needs to take place so that we never again face some of the formidable domino–effect challenges we have faced in recent times. Lack of ability to make interest payments cannot be linked to the entire stability of a country and the livelihoods of innocent millions. Perceived monetary instability in one market or in one part of the world, further, cannot be allowed to penalize other markets of parts of the world. The flow of money has to be able to reach a wider and broader range of creative individuals from many walks of life. Truly sustainable development needs to be rewarded while activity that compromises development of individuals, communities, society, and countries has to be stopped in its tracks.

Patterns in Markets

A secret knowledge will continue to remain a secret so long as one does not look in the right place for the answer. And so long as one does not look in the right place for an answer, the behavior and potential behavior of markets, the very DNA of markets, will remain a mystery.

Financial prophets, gurus, and analysts have come up with potential models that explain markets sometimes. At one end of the spectrum is the Efficient Market Hypothesis (EMH) which itself comes in different shades. But the bottom line is that prices on traded assets reflect information about that asset. Hence, financial markets are informationally efficient. On the other end of the spectrum are models that define financial markets as stochastic. Mandelbrot, the father of fractal geometry, has been a big proponent of this model. Then there are models that define price behavior as a function of human emotion, and hence, predictable within boundaries. Elliott and Prechter have built models based on this supposition. Thus, we have models that define financial markets correctly, within their prescribed limits, but fall apart when those limits are transcended. We will have occasions to delve into these models in more detail later in the book.

The great secret to understanding market behavior, however, is in understanding the DNA of markets as determined by the physical, vital, and mental strands that combine together differently to create different behavioral paradigms for markets. Each of the three market models referred to above are a function of how these basic strands combine together. With the purer vital, a Mandelbrot-type Stochastic model results. With a combination of physical and vital, the Elliott and Prechter model comes into being. When the mental strand tends to lead then EMH comes into being. Continued misapplication of these models during real-time decision-making will exacerbate dysfunction and result in crises—of the type we continue to experience globally now.

Such an analyses reveals the DNA of progress—that is, of sustainable progress—and that is the key to understanding market behavior and what the conditions must be for us to correctly apply either an Elliott and Prechter or a stochastic or an EMH type model. That is also the key to moving out of the financial mess we are in globally. Through this book we will seek to understand stock markets in these terms.

3

Pandorian Business

Business today is a central building block of society. It is one of the most active components of society that focuses on collectivities. By virtue of its central position, it has huge impact on individuals, on communities, and on larger society. It has commonly been accepted as the reason for being for each of these respective levels. In effect, this acceptance of business into the very fibers of our lives summarizes the huge impact it has had. So what really is this impact and what really does business offer us today?

I would argue that its very dynamism is what has proffered it with such a central place in today's life. It is driven by an accepted perception that to be able to live, money has to be earned. Business exists to make money, and in that process, money is also made by each of the individuals working for the business, and in that process, the community in which it exists also benefits. This central urge to make money is what has driven the centralization of business. Business in effect is the dynamo which allows money to be accessed.

The force with which the institution of business has played itself out over centuries has been so complete that this view of money, and of personal, community, and societal freedom being tied to actually having money, has become pervasive. Other filters with which to view life have effectively receded into the background and now instead the one practically omnipresent filter is that we exist for business, and business is the path of universal development. There cannot be any other way because that is the only way we can get money, which after all, in this view of things, is the only means to live.

This view that fulfillment in life depends on having money and that business is the means and way by which this precious force can be obtained is business's primary contribution to life. But it is a contribution of questionable character, and when one probes into it, it has the very characteristics of Pandora's Box. For Pandora's Box contained all the problems that humankind could possibly be faced with, and when we probe into the nature of today's business and especially its reinterpretation of life as being synonymous with accumulating money, often regardless of true cost, it is a mass of contradictions, misfortunes, and problems that we are confronted with.

For, in current-day business-mathematics, all that exists, is either an asset or a liability. The equation is simple. If something helps to make money, it is an asset. If it costs money, it is a liability. And in this mathematics, that which was once an asset can overnight become a liability. Hence, a tree is not a tree but a commodity worth only its weight in firewood. An ecosystem is not an ecosystem, built over millions of years with untold riches, but an inventory or stockpile of its constituent parts. A flowing stream is not a vein of the earth carrying precious life force but an asset to move toxic substances away from some manufacturing site while it is clean and a liability once it has become filled with toxic substances and outlived its utility. A person is not a repository of untold possibility but a machine or a cog that must play a precise role to ensure that the ruthless engines of business do not slow down for even a minute.

Further, there is a vast marginalization of concept, culture, idea, history, development, and possibility. In this marginalization, the tradable value as represented by bonds issued by city or state or country, for example, trumps any ideals or concept that exists implicit in the "product." Or debt-payments owed by such complex collectivities trump everything else that collectivity may stand for, and if payments cannot be made, then the issuers of the loan assume a right over a range of assets in that collectivity. In the continued anomalies of this mathematics, any beauty, any rare or exceptional knowledge, any extraordinary ability to organize people and resources, amongst many other possibilities from the splendor are cast aside and the tradable stock price of a company comes to represent all of that. And then it is not the context that is considered but only the opportunity for profit, as shares of the company are sold or bought on a dime.

In this mathematics, the play of assets and liabilities must create a net positive sum of money in the end or the business is dead. The whole purpose is to ensure that there is profit. that is, that the total revenues generated by the business exceed the total cost incurred by the business. There may be a reason that is attributed to the business, an ideal that all its component parts pay lip service to, but at the end of the day the ideal does not matter. That was only used to attract potential customers and soothe possibly questioning stakeholders, so that its primary purpose of making profit is preserved at the end of the day.

Here are the problems with this view. First, as has already been stated, life with its implicit creativity and base of splendor has effectively been marginalized and even assiduously replaced by a meager view of life as the accumulation of money. It is only with money that power can grow. It is only with money that a person, a corporation, a country, has meaning and say. Worth is money. Wealth is money. A useful education is that which prepares one to make money. Useful art is that which sells for more money. A good religion is that which gives people the moral knowledge that god is money. Knowledge is only useful in so far as it results in more money. All relationship is not really about strengthening bonds between person to person or collectivity to collectivity or community to community but about ensuring micro markets and customers and market segments so that more goods and services can be sold and more money be made in the bargain. Love is the facade; knowledge is the facade; service, collaboration, all the virtues are facades or one-pointed doorways leading always toward the possibility of making more money. Freedom, equality, liberty, and fraternity and every high ideal espoused through all history have now been overtaken by something much more meaningful, much more fulfilling; the true purpose of it all—and this is, to make money. Without that there is no chance of liberty. Without that there is no chance of freedom. And fraternity and equality only have meaning when one's accumulated money enters into the picture. A human is not a human unless he has money, unless he has proved his worth by accumulating money. Someone who has no money is perhaps barely human, and even access to water, basic sanitation, basic education, other basic rights, and the articles declared as necessary by human rights activists are something that must remain in question because one who has no money is perhaps subhuman. The beggar on the street is not a person but someone who has failed in the affairs of life, and therefore, hardly worthy to even be looked at or considered. The scales of judgment have been altered, not to track one's intrinsic beauty and possibility of splendor, but to weigh their worth by the amount of money they have accumulated in life. Money has become the arbiter of all transaction and the final filter for any decision worth making. Nothing else matters.

Secondly, profit is king. But in the computation of it, total costs that have actually occurred are never considered. Costs to people, to community, to environment, to humanity, and to future generations are ignored. Hence, the business continues to be subsidized by each of these entities. If one considered the level of accrued subsidization, then even from a purely financial perspective, it would perhaps be apparent that the company belongs to each of the subsidizing entities. But the company in fact acts as though it owns all these entities. It will plunder the earth for resources, resources that belong to the earth and to all inhabitants on earth and by an odd sleight of hand will assume control over it. It will spew out all manners of waste on the earth, assuming it is its privilege to do so and then move to another location once the previous has become quite barren or loaded with toxins. It will pay some wages to people and then assume control over much of their lives, and instead of nurturing the splendor resident within them, will often after using them, toss them aside in favor of newer human assets, just as it does tracts of land and water. And since profit is the primary motive, achieving economies of scale sooner or later becomes a key driving force for many companies. Thus, the bigger the company becomes, the more is its effect on each of the entities identified magnified, in effect multiplying the intrinsic subsidies it is receiving, and the more miscalculated profit it makes. The anomalies are huge.

But this urge for monopolization, driven essentially by the profit motive is especially true in the realm of finance and money where the nature of transaction is facilitated by advances in technology and creates disastrous effects in the now far more organized power of speculation. Speculation by itself when practiced in small spaces tends to reduce creativity and development to its "weight in fire-wood." When the global arena becomes the playing field, and when much larger pools of funds are available to speculate with, the effects are far more disastrous and entire countries and global ecosystems and companies can be affected in minutes. The rise of mutual funds and trading activity of all kinds facilitates this.

Further, wherever profit becomes a serious motive for organizing corporate activity, economies of scale kick in. To fund this growth, stock markets are the key vehicles. The growth and increasing proliferation of stock markets designed in a certain way promote the same long-term destructiveness.

The essential urge for profit, bolstered by the foundational belief that money is the arbiter of power and the true elixir of life, creates a number of irrational effects in its wake. These play themselves out in the perversities we see prevalent across the field of business. Let us take up some common industries to understand some of the anomalies and perversities we are currently plagued with.

Consider the Food, Beverage, and Agricultural Industry

Food is essentially a source of energy for people around the world. Its nutritional value is directly proportional to its freshness and the conditions within which it is grown. In ideal circumstances, food, to promote freshness, should be grown locally. In reality, it has today become a major global enterprise. And once it has entered the realm of global business, it means that it is now subject to a different set of criteria to make it financially viable. The creation of food has to become a business and be operated as a business, and in that translation, the essential condition for its effectiveness is cast aside. Instead of being a labor of love, with consideration for season and local ecosystem and the health of people, in its creation, it is driven by global competition and economies of scale.

This means that at every phase of the supply chain, compromise has to be made and costs have to be assumed by the locality or region within which that supply chain phase exists. Starting from the growth of the essential raw materials, we see increasing instances of ecosystems, complex forests, marshlands, amongst other natural habitats that have been built up over millennium and are embedded into the very fabric of life often in ways that we do not completely understand, being wiped aside in favor of regimented, and for that locality, unnatural growth of crops. This has huge costs to the soil and natural life in the locality, the environment, the surrounding community, the economy, and future generations. Destruction of ecosystems destroys ecosystem services provided to humanity, such as water and air filtration, carbon sequestration—essential to counteract climate change, flood control, enrichment of soil, and destruction of species—along with their effects such as creation of food, pollination, and provision of medicinal compounds, among others. None of these tremendous costs are ever considered as costs. They are taken for granted and externalized to the other entities unfortunate enough to be the context for that phase of the supply chain.

Further down the supply chain where there may be a processing plant, a whole new level of costs that are usually not considered come into being. The first order of costs is usually environmental. Hence, if water for the plant is needed, or even if water is a key ingredient in the food or beverage, then tube wells may be sunk and the underlying water table is seriously affected. This has huge effects on the lives of communities in the vicinity. If the plant has by-products, then these are often spewed into the atmosphere, sunk into the earth, or offloaded into a water supply or flowing body of water in the area. This too has serious effects on surrounding communities and is often not considered in the statement of cost. The agricultural sector is the highest user of water. Hence, it becomes very important for it to be used most efficiently and responsibly.

In the processing itself, often additives and preservatives and other questionable chemicals are employed that create a food filled with subtle poisons. Our current approach of assuming otherwise until proven beyond a shadow of a doubt is biased toward the big corporation that we have to remember is motivated primarily by maximizing its profit, often at any cost.

Further is the whole issue of Genetically Modified Foods. Nature and its output have been created over millennium. There is an inherent wisdom in the array of compounds that constitute any single herb or plant, and there is a long built-up equilibrium in which each herb or plant exists in harmony with everything else around it. To modify the genetic structure of such a construct, without considering or comprehending the huge number of interrelationships that are being changed as a result of that, is to load up the dice in random ways and hope for the best when they are thrown. One simply cannot maintain long-established equilibriums in such a manner. As Einstein has said, "God does not play dice with the universe."

Further, we really have no clue as to how the genetically modified organism (GMO) is going to interact with human bodies and what the effects on the cells are going to be. This is an irresponsible approach to production and potentially creates a whole slew of problems in its wake.

At several points in a supply chain, large work forces are often employed. Often in order to minimize total cost of production, migrant workers are employed and human rights issues compromised. Women and children are also often exploited. Employees are overworked, not subjected to decent working conditions, and have fewer rights than the normal citizens of a country.

The point of view that an agricultural company or a global food company is doing humanity a service by providing food or beverages globally is flawed. It counteracts the very need for growth and creation of food to become a community-strengthening activity. Contact with, nurturing, and respecting the land is essential in the scheme of things. A community or a country that loses touch with its land has lost its sovereignty. Sooner or later it becomes entirely dependent on external flows and then easily can succumb to one of many external or global threats. Today's global agricultural and food industries promote loss of contact by individuals, communities, and countries with local lands. This is a huge cost that is never considered in the simplified, short-term mathematics of asset and liability that animates business today.

Every piece of land is essentially creative. The very fact that all life emerge from this matrix is proof enough. Sometimes the secret of its creativity needs to be teased out, and in working to make this happen, communities can be built and strengthened. Creative land lies at the basis of strong, local cultures and economies. A vast range of products and services that are today artificially created through remote processing can be localized. Livelihoods can be enhanced through mastering the creation and exchange of these products and services. In today's push to create profit, often at any cost, today's global agricultural, food, and beverage industries continually negate all this possibility.

Consider the Pharmaceutical Industry

At its core, the pharmaceutical industry exists to develop and produce drugs that can assist the healing and regeneration of the body. If we exist in a world with splendor at its base, and if we are all constructs of that incredible possibility that seeks continually to express and enhance itself, there are a few things that are very possible. First of all, the healing power is likely not something that has to be imported into the body but probably exists resident in the body itself. If we can grow and self repair through childhood and adolescent years, then it stands to reason that the same ability should continue to exist in adult and later years. If it does not, then perhaps that is the case because certain abilities are being switched off or negated through lifestyle. If this is the case, then the purpose of drugs should be to help this natural healing ability to come alive once again.

Today's common thought on disease though, is that it is caused by external agents such as microbes, pathogens, bacteria, and virus that invade and compromise the functioning of the body. Health is a function of keeping disease away, or if it invades the body, not so much of invigorating the natural healing ability of the body, as killing the invading agents. If this were true though, that is, if it were the strains that create disease, then disease should be rampant because the fact is that some microbes, pathogens, virus, bacteria exist in every intake of breath. All air is like a cocktail mixture with the good and the bad mixed in it. This cannot but be the case since we live in a greenhouse in which all types of agents are free to mix and roam the greenhouse with impunity. The fact that we are for the most part not filled with diseases means that it cannot be the external agents that are the sole cause of disease. There has to be something else in our way of being that gives its consent to the potentiality of disease.

Many of today's drugs though are created to kill these various strains that supposedly create disease in their wake. If disease is not created by these external agents and if these drugs are now freely moving through our entire bodily system once we ingest or inject them, then the question is what are they really doing within us? If the determining factor behind the expression of disease in ourselves is our power of assent, however subtle this may be, and if our cells and fantastic bodily systems themselves have the power to heal, then what we are injecting or swallowing cannot but have a detrimental effect on our systems since they are based on a false or ignorant set of premises.

But today's emphasis on profit-making has a great masking effect, and the truth of healing is veiled by evoking fear in its place. Pharmaceutical companies resort to advertizing campaigns that strike fear in people, and through fear, people now take a whole slew of "medicines" to combat or keep away disease. One of the most questionable practices is that of vaccination. In truth, vaccinations are the very diseased potion injected into us so that we may create antibodies if the real disease enters into us. But why take in darkness to fight darkness. Darkness must be met with light, and true light is generated when the cells are allowed to release the healing powers inherent within them.

While vaccinations stand at one extreme of portfolio of products offered by pharmaceutical companies, at the other end of the portfolio are compounds that are made from plant extracts. But the truth that these compounds are derived from some thriving, living plant is veiled by tremendously complex chemical names. This makes it impossible to realize that the compound could be commonly grown in one's backyard. Regardless, the complication though is that the active ingredient from the plant in the compound is not harmonized with the plethora of other plant ingredients that it naturally exists with but isolated and magnified, so that it in effect it is now out of proportion from how nature intended it to exist, and because of that, it will likely have a more caustic effect than necessary on the body.

Pharmaceutical companies claim that they are involved in drug discovery. But everything of use that they have come up with exists in a more balanced form in nature. So what exactly have they been discovering? Further, much of the biotech industry replicates drug-formation processes in nature and then patents the process. If the process already exists in nature then what right does a company have to now patent the process for its own? If the real power of healing is something within each individual being, then the real value of drugs would be in allowing this automatic or profound ability to take effect without in anyway compromising any portion or system of the body. Instead drug use usually has many side effects, and mixing drugs can be lethal. So under the aegis of profit-making, the pharmaceutical companies, like the food, beverage, and agricultural industry, have pushed something that should be local and in the immediate and accessible province of every individual into a falsely unattainable realm. It has mystified natural processes of healing and in effect claimed to be the sole intermediary of nature's magnificent processes. It has at best inadvertently covered up man's natural ability to heal himself and in that regard continues to do a great disservice to humanity. Meanwhile, it continues to grow rich on plundered money.

Consider the Energy Industry

Energy is existent in every micro measurement of life. It is present in the atoms that exist all around us. It is present in the light that makes everything visible. It is fair to say that it is present in every fiber of existence. Energy is in fact abundant. It is only the paucity of our own perception that has made energy scarce and burdened humankind with the exorbitant costs that our mishandling of energy continues to create. Even as I write this, the biggest oil-spill in history with its disastrous long-term effects is in process of unfolding.

Our primary source of energy today is oil. When energy is available locally at every point of the earth, why we have to lay pipelines that move a deadly substance across the earth and which is really meant to remain in the bowels of the earth, is one of those astounding questions posterity will be forced to ask. Why did we continue to extract a poison to fuel every manner of system is the big question? Why did we play with an eons-old equilibrium of earth's fluids? And even if we did do so, and extracted these fluids to be used on the surface, what right did a single company or even a group of companies have to claim something that belongs to the earth and to all humanity as its own and charge extraordinary prices for the use of it? The simple answer, of course, is that in doing just this, in externalizing all these costs and in being subsidized by current and future generations, communities, environment, and nature, the few have been able to maximize profit to get rich at the expense of the many. That in itself is a lure too seductive to turn aside from. And naturally, once it is being done, then economies of scale might as well be the arbiter of future decision-making and make the whole enterprise bigger, faster, and far uglier than before.

Modern times have seen huge wars being fought for access to oil. Countries have reportedly been invaded in the name or the lure of oil, and millions of innocent people have suffered from the disastrous social disorder that resulted because of such wars. Dislocated and disenfranchised youth who once had a chance at a normal life have had their lives marginalized and become targets for terrorist groups. Terrorist groups, acting as parasites, have sought to destroy the invading hosts in all its forms. The cycles of destruction are huge as local cultures, society, and centuries' old ways of being are tossed aside in the pursuit of a deadly poison that ultimately destroys its very users. Why has such madness been allowed to exist? Why has the work of centuries been destroyed in a few short years?

Oil causes havoc at every step of the supply chain. At the point of extraction, as just stated, the natural equilibrium of the earth is altered as now deeply embedded fluids are extracted from its very being. Imagine a similar procedure being done on the human body where a deeply embedded fluid is continually extracted. It will likely result in instability that we do not rightly understand or foresee. Then during transportation of the oil through pipes and in storage facilities, there is continual seepage, and the fluid that once existed in a natural equilibrium deep in the earth is now randomly distributed in a completely different environment than what is natural for it. The chemistry of the different environment has been altered and species introduced to a substance that is completely foreign to them. In the absence of precise knowledge and balancing action, there cannot but be an adverse effect in which the natural equilibrium of the environment is altered. Further downstream, there will be processing and refining plants. This means that water will be extracted and waste products spewed out where it once belonged and in the air and general environment around it. Storage facilities for processed oil will inevitably leak the oil into the water and air supply. Carcinogens and a deadly host of toxic substances are now distributed into communities of all kinds. Health of people deteriorates in different ways. People's very cells are now infiltrated with the unnatural and deadly substance which compromises the workings of all the bodily systems. Ecosystems get affected, and we are back to the very basis of modern civilization being threatened at its very foundation. But further, the oil is now also widely distributed through vehicles. It now spreads across civilization, and when burnt, introduces further toxicity into life.

As though all this is not sign enough that we have embarked down an incorrect avenue, we have continued to build our systems and cities such that they are fueled by this source. This is a contradiction in terms, and like the food and agricultural industry, and the pharmaceutical industry, this pushes away the wealth and wholeness that must be a natural part of our lives. Sunlight has energy and is available for the asking. We do not have to extract and pull anything out of its natural place and way of being. So powerful is sunlight that all life moves naturally toward it and yearns for it. Life does not shrivel, coil up, and get poisoned as a result of contact with it. How out of touch with reality are we when we refuse to see the signs that are so detrimental to us? We have been brainwashed and programmed to accept oil as a natural part of life. It is unnatural. If it were natural, everything would yearn for it as it does sunlight.

The trillions of dollars that have been spent on the oil industry and the ways of life that have emerged from the use of it, need now to be focused on the storage and utilization of solar-based products.

Consider the Water Industry

Water is essential to life. It is not only a profound matrix from which life supposedly arose, but it also renews and replenishes life and even holds the essence or quality of substance or even of a vibration put into it. There have been some remarkable experiments to this effect conducted by Masaru Emoto. It is a truly universal medium interchangeably existing in gas, liquid, and solid state and is intimately connected together with all other water the world over. This is so because there are not a thousand sources or cycles of water but only one source and cycle of water for the whole planet. But also, water exists wherever life is to exist. It is in every cell of a living being, be it plant, animal, or human. One person's conscious relationship with water, putting into it vibration of a pure kind, can, by the intimate contagion shared between water and water, alter the vibratory pattern of a much larger body of water. There is a fractal effect so that a small pattern tends to ripple out. Conversely, the misuse of water and the putting into it of negative or irresponsible patterns will have a much larger negative and irresponsible effect on life.

Wherever life needs to exist, there water needs to exist. Wherever water seizes to exist, there life seizes to exist. Wherever water is held as sacred, there life becomes sacred. Wherever water is desecrated, there life is desecrated.

So how is water treated today? It is treated as a discrete, forever available substance existing primarily for commercial use. It is used to build product and more products. It is irresponsibly pumped from the earth as though it exists in infinite measure in the small confines of a locality. It is treated as a convenient mechanism to whisk away waste. It is dammed by local or regional authorities and not allowed to complete its natural course across the body of the earth where it was providing the gift of life wherever it was flowing. The rhythm of its global cycle is neither understood nor respected. The effects of breaking its global flow or of altering it are also not understood. Water acts intimately with the earth and the natural mechanisms of the earth to renew itself through the cycle of evaporation, condensation, and filtration. The limits of this cycle need to be respected if life is to continue in a sustainable state. The rhythm, however, through aggressive, one-sided, and incomplete processing of water is broken again and again, which ultimately means that the bases of our life is being broken again and again.

Because of the paradigm of profit maximization, often at any cost, industry the world over will in usual fashion externalize the tremendous cost by its continued mistreatment of water. Communities, the environment, numerous life forms, society, and future generations are therefore subsidizing industry with their lives. The can of popularly available soft drink has the names of dying beings imprinted in it. So long as the treatment of water continues in the irresponsible manner in which it exists today, that drink must be treated as what it is—an obituary sung to those unknown beings who have sacrificed or who are soon going to sacrifice their lives for this moment's enjoyment.

Water is a universal right because it is linked with universal life. Business and society need to treat it as such.

Consider the Retail Industry

Abundance is the law of life. It manifests in myriad forms in nature. We see it in the wealth of species. We see it in the raw beauty of nature. We see it in the eyes of children and sometimes in the lives of adults. There are natural rhythms and cycles that if respected, if understood, and if worked in alignment with will keep this universal law of abundance alive. As humans we like to see abundance. It is encoded in our DNA. We unconsciously always strive to increase abundance in our lives.

Our approach for arriving at this abundance and our very meaning of abundance, however, is based on our perception. And more often than not, and under the rush of everyday events, we will perceive abundance by what appears on the facade and not by all that occurred behind the facade to make the image on the facade possible. And more often than not, there was a tremendous alteration and lack of observance, and even an outright opposition to the great and natural rhythms of life to create the products and services that appear in one of the most commonly available facades of our times—the retail store. And more often than not, the very use of all these products also has a detrimental effect on the natural laws and rhythms of our bodies so that day-after-day the natural healing abilities of the body are compromised until one day we realize we are ridden with some devastating disease that we never quite comprehend was the result of our facade-based choices and facade-based way of life.

The cosmetics in the retail store have been projected as making us more beautiful, desirable, as bringing out our youth, and as making us feel better. Often though, these very cosmetics are laced or simply comprised with a cocktail of toxins. When applied year after year, they seep into the very cells and change the condition of alkalinity necessary for normal, healthy functioning to a condition of acidity so that the natural functioning of the cell is severely compromised and key functions of the body are not able to fulfill themselves. The same is true of a whole variety of consumer products.

Household cleaning products, detergents, toiletries, toys, upholstery, textiles, plastics are also similarly comprised of a host of toxic substances and chemicals. These compromise the functioning of our bodies. Nena Baker's *The Body Toxic* (2008) illustrates so with clarity. Numerous studies now show how certain chemical compounds in these consumer products have the right molecular configuration to bind into hormone receptor cells in the body, to thereby disrupt normal hormone functioning. Deep, underlying laws that we take for granted are compromised as a result of this and different rhythms as basic as the development of human sexuality are affected as a result. Some common and destructive chemicals in use in common cosmetics include the likes of synthetic musks such as Galaxolide and Tonalide, which are hormone disruptors; Pthalates, another hormone disruptor; Formaldehyde, Dioxane, Hydroquinone, and Parabens, which are carcinogens; amongst a host of other chemicals.

These are manufactured in high quantities, and since they exist in the most common products, create widespread human exposure and environmental degradation (Campaign for Safe Cosmetics, 2010). Another common and widespread metal which is stunningly toxic is lead. A long list of problems has been linked to lead exposure: lowered intelligence, behavior problems, cancer, strokes, high blood pressure, kidney problems, anemia, cavities, and delayed puberty. While lead is a mineral that occurs naturally in our soils, people's activities have caused our exposure to lead to dramatically increase. Levels in our environment are about thousand times what they were a few hundred years ago (Center for Environmental Health Report, 2008). Children are particularly sensitive to lead poisoning. According to the U.S. Department of Health and Human Services, "no safe blood level in children has been determined" (cited in Anderson, 2007). Yet in recent decades, children have been exposed to lead through products that we all use regularly. Lead has been removed from some of these products (gasoline and household paint) but children continue to be exposed to lead in candy, jewelry, vinyl lunchboxes, and other everyday items.

Telecommunication and computer-related products set up their own electromagnetic fields. Since human beings are essentially electromagnetic entities, there is a disturbance and the deep electromagnetic balance that must exist for normal functioning of our bodies is compromised. The ease of availability and the pervasiveness of use of these products similarly compromise the functioning of the human body.

What Fractal Pattern Is Being Displayed by Business Today

Today businesses operate at the vital level. They exist to aggrandize their narrowly defined version of wealth and worth. The result of such operation is that the world, like everything else in it, is viewed as a valid object of exploitation. That is the reason for its existence—to be happily exploited by anything else with the power to do that. The unwritten law is eat or be eaten. This way of being, as we have seen, externalizes costs to other stakeholders, to the environment, and to society in general. The very basis for its current way of operation is destroyed through the current way of operation. Sooner or later the business or the industry has to awaken to the fact that it requires another way of operating. Usually the pressure for change, especially so long as the business continues in its current vital paradigm, is from external stakeholders—those who have been forced to awaken and forced to voice themselves because of the continuous exploitation they are subjected to at one or the other level.

The vital level is an expression of energy but of displaced energy that does not take guidance from a mental light. Such a light would be one of holism and of considering several points of view in the process of decision-making. At the vital level, the decision-making is myopic and self-serving. The thought is overpowered by the sense of preservation and aggrandizement of small self limits.

As a result, a contrary of the implicit impulse behind different industry comes into being. Our connection with the land is replaced by a callous disconnection in which our source of nutrients is progressively stripped away from us. Inherent health is replaced by impulses of constant debilitation that destroy even our ability to self-heal at its very core. Energy is replaced by a dark and poisonous binding chain that has wound itself into all aspects of life, breathing its poisonous fumes as it draws us into the lures of lethargy and self-annihilation. Our very source of material life is polluted and bastardized and becomes a source of material death. Our connection with abundance is replaced by a reality of a lack of abundance as we become slaves to objects that lure us into cycles of destruction. Our very psychology is altered so that our notion of self-worth is now dependent on the number and variety of objects we possess.

So why do we continue down this track? What can we do, practically speaking, to alter these destructive trends? This is where the redesign of stock markets is critical and that is what this book is about.

Before we begin to address this critical issue at its core, we need to become clear on the role stock markets have played in reinforcing trends of destruction. We also need to become clear on what trends we would like to have seen in the place of the ones we observe. This then will launch us better into what may need to be done to not allow our close call with death to fructify but to allow a vivacious affair with life to unquestionably come into its place instead.

4

Stock Market Role

In the last chapter, we had studied disturbing trends that have manifested through the course of the vital-level business-as-usual paradigm. While we did not look into all trends across all industries, we studied trends in representative industries to cover a spectrum that included the food and beverage industry, the agriculture industry, the pharmaceutical industry, the energy industry, the water industry, and the retail industry. We considered the inherent possibility of each of these industries and saw too the play out that is continuing to result in the opposite of these very possibilities. Quite simply, this leaves us with the overarching questions: what role has the stock market played in creating the current manifestation of business operation with its detrimental effects and what role should the stock market play in creating and perpetuating fully sustainable business? In this chapter, we will focus on the first question. Ideally we would like the future of business to approach the vision we canvassed in Chapter 1. We may never get there, but to the extent that we can get closer to that, the world and all our institutions will be better-off.

For, it is nothing short of perturbing as to how ardently we all seem to be engaged in destroying our very bases of life. Few care anymore on the real effects of investments. Housewives and students, let alone that corporate shark whose perspective is in any case twisted out of proportion, talk about the quick bucks they made through trading between preparing meals these days. Perhaps little do they realize that each of those trades is most likely contributing to the slow and sure destruction of civilization.

In this chapter, we will look at stock market trends in some of the industries identified. In particular, we focus on the growth of stock market activity for a leading company or two in that industry and further look at what detrimental environmental, social, and governance practices that money is contributing toward. As a result, what is the massive funding that took place over the last few decades really achieve?

Energy Industry: ExxonMobil

Let us start the examination of the flow of funds generated from stock market into a segment that comprises some of the largest companies as per the Forbes Global 2000 ranking—the oil industry. First of all, it is perhaps fair to say that the creation of the supermajors was facilitated by the vast funds flowing into this sector that allowed mergers and acquisitions to take place. Supermajors are the six largest, non state-owned energy companies. Namely, ExxonMobil (US), Royal Dutch Shell (Netherlands/UK), BP (UK), Chevron Corporation (US), ConocoPhillips (US), Total S.A. (France). The supermajors began to appear in the late 1990s. This is also about the time when stock–market-based funding began to increase for these companies (refer to Figure 4.1, where it can be seen that there is an order of magnitude increase in stock activity for ExxonMobil, for example). Large petroleum companies began to merge, often in an effort to improve economies of scale, hedge against oil price volatility, and reduce large cash reserves through reinvestment (Lehrer, 1998).

As of December 10, 2010, ExxonMobil ranks first among the supermajors in terms of market capitalization, assets, revenue, and profits (Forbes.com, 2011a, 2011b). Figure 4.1 illustrates the incredible rise in stock trading activity, stock price, and consequently market capitalization for ExxonMobil.

As such a corporation receives more funding through the stock market, naturally the question is what kinds of activities does this funding, in part, contribute to. Since public companies of this size have an increasing number of global shareholders, it stands to reason that it needs to be held accountable to a more comprehensive set of global environmental, social, and governance standards. Questionable environmental, social, and governance practices have to be much more carefully monitored and changed

Figure 4.1: ExxonMobil Common Stock

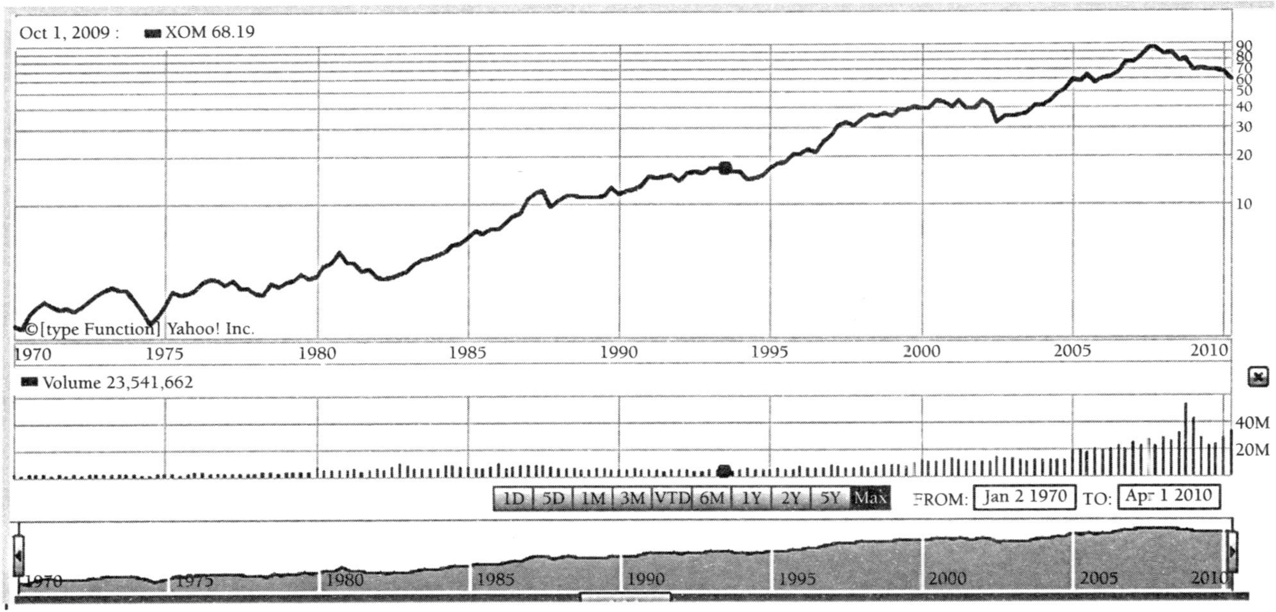

Source: Yahoo! Finance, 2010.

since failure to do this will cause such practices to multiply because of the global influence and leverage available to the company. The following are the controversial environmental, foreign business practice, and human rights practices of ExxonMobil that must be reversed (Wikipedia, 2010m). These are organized chronologically, and one cannot help but notice that there appears to be a correlation between the influx of stock-based funds and the apparent impunity with which ExxonMobil conducts highly questionable vital-centered practices.

- **Oil Spill and Manipulation (1989–2010):** The March 24, 1989, Exxon Valdez oil spill resulted in the discharge of approximately 11 million gallons of oil (240,000 barrels) into Prince William Sound, oiling 1,300 miles of the remote Alaskan coastline. The State of Alaska's Exxon Valdez Oil Spill Trustee Council stated that the spill "is widely considered the number one spill worldwide in terms of damage to the environment" (State of Alaska's Exxon Valdez Oil Spill Trustee, 2010). Exxon was widely criticized for its slow response to cleaning up the disaster. John Devens, the mayor of Valdez, said his community felt betrayed by Exxon's inadequate response to the crisis (Baker, 2008). Exxon later removed the name "Exxon" from its tanker shipping subsidiary and renamed it as "SeaRiver Maritime." The renamed subsidiary, though wholly Exxon-controlled, has a separate corporate charter and board of directors, and the former Exxon Valdez is now the SeaRiver Mediterranean. The renamed tanker is legally owned by a small, stand-alone company which would have minimal ability to pay out on claims in the event of a further accident (Little, 2002). After a trial, a jury ordered Exxon to pay US$5 billion in punitive damages though an appeals court reduced that amount by half. Exxon appealed further, and on June 25, 2008, the United States Supreme Court lowered the amount to US$500 million (*Seattle Times*, 2007).
- **Human Rights Violations (1992–2010):** ExxonMobil is the target of human rights activists for actions taken by the corporation in the Indonesian territory of Aceh. In June 2001, a lawsuit against ExxonMobil was filed in the Federal District Court of the District of Columbia under the Alien Tort Claims Act. The suit alleges that ExxonMobil knowingly assisted human rights violations, including

torture, murder, and rape by employing and providing material support to Indonesian military forces who committed the alleged offenses during civil unrest in Aceh. Human rights complaints involving Exxon's (Exxon and Mobil had not yet merged) relationship with the Indonesian military first arose in 1992; the company denied these accusations and filed a motion to dismiss the suit which was denied in 2008 by a federal judge (O'Reilly, 2008). This was then dismissed in August 2009 by a different federal judge. The dismissal is currently under appeal.

- **Climate Change Crimes (2003–2010):** In 2003, Greenpeace listed Exxon as #1 Climate Criminal. Exxon's alleged crimes include the sabotage of efforts to deal with climate change (Adam, 2008), the fraudulent manipulation of peer reviewed scientific studies and organizations; and misleading and outright lying to the population of the USA, its government officials and the global community in general (*The Australian*, 2010). Further, ExxonMobil has been accused of paying to fuel skepticism of anthropogenic global warming (Union of Concerned Scientists, 2007). According to *The Guardian*, ExxonMobil has funded, among other groups skeptical of global warming, the Competitive Enterprise Institute, George C. Marshall Institute, Heartland Institute, Congress on Racial Equality, TechCentralStation.com, and International Policy Network (Adam, 2006).
- **Global Corruption (2003–2010):** Investigative reporting by *Forbes* Magazine raised questions about ExxonMobil's dealings with the leaders of oil-rich nations. ExxonMobil controls concessions covering 11 million acres (44,500 km^2) off the coast of Angola that holds an estimated 7.5 billion barrels (1.2 km^3) of crude oil (Wikipedia, 2010m; Foley & Lardner, LLP, 2003). Further, in March 2003, James Giffen of the Mercator Corporation was indicted, accused of bribing President Nursultan Nazarbayev of Kazakhstan with US$78 million to help ExxonMobil win a 25 percent share of the Tengiz oil field, the third largest in the world. On April 2, 2003, former Mobil executive, J. Bryan Williams was indicted on tax charges relating to this same transaction. The case is the largest under the Foreign Corrupt Practices Act. This series of events is depicted in the film *Syriana* (Foley & Lardner, LLP, 2003).

- **Airborne Pollution (2005–2010):** The Political Economy Research Institute ranks ExxonMobil sixth among corporations emitting airborne pollutants in the US. The ranking is based on the quantity (15.5 million pounds in 2005) and toxicity of the emissions (PERI, 2010).
- **Lack of Appropriate R&D (2005–2010):** In 2005, ExxonMobil had committed less than 1 percent of their profits towards researching alternative energy (Mufson, 2008) which is less than other leading oil companies (The Heat is Online, 2006).

The question is why should public money be used to fund a corporation that indulges in such practices as above? Is it not clear that continued funding of organizations engaged in such practices is in fact slowly but surely destroying the very bases of civilization? Consequently, what can be done to reverse this? To what degree can the stock market be redesigned to alter destructive behavior? That is the focus of this book.

Agriculture: Monsanto Company

The Monsanto Company is a US-based multinational agricultural biotechnology corporation. It is the world's leading producer of the herbicide glyphosate, marketed as "Roundup." Monsanto is also the leading producer of the genetically engineered (GE) seed. It is headquartered in Creve Coeur, Missouri. Monsanto has a market capitalization of US$26.33B.

Since it too has been the recipient of major funds through the stock market, as Figure 4.2 indicates, questionable practices that have likely continued because of increased money power need to be reversed. Many of these practices are marked by arrogance (Wikipedia, 2010p). Practices include poisoning through superfund sites, destruction of farming society, destructive company regulatory policies, artificial seed dependency, cancer crimes, GE induced poisoning, coercion of democracy, amongst others. These too are organized chronologically and one cannot again help but conclude that the level of vital-level arrogance is correlated with increase in money power as indicated by the increased company stock-market activity in Figure 4.1.

Figure 4.2: Monsanto Common Stock

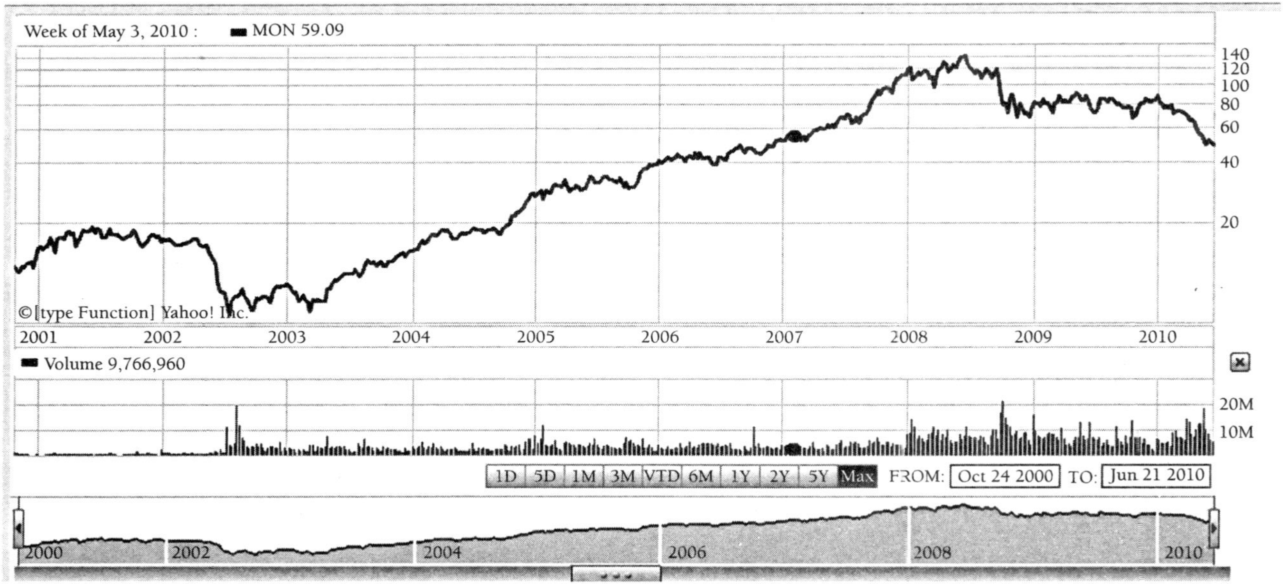

Source: Yahoo! Finance, 2010.

- **Poisoning through Superfund Sites (1960s–2010):** According to an anonymous 2001 document obtained by the Center for Public Integrity (2001), Monsanto has been identified by the US Environmental Protection Agency (EPA) as being a "potentially responsible party" for 56 contaminated sites (superfund sites) in the US. Monsanto has been sued, and has settled, multiple times for damaging the health of its employees or residents near its superfund sites through pollution and poisoning (Grunwald, 2002).
- **Destruction of Farming Society (1995 [at least]–2010):** Since the mid-1990s, Monsanto has sued some 150 individual US farmers for patent infringement in connection with its genetically engineered seed (Monsanto, 2010). The usual claim involves violation of a technology agreement that prohibits farmers from saving seed from one season's crop to plant the next, a common farming practice (Sierra Club of/du Canada, 2010) . One farmer received an eight-month prison sentence for violating a court order to destroy seeds (Shinkle, 2003). "Farmer who lied in dispute with Monsanto will go to prison" (Shinkle, 2003), in addition to having to pay damages, when a Monsanto case turned into a criminal prosecution (Meek, 2006).
- **Destructive Company Regulatory Policy (1998–2010):** Phil Angell, Monsanto's director of corporate communications (referring to the US Food and Drug Administration), explained the company's regulatory philosophy to Michael Pollan in 1998: "Monsanto should not have to vouchsafe the safety of biotech food. Our interest is in selling as much of it as possible. Assuring its safety is FDA's job" (Pollan, 1998).
- **Artificial Seed Dependency (1999 [at least]–2010):** In June 2007, Monsanto acquired Delta & Pine Land Company, a company that had patented a seed technology nicknamed Terminators. This technology, which was never known to have been used commercially, produces plants that have sterile seeds so they do not flower or grow fruit after the initial planting. This prevents the spread of those seeds into the wild; however, it also requires customers to repurchase seed for every planting in which they use Terminator seed varieties. Farmers who do not use a Terminator seed could also be affected by his neighboring farmer that does through natural pollination.

In recent years, widespread opposition from environmental organizations and farmer associations has grown, mainly out of the concerns that hypothetical seeds using this technology could increase farmers' dependency on seed suppliers. Despite the fact that in 1999, Monsanto pledged not to commercialize Terminator technology (Vidal, 1999), Delta Vice President, Harry Collins, declared at the time in a press interview in the Agra/Industrial Biotechnology Legal Letter, "We've continued right on with work on the Technology Protection System (TPS or Terminator). We never really slowed down. We're on target, moving ahead to commercialize it. We never really backed off" (Warwick, 2000).

- **Cancer Crimes (2000 [and before]–2010):** Monsanto sparked controversy with the introduction of Bovine somatotropin, abbreviated as rBST and commonly known as rBGH. It is a synthetic hormone that is injected into cows to increase milk production. IGF-1 is a hormone stimulated by rBGH in the cow's blood stream, which is directly responsible for the increase in milk production. IGF-1 is a natural hormone found in the milk of both humans and cows causing the quick growth of infants. Though this IGF-1 occurs naturally in mothers' milk to be fed to their infants, it produces adverse effects in non-infants, behaving as a cancer accelerator in adults and non-infants; this biologically active hormone is associated with breast cancer (correlation shown in premenopausal women) (Warwick, 2000).
- **GM Induced Poisoning (2009 [and before]–2010):** Much of Monsanto's seed products are specifically genetically modified, to make them resistant to Monsanto produced agricultural chemicals such as "Roundup" herbicide. In a study published in the *International Journal of Biological Sciences*, researchers applied a different statistical analysis on raw data obtained from Monsanto and concluded that these GM corn (maize) varieties induced a state of hepatorenal toxicity. They suggested that the presence of the new pesticides associated with the inserted genes were responsible, although the possibility that this could be due to a mutation during the transformation process was not excluded (De Vendômois et al., 2009).

- **Coercion of Democracy (2003 [at least]–2010):** In 2003, Monsanto sued Oakhurst Dairy in Maine for advertising that its milk products did not come from cows treated with bovine growth hormone, claiming that such advertising hurt its business. The president of Oakhurst responded by saying, "We ought to have the right to let people know what is and is not in our milk" (*Democracy Now*, 2003).

Clearly such practices as pursued by Monsanto are of even a different flavor than those pursued by ExxonMobil. There is a degree of passivity, almost, in ExxonMobil's business in that one can see a definite end dictated by peak-oil. It is a slave to pumping and distributing a finite resource from the earth and its days are numbered. In the case of Monsanto, there appears to be a much higher degree of vital-level arrogance. Monsanto is playing a game of patenting slightly altered natural processes that occur in nature. There is no end to that, and it is not inconceivable from its practices that rather than planet Earth, it would perhaps like to see a planet Monsanto in which it is the owner of all natural processes and all are forever paying it rent to drink, eat, and soon even to breathe. How this is different from the most dangerous isms the world has ever experienced, is the question to be asked. Why an organization of such a type should continue to receive public funding is the second question. Clearly the stock market must be redesigned to more intelligently distribute funds.

Pharmaceuticals: Pfizer

Pfizer Incorporated is a pharmaceutical company, ranking number one in sales in the world. The company is based in New York City with its research headquarters in Groton, Connecticut. Like ExxonMobil and Monsanto, it too has been a recipient of major funding through the stock market as Figure 4.3 suggests.

The question, therefore, is what kinds of questionable environmental, social, and governance practices has Pfizer been involved in (Wikipedia, 2010q). Some of these practices include questionable acquisition strategies, unapproved human testing, excessive environmental emissions, being too big to fail, illegal marketing of drugs which are illustrated chronologically:

Figure 4.3: Pfizer Common Stock

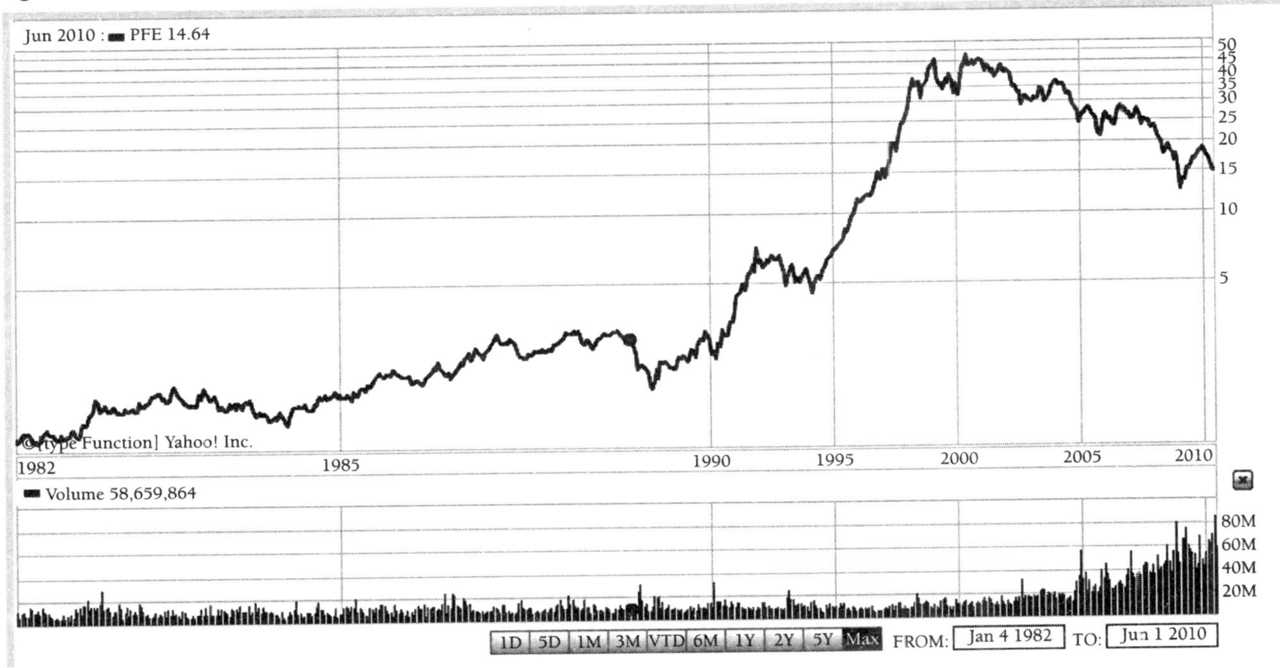

Source: Yahoo! Finance, 2010.

- **Questionable Acquisition Strategy (1960s–2010):** Pfizer acquired Quigley in 1968 and the division sold asbestos-containing insulation products until the early 1970s. Asbestos victims and Pfizer have been negotiating a settlement deal which calls for Pfizer to pay US$430 million to 80 percent of existing plaintiffs. It will also place an additional US$535 million into an asbestos settlement trust that will compensate future plaintiffs as well as the remaining 20 percent of current plaintiffs with claims against Pfizer and Quigley. Further, Pfizer purchased Shiley in 1979 at the onset of its Convexo–Concave valve ordeal, involving the Bjork–Shiley heart valve. Approximately 500 people died when defective valves failed and, in 1994, the US ruled against Pfizer for US$200 million (Blackstone, 2005).
- **Unapproved Human Testing (1996 [and before]–2010):** In 1996, an outbreak of measles, cholera, and bacterial meningitis occurred in Nigeria. Pfizer representatives traveled to Kano, Nigeria, to administer an experimental antibiotic, trovafloxacin, to approximately 200 children. Local Kano officials report that more than 50 children died in the experiment while many others developed mental and physical deformities (Murray, 2007). In 2001, families of the children as well as the governments of Kano and Nigeria, filed lawsuits regarding the treatment (BBC News, 2001). Representing the government was Babatunde Irukera. According to the lawsuits, Pfizer administered the trovafloxacin (now marketed as Trovan) without parental consent. The lawsuits also accuse Pfizer of using the outbreak to perform unapproved human testing as well as allegedly under-dosing a control group being treated with traditional antibiotics in order to skew the results of the trial in favor of Trovan. Pfizer denied these claims, and subsequently, produced an approval letter for testing from the Nigerian Ethics Committee. The Nigerian government insisted that it was a fake and a panel of Nigerian medical experts agreed that the letter had been concocted and backdated by the company's lead researcher in Kano. They went on to conclude that Pfizer never obtained authorization from the Nigerian government to give the unproven drug to children and infants (Stephens, 2006).

- **Environmental Emissions (2005 [and before]–2010):** According to the EPA, Pfizer is among the top ten companies in America with the most numerous emissions sources (KLD, 2011).
- **Too Big to Nail (2007–2010):** CNN reported that Pharmacia & Upjohn, not Pfizer itself, pleaded guilty because prosecutors thought Pfizer was "too big to nail." Companies convicted of major health-care fraud are automatically barred from billing Medicare and Medicaid for their products. Prosecutors feared that Pfizer would collapse if it pleaded guilty and felt that the risk of harm to patients was too great. A CNN investigation revealed that Pharmacia & Upjohn is little more than a shell corporation Pfizer uses to plead guilty; it was first created in 2007 as the defendant in a kickback case (Griffin and Segal, 2010).
- **Lobbying Health Care Reform (2009 [and before]–Current):** Pfizer is one of the single largest lobbying interests in the US politics. For example, in the first 9 months of 2009, Pfizer spent over US$16.3 million on lobbying the US congressional lawmakers, making them the sixth largest lobbying interest in the US (following Pharmaceutical Research and Manufacturers of America [PhRMA], which ranked fourth but also represents many of their interests). A spokeswoman for Pfizer said the company "wanted to make sure our voice is heard in this conversation" in regards to the companies expenditure of US$25 million in 2010 to lobby health-care reform (Steinbrook, 2009).
- **Illegal Marketing of Drugs (2009 [and before]–2010):** In September 2009, the United States Department of Justice announced that Pfizer had agreed to pay US$2.3 billion to settle civil and criminal allegations that it had illegally marketed four drugs: Bextra, Geodon, Zyvox, and Lyrica "with the intent to defraud or mislead" by promoting the drugs for non-approved uses. This marks Pfizer's fourth such settlement in a decade (Harris, 2009). Further, health insurance company Blue Cross Blue Shield (BCBS) filed a lawsuit against Pfizer for reportedly illegally marketing their drugs Bextra, Geodon, and Lyrica. BCBS has reported that Pfizer used "kickbacks" and wrongly persuaded doctors to prescribe the drugs (Edwards, 2010). FiercePharma reported that,

> According to the suit, the drugmaker not only handed out those "misleading" materials on off-label uses, but sent doctors on Caribbean junkets and paid them US$2,000 honoraria in return for their listening to lectures about Bextra. More than 5,000 health-care professionals were entertained at meetings in Bahamas, Virgin Islands and across the U.S., the suit alleges. (Staton, 2010)

As with the other corporations reviewed, Pfizer too has received a huge inflow of funds from the stock market. This has in effect made it "too big to nail" and offered it immunity against very questionable practices. If stock market mechanisms are to remain the same, then there is no reason why Pfizer, and many other companies like it, should not become too big to fail and nail. There is tremendous moral hazard associated with such a state, and at the very least, it reinforces the destructive vital-level dynamics. It is, therefore, a necessity that the stock market be redesigned so that the size of a corporation is more intelligently determined.

Retail: Wal-Mart

Wal-Mart Stores, Inc. is an American public corporation that runs a chain of large discount department stores and a chain of warehouse stores. In 2010, it was the world's largest public corporation by revenue, according to the Forbes Global 2000 for that year. Wal-Mart has 8,500 stores in 15 countries with 55 different names (Daniel, 2010). The company operates under its own name in the US including the 50 states. It also operates under its own name in Puerto Rico. Wal-Mart operates in Mexico as Walmex, in the UK as Asda ("Asda Wal-Mart" in some branches), in Japan as Seiyu, and in India as Best Price. It has wholly owned operations in Argentina, Brazil, and Canada.

Wal-Mart's ability to expand globally is in no small measure determined by the popularity of its stock as indicated in Figure 4.4.

Wal-Mart's low-price paradigm and huge customer base has huge effects on the planet. Consider USA itself. Each week, about 100 million customers, nearly one-third of the US population, visit Wal-Mart's US stores (Zimmerman and Hudson, 2006) . Wal-Mart customers give low prices as the most important reason for shopping there, reflecting the "Low prices, always" advertising slogan that Wal-Mart used from 1962 until 2006 (Barbaro, 2007).

Figure 4.4: Wal-Mart Common Stock

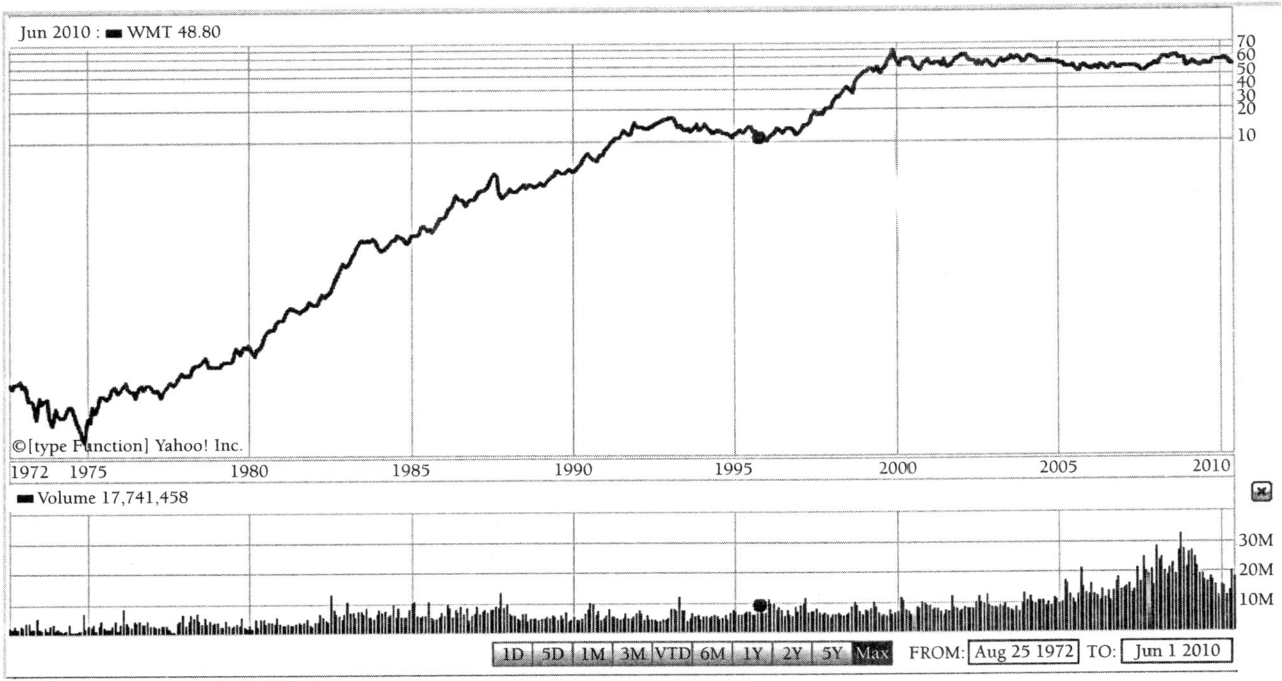

Source: Yahoo! Finance, 2010.

Wal-Mart's success to date has been driven by consumer desire for an increasing array of diverse product offered at low prices. Wal-Mart leverages its tightly managed global supply chain to offer just such a mix. But what are the hidden costs of this equation? Insight into this is gained by dwelling further on the nature of the driver behind Wal-Mart's success (Malik, 2009a):

1. This driver is consumer desire, a vital-level dynamic. Such a dynamic seeks for satisfaction of its want immediately without considering the factors that have allowed the product to be supplied in such a manner. The cost, hence, tends toward a marginalization of all longer term and more sustainable solutions.
2. As this dynamic becomes more real, there is a ripple effect and the vital-level dynamic is reinforced at the local, national, and global levels for a number of related fractals. These include the consumer-fractal, the business-fractal, the supply-chain fractal, the culture-fractal, and the society-fractal. In other words, the progressive realities possible to each of these entities are stalled, resulting in a slew of additional costs. Cycles of conspicuous consumerism, of business-as-usual, of questionable supply chains, of stalled culture, and of misplaced society, respectively, are reinforced. To illustrate some of these:

    a) Vital-level consumer desire reinforces and strengthens vital-level global supply chains. Such vital-level supply chains often operate at suboptimal levels increasing the social and environmental costs to humanity in their wake. These costs remain unfactored in the final price of the product and are borne by the locality that has come into contact with the ever-expanding supply chain. Ironically, as the companies managing such supply chains show increasing profits, they are rewarded by investors, and the very dynamic that it would make most sense to move away from is given additional impetus to continue with its questionable effects.
    b) As local communities become part of these supply chains, their dependence on continuing to be a part of the supply chain increases, and a balanced investment in their own communities often decreases. As a result, local and, hence, regional

development at multiple levels is compromised, and then all must become part of the global business machinery in order to survive. There are, hence, huge costs at the community and regional levels.

c) The culture-fractal and the society-fractal are also hence compromised, and instead of growing to express their own uniqueness and possibilities, outcomes of journeying to the mental phase in their own trajectories continually circle at a standardized level because the basis of creativity has been marginalized by assimilation into a strong global machinery.

3. By the nature of the unrefined vital consciousness, the costs to humanity of remaining at that level increase much faster than if corresponding shifts were made to the mental levels of the respective fractals. Recall that mental-level dynamics are by their very nature more inclusive of a wider set of issues and, hence, more balanced in resulting action. Consideration of such balance has a longer-term positive effect that lowers hidden costs to humanity. By failing to shift to this level, there are rapidly escalating opportunity costs.

Some of the dynamics pointed to are reinforced by the following (Wikipedia, 2010v):

- **Aggressive Vital-level Expansion:** 'In 2006, Wal-Mart took steps to expand its US customer base, announcing a modification in its US stores from a "one-size-fits-all" merchandising strategy to one designed to "reflect each of six demographic groups—African-Americans, the affluent, empty-nesters, Hispanics, suburbanites and rural residents" (Associated Press, 2006). Around six months later, it unveiled a new slogan: "Saving people money so they can live better lives." This reflects the three main groups into which Wal-Mart categorizes its 200 million customers: "brand aspirationals" (people with low incomes who are obsessed with names like KitchenAid), "price-sensitive affluents" (wealthier shoppers who love deals), and "value-price shoppers" (people who like low prices and cannot afford much more) (Barbaro, 2007).'

- **Negative Impact of Community Economics:** 'Kenneth Stone, Professor of Economics at Iowa State University, in a paper published in Farm Foundation in 1997, found that some small towns can lose almost half of their retail trade within 10 years of a Wal-Mart store opening (Stone, 1997). Further, a Loyola University Chicago study suggested that the impact a Wal-Mart store has on a local business is correlated to its distance from that store. The leader of that study admits that this factor is stronger in smaller towns and does not apply to more urban areas saying "It'd be so tough to nail down what's up with Wal-Mart" (Mui, 2008). Another study found Wal-Mart's entry into a new market has a profound impact on its retail competition. When a Wal-Mart opens in a new market, median sales drop by 40 percent at similar high-volume stores, by 17 percent at supermarkets and by 6 percent at drugstores, according to a June 2009 study by researchers at several universities and led by the Tuck School of Business at Dartmouth College (Wernau, 2010). Dr Raj Patel, author of *Stuffed and Starved: Markets, Power and the Hidden Battle for the World Food System* (2008), claims that a study in Nebraska looked at two different Wal-Marts, the first of which had just arrived and "was in the process of driving everyone else out of business but, to do that, they cut their prices to the bone, very, very low prices." In the other Wal-Mart, "they had successfully destroyed the local economy, there was a sort of economic crater with Wal-Mart in the middle; and, in that community, the prices were 17 per cent higher" (Patel, 2007).'
- **Community Opposition to Wal-Mart:** 'When Wal-Mart plans new store locations, activists sometimes oppose the new store and attempt to block its construction. Opponents to the new Wal-Mart cite concerns such as traffic congestion, environment problems, public safety, absentee landlordism, bad public relations, low wages and benefits, and predatory pricing. Opposition sometimes includes protest marches by competitors, informed citizens, activists, labor unions, and religious groups. In some instances, activists demonstrated opposition by causing property damage to store buildings or by creating bomb scares. Some city councils have denied permits to developers if they plan to include a Wal-Mart in their project. Those who defend Wal-Mart cite consumer choice and supposed

overall benefits to the economy and object to bringing the issue into the political arena (Wikipedia, 2010h).'

- **Negative Wal-Mart Labor Practices:** 'In January 2004, *The New York Times* reported on an internal Wal-Mart audit conducted in July 2000, which examined one week's time-clock records for roughly 25,000 employees. According to it, the audit, "pointed to extensive violations of child-labor laws and state regulations requiring time for breaks and meals," including 1,371 instances of minors working too late, during school hours, or for too many hours in a day. There were 60,767 missed breaks and 15,705 lost meal times. Wal-Mart's vice president for communications responded that company auditors had determined that the methodology used was flawed and the company "did not respond to it in any way internally" (Greenhouse, 2004).'

Financial Services: Citigroup

Citigroup Inc. is a major American financial services company based in New York City. Citigroup was formed from one of the world's largest mergers in history by combining the banking giant Citicorp and financial conglomerate Travelers Group in 1998. Citigroup Inc. has the world's largest financial services network, spanning 140 countries with approximately 16,000 offices worldwide. The company employs approximately 260,000 staff around the world and holds over 200 million customer accounts in more than 140 countries. See Figure 4.5 for Citigroup's stock trends.

Controversies (Wikipedia, 2010e) that surround Citigroup include money laundering, deceiving investors with biased research, manipulation and disruption of European Bond Market, customer account theft, and gross and continued mismanagement of its business.

- **Money Laundering (1998):** 'In 1998, the General Accounting Office issued a report critical of Citibank's handling of funds received from Raul Salinas de Gortari, the brother of Carlos Salinas, the former president of Mexico. The report, titled "Raul Salinas, Citibank and Alleged Money Laundering," indicated that Citibank facilitated the transfer of millions of dollars through complex financial transactions

Figure 4.5: Citigroup Common Stock

Source: Yahoo! Finance, 2010.

to hide the paper trail of funds. The report also indicated that Citibank took on Raul Salinas as a client even though they did not make a thorough inquiry as to how he made his fortune (Day, 1998).'

- **Deceiving Investors with Biased Research (2002–2003)**: 'In December 2002, Citigroup paid fines totaling US$400 million, with the amount split between the states and the federal government. The fines were part of a settlement involving charges that 10 banks, including Citigroup, deceived investors with biased research. The total settlement with the 10 banks was US$1.4 billion. The settlement required that the banks separate investment banking from research and ban any allocation of IPO (Initial Public Offering) shares (Beltran, 2002). Further, Citigroup paid out over US$3 billion in fines and legal settlements for their role in financing Enron Corporation, which collapsed amid a financial scandal in 2001. In 2003, Citigroup paid US$145 million in fines and penalties to settle claims by the Securities and Exchange Commission and the Manhattan district attorney's office. In 2005, Citigroup paid US$2 billion to settle a lawsuit filed by investors in Enron (Johnson, 2005).'
- **Disruption/Manipulation of European Bond Market (2004–2007)**: 'Citigroup was criticized for disrupting the European Bond Market by rapidly selling 11 billion worth of bonds on August 2, 2004, on the MTS Group trading platform, driving down the price and then buying it back at cheaper prices (*EuroWeek*, 2004). Further, in November 2007, it became public that the Citigroup is heavily involved in the Terra Securities scandal, which involved investments by eight municipalities of Norway in various hedge funds in the US bond market (Landler, 2007). The funds were sold by Terra Securities ASA to the municipalities while the products were delivered by Citigroup. Terra Securities ASA filed for bankruptcy November 28, 2007, the day after they received a letter from The Financial Supervisory Authority of Norway announcing the withdrawal of permissions to operate (Kredittilsynet, 2007). The same letter also stated, "The Supervisory Authority contends that Citigroup's presentation, as well as the presentation from Terra Securities ASA, appears insufficient and misleading because central elements like information about potential extra payments and the size of these are omitted."'

- **Customer Account Theft (2008):** 'On August 26, 2008, it was announced that Citigroup agreed to pay nearly US$18 million in refunds and fines to settle accusations by California Attorney General Jerry Brown that it wrongly took funds from the accounts of credit card customers. Citigroup would pay US$14 million of restitution to roughly 53,000 customers nationwide. A three-year investigation found that Citigroup from 1992 to 2003 used an improper computerized "sweep" feature to move positive balances from card accounts into the bank's general fund without telling cardholders. Brown said in a statement that Citigroup "knowingly stole from its customers, mostly poor people and the recently deceased, when it designed and implemented the sweeps ... When a whistleblower uncovered the scam and brought it to his superiors, they buried the information and continued the illegal practice" (Stempel, 2008).'
- **Gross and Continued Mismanagement of Business (2008 [and earlier]):** 'On November 24, 2008, the US government announced a massive bailout of Citigroup, designed to rescue the company from bankruptcy while giving the government a major say in its operations. The Treasury will provide another US$20 billion in Troubled Asset Relief Program (TARP) funds in addition to US$25 billion given in October. The Treasury Department, the Federal Reserve, and the Federal Deposit Insurance Corporation (FDIC) will cover 90 percent of the losses on its US$335 billion portfolio after Citigroup absorbs the first US$29 billion in losses. As the subprime mortgage crisis began to unfold, heavy exposure to toxic mortgages in the forms of collateralized debt obligation (CDO) compounded by poor risk management led the company into serious trouble. Further, according to New York Attorney General, Andrew Cuomo, and as reported by the *Wall Street Journal*, after having received its US$45 billion TARP bailout in late 2008, Citigroup paid hundreds of millions of dollars in bonuses to more than 1,038 of its employees. This included 738 employees each receiving US$1 million in bonuses, 176 employees each receiving US$2 million bonuses, 124 each receiving US$3 million in bonuses, and 143 each receiving bonuses of US$4 million to more than US$10 million (Grocer, 2009).'

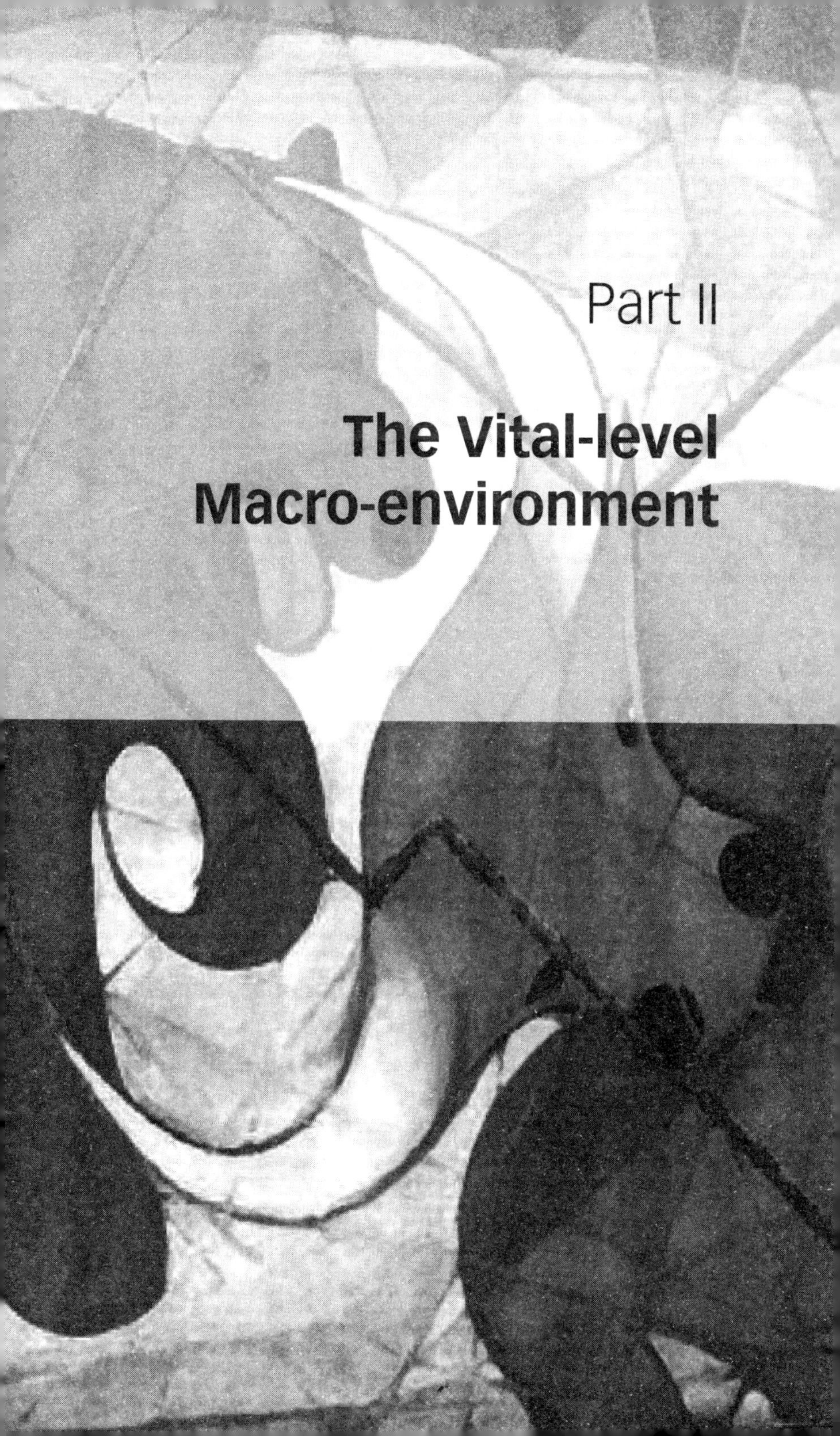

Part II

The Vital-level Macro-environment

5

Evolution of the Macro-environment

In examining corporate funding over the last couple of decades one can see the massive increase in share trading volume. Figure 5.1 illustrates this. From a global level of US$55 trillion in 2000, the volume has increased to US$120 trillion in 2006. It is no wonder that that massive increase resulted in the global financial crises. This is much like massive flows of water being forced into pipes and reservoirs that are not quite ready for that flow. The pipes and reservoirs were made for another reason: to facilitate a predictable, efficient market type, rise in funding. The rise in funding, as the previous chapter's analyses and Figure 5.1 in indicates, has been anything but gradual. Stoked by the vital-dynamic of making it rich in the short term, often at any cost, the source of funding from would-be millionaires has increased dramatically.

But this rise has not occurred in a vacuum. The expectation and the possibility of such an outcome has been built over decades. John Authers, in his insightful book, *The Fearful Rise of Markets* (2010), has traced the milestones that have made such a reality possible.

Starting from 1954, in the US stock market recovery from the Great Crash, post-Depression regulation forced commercial banks to be covered by deposit insurance. Further, commercial banks were barred from investment banking. Fixed exchange rates were linked to gold under Bretton Woods. There was a clear division in the financial playing field with banks dominating finance and investment dominated by individuals using their own money. As Authers reinforces, mainstream investors had

Figure 5.1: Evolution of Share Trading Volume: 2000–2009 (US$ billion)

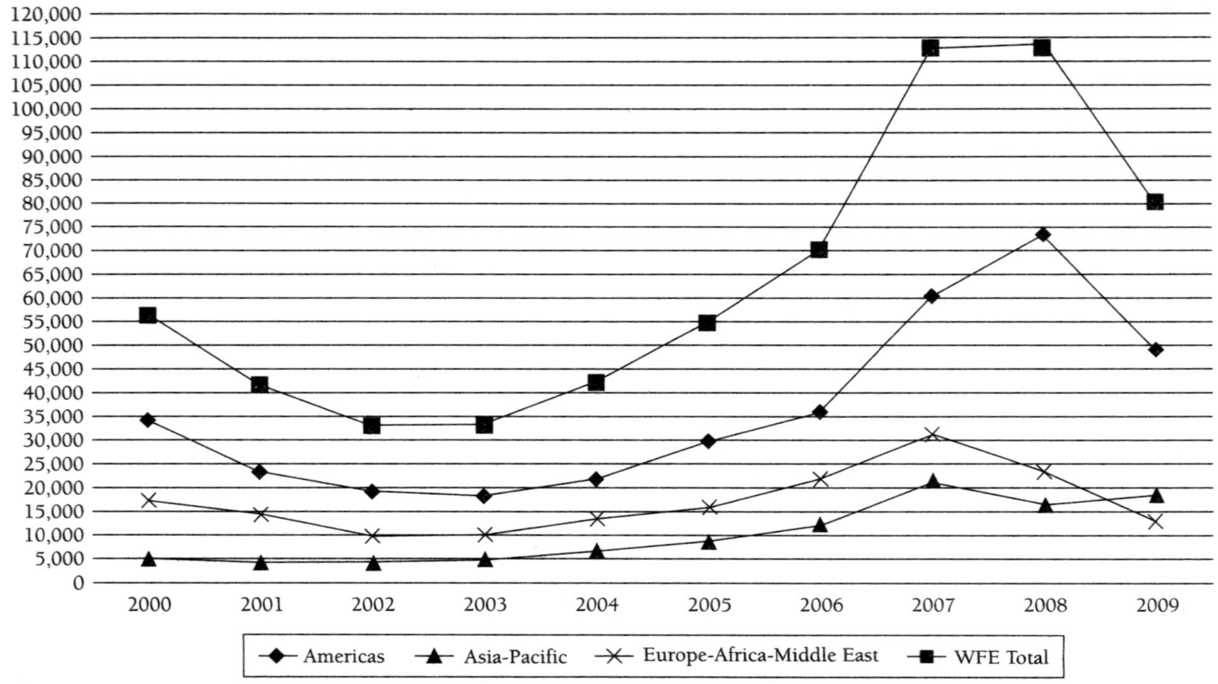

Source: World Federation of Exchanges, 2010.

no access to investing in commodities, foreign exchange, credit default risk, or emerging markets. However, all these conditions changed over the next 50 years to create the conditions for unrelated markets to overheat and move as a synchronized bubble.

Another way to look at this is to equate each bubble and the global synchronized bubble as similar to atomic bombs. At its basis, the atomic bomb breaks the bonds at the atomic level to destroy the fabric of matter-based development. When atoms are split, then atom cannot combine with atom to form molecule. Molecule cannot combine with molecule, and therefore, the entire basis of creation is toppled. In this way of seeing, the atomic bomb really helps us to understand the effect of modern-day finance. For just in the case of the action of an atomic bomb, where complex matter is reduced to simple denominations of it, in modern-day finance, all value and development is reduced to a simple denominator in which value and development effectively lose their meaning. When completely unrelated markets that have a different meaning for existing begin to synchronize their movements, it means that the meaning, the value, the raison d'être has been stripped away and something baser, of less value has become the means for moving those markets. In effect, those markets have been standardized. And the very fact that today the movement of even what should be fundamentally different markets—such as emerging markets on the one hand and developed markets on the other—move in synchronized manner means that money is not being used to develop the market in accordance with the opportunities and challenges there, as it should be, but is being used to develop something entirely different—the myopic and selfish need of an even distant and completely indifferent speculator.

This has to be the case since speculators do not care how they are making money. They just care that they do. Since money is the end result or the common denominator, it is immaterial whether that money comes from the construction or destruction of culture and civilization. It is immaterial if they are supporting the funding of the social destruction of an innocent people so long as a multinational now has access to raw materials it may need. So long as they pocket money in the end, it is irrelevant if this is done through the destruction of complex ecosystems such as rain forests, wetlands, marshes that provide numerous and irreplaceable ecosystem services. In the atomic bomb analogy, this is like reducing beautiful scenery and profound architecture to a coarser and valueless denominator of itself by breaking the bonds that hold matter together and then imagining that we have gotten richer because now we have the stream of particles or other such denominators from which all is created, in our possession. If this were true, then there would be value in destroying everything with atomic bombs. This is clearly not true. The basis of modern-day finance is therefore perverse and it is necessary to alter it immediately. Let me reemphasize: it is perverse because the very reason that money exists, to engender beautiful creation, is being reversed, and the beautiful creation that should be the end has now become the means to amass the intermediary—money—whose meaning is, in the final analyses, lost when it does not support meaningful creation.

Financial dashboards and metrics that are tracked today are standardized to meaningless indicators. Consider the consolidated statistic reported by the World Federation of Exchanges (Table 5.1):

Table 5.1: Twenty Major Stock Exchanges*

Economy	*Stock exchange*	*Trade value (US$ billions)*	*Market capitalization (US$ billions)*
United States	New York Stock Exchange	17,521	11,838
Japan	Tokyo Stock Exchange	3,704	3,306
United States	NASDAQ	13,608	3,239
Europe	Euronext	1,935	2,869
United Kingdom	London Stock Exchange	1,772	2,796
China	Shanghai Stock Exchange	5,056	2,705
Hong Kong	Hong Kong Stock Exchange	1,416	2,305
Canada	Toronto Stock Exchange	1,245	1,677
Spain	BME Spanish Exchanges	1,259	1,435
Brazil	BM&F Bovespa	645	1,337
India	Bombay Stock Exchange	264	1,307
Germany	Deutsche Börse	1,517	1,292
Australia	Australian Securities Exchange	799	1,225
India	National Stock Exchange of India	792	1,225
Switzerland	SIX Swiss Exchange	740	1,065
China	Shenzhen Stock Exchange	2,772	868
Korea	Korea Exchange	1,570	835
Nordic Countries	NASDAQ OMX Nordic Exchange	697	817
South Africa	JSE Limited	271	799
Taiwan	Taiwan Stock Exchange	905	658
Italy	Borsa Italiana	948	656

Source: World Federation of Exchanges.
Note: *Year ended December 31, 2009.

What is the value in knowing the trade value and market capitalization of the global stock exchanges unless we can also see how this money is actually being used? What are companies and the industry doing with the money, and what real value of creation and what costs of destruction are being incurred because of these flows of funds? This is what needs to be tracked, and this is what needs to influence potential investors to invest or not. But we will come back to this critical theme in a later chapter.

Such indicators that are currently being tracked give us the impression that all is hail and hearty and that world development is proceeding in a completely sustainable way. Consider this typical article by Reuters (2007) on the eve of the global crash that paints a picture of solid health and financial well-being:

Global stock values top $50 trln: industry data

LONDON | Wed Mar 21, 2007 7:57am EDT

(Reuters)—The value of companies listed on global stock markets rose to a more than $50 trillion record in January, after jumping by almost a third in the past year, according to data from the World Federation of Exchanges.

The global trade association for stock exchanges said the total market capitalization of companies listed on its 54 member bourses reached $51.225 trillion at the end of January, up from $49.924 trillion a month before.

By comparison, world gross domestic product was around $44 trillion in 2005, according to the International Monetary Fund.

The value of global stocks was some 31.8 percent higher in U.S. dollar terms than a year earlier, while gains in local currency terms were a still-healthy 20.2 percent, WFE said on its Website.

Market performance drove most of the gains, with global stocks enjoying a spectacular run in 2006 and into January.

WFE members weighted by market capitalization rose an average 19.1 percent in local currency terms in 2006 and 23.8 percent in U.S. dollar terms.

Global stocks tumbled at the end of February and into March, with MSCI's All Country World Index, MSCIWD, shedding almost 7 percent, but the index has since recouped around half that loss.

> The value of shares traded on exchanges is also trending higher, with nearly $7 trillion in stocks changing hands in January compared with average 2006 monthly turnover of $5.8 trillion.
>
> However, the scale of stock market trading is still dwarfed by activity in foreign exchange markets, where turnover is well in excess of $2 trillion per day and is forecast to rise to $3 trillion a day this year.

It is clear that a different set of developmental metrics need to be tracked. But it is also clear that these metrics need to factor in at the time of the very act of trading itself and become filters by which trades are allowed or not. This will be discussed in more detail subsequently.

But let us go back to Auther's time line to examine how such atomic bomb like conditions where value is so easily destroyed through modern-day trading and finance came into being in the first place. In 1962, for the first time, markets were now driven by people using other people's money. This was a huge departure from the norm of individuals investing their own money. This departure was facilitated by the launch of funds such as Fidelity's Magellan Fund and increased the appetite for risk taking since it was always someone else's money at stake. Further, such funds managers were paid a percentage of assets they managed and judged against their peers, which had the perverse effect of causing funds to move in herds, thereby creating the foundation for a massive standardization in investment and the disastrous atomic bomb like effects.

For money always then sought out the same destination regardless of whether money was needed there or not and regardless of whether the target hot-spot was even able to effectively and meaningfully assimilate such increased flows of funds. Such standardization with their meaningless flows is one of the prime reasons that bubbles are created and consequently burst. The herd mentality was further exacerbated by the rise of independent ranking organizations that started publishing league tables comparing fund's short-term performance. This also had the effect of beginning to orient the market toward the short term as opposed to the more important and sustainable long-term.

In 1969, the first money market fund was created. In effect, what this meant was that capital markets began to strip banks of many core functions. Regulations that had been created to uphold people's wealth was in effect marginalized. For money market funds did not require deposit insurance. Decisions to lend money that had a higher level of due diligence when conducted by bank's lending officers were now being made by markets that had a different incentive to operate. Money market funds even began issuing checkbooks. As a result, not only were inbuilt mechanisms to keep the irrational flow of funds in check removed but to survive, banks themselves now had to seek out riskier lines of business. The move from a physical orientation or mind-set where yesterday's world must be reinforced to a vital orientation or mind-set where energetic initiatives, not necessarily ordered by a sense of longer-term sustainability, were commonplace and often at loggerheads with one another, was thus being surely put in place.

But the lynchpin, the support stone of the old arch of financial operation, was surely removed in 1971 when the gold standard was exited. Gold is an inert metal that does not lose its luster over time. Further, only 20-cubic meters of gold have been mined through human history (World Gold Council, 2010). This is the consummate symbol of the physical phase of financial evolution; physical implying that the world and its laws are fixed, determined by what the eye can see. Under the Bretton Woods system, the gold price was fixed in dollars at US$35 per ounce and other currencies' exchange rates were fixed to the dollar. Hence, gold anchored all currencies. This meant that the money supply was limited. This also meant that it was hard for inflation to rise. It also meant that bubbles of all kinds would largely be avoided. Additionally, it also meant that the US was in effect the banker for the entire world. By removing the gold standard, the rules of world trade changed overnight. The price of gold rose, which meant that governments and traders who had been piling onto dollars found that their dollars purchased substantially less gold. Currencies began to float. Exchange rates began to diverge. But most significantly, oil exporters, represented by Organization of the Petroleum Exporting Countries (OPEC) now received far less gold for oil. This caused OPEC to raise the price of oil. This triggered inflation in the US and a weakening of the dollar, which led to a further increase in oil prices. The US, hence, and the rest of the world, thus found itself tied to a new Oil Standard.

Symbolically, oil is a flowing source of energy—that is, it is representative of the vital phase. And this is precisely what this shift really signifies. However, it is not openly and easily available energy, such as exists in the sun, but the result of dead and crushed plants and animals existing now as fluid in the depths of the earth. The energetic possibility contained in this crushed material is in the first place obtained from solar energy. Hence oil is, symbolically, a derivative energy obtained from the past, made up from essentially physical-vital beings that once existed on the surface of the earth. Its utility has to be finite, and this is borne out by the phenomena of peak oil, which suggests that once the extraction of oil has peaked, there is less of it available in the earth. In other words, oil as a medium of energy, and even as a symbol of financial operation, has only a finite life. But during that life, symbolically speaking, being of the essence of the physical-vital, we can expect its era to be characteristically physical-vital—that is, an increasing energy driven by myopia rather than order, driven by selfishness rather than selflessness, and driven by destruction rather than creation.

This also has an implication for what kind of standard should be created next. Following the notion of the fractal for progress, with base orientation shifting from the physical to the vital to the mental, it is clear that an attempt to create a "mental" standard is next. It is something that should shift us away from the control and rigidity of the physical, embodied in the gold standard, and the recklessness and irrational monopolies of the vital, embodied in the oil standard, to the encouraging of bottom-up and globally distributed innovation, perhaps embodied in a "solar energy" standard. Solar energy is globally distributed and available forever. Money flow and creation of wealth could be tied to the ability to harness this energy, which in effect is infinite, which means that progress and development can in effect become infinite. Solar energy already fosters many ecosystem services. It therefore has a profound influence on commerce, whether we realize it or not. If it could also more consciously actively be harnessed then a new standard of wealth, that is non-monopolistic and available to all through acts of creativity, would come into being. This creativity measured in how solar energy is being harnessed, stored, and used could be the basis of new money creation and in effect become a new standard for ordering global commerce. Alternatively, as suggested by Thomas Greco, author of *The End of Money and the Future of Civilization* (2009), money should be created and monitored at the community level through the creation of local credit clearing systems. Current systems of money create conditions of artificial scarcity. Banks in their capacity to create money, charge interest in doing so and, therefore, debt increases exponentially and is at the end of the day unsustainable.

The exponential growth of debt creates expectations and societal norms engendering exponential growth, which is of course, given a finite resource base, impossible. Such dynamics reinforce the vital level in which there is never really a win-win scenario. For someone to win, someone else must lose. Hence, competition rather cooperation will prevail, and the nature of the economic system will always have a rough edge to it. At the end of the day everybody loses. The solution requires moving to the mental level, in which idea, and therefore uniqueness and possibility become the source of wealth. In such a world money is not the end but the means.

That such a scenario will be used as the standard to anchor all commerce is inevitable. The sooner we realize this and take steps to reorient our systems of business and economy around this, the sooner will truer sustainability come into being.

Authers time line, which I will continue to elaborate all the way up to the start of the global financial crises in 2006, shows how the elements of such a myopic, selfish, and destructive energy continued to be inadvertently put in place. In 1975, the first S&P 500 index fund was launched. It was based on the idea fielded by Jack Bogle that fund managers could never beat the market. The market was efficient and hence stock prices incorporated all known information into them. Stock prices follow a "random walk" and cannot be predicted from one day to the next. It is therefore pointless to do expensive research to build portfolios of stock. Index funds were therefore cheaper to manage and to buy into. This became a magnet that drew a larger number of people into the activity of investing. The company that Bogle founded, Vanguard, grew to be worth more than US$100 billion and overtook Magellan as the world's biggest fund in 2000. As they grew more successful, they made the market less efficient. More money was poured in to heating areas and more money was pulled out of cooling areas. The means of this decision-making was the market itself. There was no active management in the index approach. The lack of active management provides an opportunity to beat the market, but because of the way fund managers were paid, this prompted them to keep close to the index. Portfolio theory is based on trying to keep completely uncorrelated stocks that have different levels of volatility together to optimize overall return. By keeping a portfolio of such stocks together, the irony is that the uncorrelated stocks or markets become correlated.

The year 1982 saw the launch of the first Emerging Markets Fund focused on investing in companies in the third world. Prior to that, banks in the western world invested at the country level only in the belief that countries would never go bust as companies do. In his book, *Confessions of an Economic Hitman*, Perkins (2006) suggests that such macro-level investing was in fact a ploy by the USA to gain control over key areas of the world. Typically, incoming dollars would stoke inflation, and being that loans were based on variable interest rates, the weakening lower local currency exchange rate made it difficult for countries to repay debt. Countries would inevitably default and would need to fulfill on a number of austerity measures and provisions that left the lender nation better off and with special privileges in the debtor nation. Latin America suffered greatly as a result of this and is known to have gone through the Lost Decade in the 1980s.

But now the Emerging Market Fund, the brainchild of the World Bank, would refocus investment on the company as opposed to the country level. While the macro-level strategy caused debtor countries to in a sense become extensions of lender countries, the company-focused or micro-level strategy caused emerging markets to become more intricately entwined with developed markets. The fund essentially provided another focal point, and therefore, avenue for creating hot spots, by funneling massive amounts of funds into more micro-level regions of the world. Like the macro-level strategy that preceded it, this too is an essential dynamic characteristic of the vital phase. Even though the developmental needs of emerging markets are fundamentally different than that of developed world markets, driven by the same investors seeking high return on investment, emerging markets also began to move in lock-step with developed markets. That is the very nature of the vital phase—it is even better fulfilled if hot-spots move in unison to create a mega bubble. Tying emerging market volatility to developed market volatilities did just this. In 1988, Morgan Stanley Capital International (MSCI) started its emerging markets index fund. Like previous indices, the MSCI soon became an active guide to investing, funneling even more money into areas that were deemed as hot. As a result of this, there were further tight correlations not only between the developed and emerging worlds but also between different countries in the emerging markets umbrella.

In 1984, the Reagan administration allowed banks to package mortgage loans into bonds and sell them to investors. This created a liquid market where mortgages could be traded and moved power over housing finance into markets. This was yet another substantial shift from the physical phase to the vital phase of financial evolution. In the physical phase, the emphasis in housing finance was very much around building societies—creating concrete value measured by what the eye can see. Typically savings and loans type organizations took in savings and made loans that were monitored carefully. Such a prudent approach meant that the risk of default was minimized and lending organizations could invest money elsewhere. With the shift to a liquid market where mortgages could be traded, the fundamental approach to building society was cast aside in favor of speculation and making profit often at any cost. The meaning behind things was again cast aside, and mortgages of varying risk class were clubbed together and used to back bonds. Risk is thus being piled onto risk, and in the bargain, the very foundation of prudent building is cast aside. As the vital appetite grows, financial institutions become even more risky and venture into previously taboo areas such as subprime mortgages for people with bad credit histories. Further, the risk of default was no longer borne by those who decided to make the loan. The risk was now sold to someone else. Hence, this stoked even more risk taking and unsubstantiated loan making. Further, the money from the sale of the bonds was used in further unsubstantiated risk taking.

Authers points out that about the same time there was another financial innovation—the Junk Bond—attributed to Michael Milken. Like the theory behind index funds, this too was based on spreading risk through creating a portfolio of low-grade corporate bonds. Research had supposedly shown that such a portfolio out-performed higher-quality blue-chip bonds. Authers points out that this research was flawed, but the point is that in the vital milieu, it is just the promise of making higher returns that was more important even though it should be obvious that a blue-chip company is going to have more of its ducks in a row in general. Nonetheless, it was hugely successful because a market was created for it where enough investors and enough sellers were convinced that the whole proposition made sense. These junk bonds supposedly democratized markets by making it easier for small companies to raise finances. Time, however, proved this otherwise. This is to be expected from any vital-level dynamic.

In 1990, the crash of Japan led to the yen carry trade. "Carry" refers to the price of holding a security. The crash of Japan led to low interest rates and therefore a low cost to hold on to yen. A carry trade creates cheap money by borrowing in a currency with low interest rates, putting money into currencies with high interest rates and pocketing the difference. This can only continue so long as nothing changes in the carry's favor. It is, hence, not arbitrage. When Japan's bubble burst in 1990, low rates in yen created a carry trade. The irony is that this situation could have been reversed at any time. That is, the yen could have been strengthened and the carry trade stopped if citizens would value their own country more. However, with the vital mind-set it was not the country and the culture that was important but the promise of making money. This was yet another way in which true value was being bastardized. To top this off, equity investors then used this carry trade to finance their purchases in stocks. As a result, the yen started to move in line with stocks. Like the Borg in *Star Trek*, more and more markets were assimilated into an essentially meaningless playing field.

In the 1990s, a series of currency coups caused investors to treat foreign exchange as its own asset class. This was in spite of the fact that foreign exchange is supposed to be a series of zero-sum games that creates no value. George Soros, the currency investor, was reported to have broken the Bank of England and made US$1 billion in the bargain on Black Wednesday in 1992. The Bank of England raised interest rates on that day to strengthen the value of the pound. In spite of several increases to the interest rates amounting to a 5 percent increase, the pound still dropped in value. George Soros had exchanged US$10 billion in British Pound for Deutsche Mark. This forced the pound down. He then converted back into pound and made a 10 percent profit in the bargain. This act likely stoked the greed of vitally oriented speculators the world over and caused investors to begin to treat foreign exchange as its own asset class. Once it had become so, then driven by speculation it began to synch up with the stock market. Thus, one more asset class was added to the vital playing field of speculators. Like other classes before it, it also had the effect of marginalizing true value as fortunes could be made and won in a day, regardless of effort or true work in the areas at hand.

The late 1990s saw the rise of hedge funds. Hedge fund refers to a class of funds that are loosely regulated so that they do not obey restrictions that regulators put on investments aimed at the general public. As the name implies, hedge funds often seek to hedge some of the risks inherent in their investments using a variety of methods, most notably short selling and derivatives. However, the term "hedge fund" has also come to be applied to certain funds that do not hedge their investments, and in particular, to funds using short selling and other "hedging" methods to increase rather than reduce risk with the expectation of increasing the return on their investment. Typically hedge funds are open only to a limited range of professional or wealthy investors who meet certain criteria set by regulators. The regulations thus exempted typically include restrictions on short selling, the use of derivatives and leverage, fee structures, and on the liquidity of interests in the fund. Light regulation and the presence of performance fees are the distinguishing characteristics of hedge funds. The net asset value of a hedge fund can run into many billions of dollars, and the gross assets of the fund will usually be higher still due to leverage. Hedge funds typically make money by chasing trends and finding pricing discrepancies and trying to profit from them using leveraged money. Because their membership is comprised of wealthy investors and banks, they typically have a huge effect on markets they focus on. Hedge funds tend to bet on removing market inefficiencies by forcing different investments to converge. Sometimes this does not happen and then the price for regaining normality becomes huge. Hedge funds are therefore a magnifier. They tend to create systemic risk and to be able to bring large parts of the financial market down. Again, in the interest of making money, truer value is destroyed.

In 2004, commodities also became an asset class. Prior to this, mainstream investors avoided them because it required detailed knowledge of capacities and conditions in each commodity market. Following academic research that showed that commodity futures could offer strong returns uncorrelated to stock markets, a lot of big institutions poured money into this area. Further, a lot of the investing was in passive manner through indices of futures in different commodities. This new money of course made commodities correlate more with stocks. Historical correlations were overturned. As oil prices rise, stock prices should reduce. This is how it has always been—now this correlation was reversed.

In 2005, default risk became an asset class. Credit derivatives opened the world of credit and loans to mainstream investors. Credit started to correlate closely with equities, bonds, and commodities and drove the rise in US house prices and the subprime mortgage boom.

Hence, from 1950 through 2005, more asset classes began to synchronize, and the playing field became decisively vital. That is, the notion of true value was overtaken by another notion of surface value which in effect reversed the buildup of sustainable wealth by atomized images of it.

6

Where in the Fractal Journey Is the Stock Market?

Ultimately, the purpose of any financial instrument or transaction is to further the effective use of money so that the world, its people and myriad species, communities, and societies are positively and sustainably benefited from this. In Chapter 1 we described what we would really like from the business world. The reality of what we continue to create, however, is vastly out of sync with the dream and true purpose of business. We had reviewed many aspects of the current reality of business-as-usual in Chapters 2 and 3. Ideally we want the stock market, as a primary conduit of funds, to exist to create a scenario closer to that described in Chapter 1 than that of the reality as described in Chapters 2 and 3. This aim is the crux of this book.

How do we actually get the stock market to begin to funnel funds in a manner that will create a beautiful, sustainable world, no matter from which angle we look at it? The role the stock market plays in such a possible creation is actually critical. Chapter 4 looked at the effects of funding at a micro level. That is, in the actual growth of companies and the actual intrigues, such companies continue to be involved in. As illustrated, the funding for all industries, and for leaders in those industries, has increased dramatically in the last decade. The quote "Power tends to corrupt, and absolute power to corrupt absolutely," attributed to Lord Acton, seems to be very appropriate when we see what many of these companies tend to use money for. The truth is, if the means of these companies was not as vast as they have become through stock market funding, they would tend to operate differently. Alternatively, if there was more due diligence at the time of the funding, and further, if there were conditions attached to the funding, perhaps that too would have a dampening effect on such outcomes. Then there is also the cumulative effect of funding companies and industries in this manner that has disastrous systemic environmental and social effects. So, the micro affects, in a fractal manner, the macro in this way.

But there is also a direct and disastrous macro effect that stock market action has had on the macro-financial environment. The stock market has been an attractor and device to focus funds and to change the very meaning and use of funds. That is, it has been instrumental in changing the field of finance itself. It has played a primary role in bastardizing value and in atomizing markets so that they are arranged or reorganized by a common denominator of least value the world over. In Chapter 5, we began to look at this effect of the stock market. In its role as attractor of funds, it has had the effect of monopolizing global flows of money, which like huge tidal waves, have gone about their business of destruction regardless of the relative intricacy in development of the target. It is not that it strove for that outcome—of monopolizing flows of money. But that is what has happened as a result of the way in which it has been structured, developed, and managed.

The macro-financial environment historically consisted of a number of unrelated asset classes. The movements of individual commodity markets, whether of oil, grain, or metals, were completely unrelated and investors were required to have expertise in those areas to play in them. Similarly there was no correlation between commodity markets and stock or bond markets. Stock markets themselves were distinct as companies in one region of the world had different requirements and possibilities than companies in other parts of the world. Governments themselves were stewards of uniqueness, expressed by vast difference in culture from one country to the next. But now these separate developments were all cast aside, and the means for these separate developments to continue through wise use of funding was all cast aside as everything began to correlate. Further, stock and bond markets were unrelated to emerging markets and to foreign exchange markets. However, as the recent synchronization of bubbles across the world has shown, these markets are now fundamentally in sync. Another way of expressing this is to say that market-specific flow of funds, focused on relatively unique development, have been replaced by monopolized flow of funds that cares little for unique and differentiated development. This is a seriously disastrous outcome.

Nature and history, both great teachers that should never be ignored, have shown us that differentiation and uniqueness are the cornerstones of sustainable development. Where standardization is the focus, there rebellion in one form or the other, is soon to follow and wipe clean the erroneous foundation. That today our very means and source of funding in so many parts of the world have lost sight of this fundamental principle of development means that we have only begun to experience the global crises that we keep hoping will be over.

But coming back to the stock market: How has this been the critical devise in precipitating today's reality of a monopolized flow of funds that marginalizes true development? This is essentially and basically because it has whetted our appetite for what seems like quick and painless return on investment. As a result, it has mobilized the common man to invest in companies and movements that he does not completely understand. It has caused institutions to take those increasing flows of funds and amplify the quantity of investment focused on hot-spots pointed to by the stock-market. The accumulation and flow of funds into such institutions has resulted in financial engineering to make asset classes of fundamental building blocks of development. Company stock has become an asset class. Commodities have become an asset class. Government bonds have become an asset class. Emerging markets have become an asset class. Foreign exchange has become an asset class. Credit, itself, has become an asset class. This means that their inherent differentiation has relatively speaking been marginalized and they have all essentially become means for making money, usually at any cost.

In this chapter, we will take a deeper look at the stock market itself. This will position us to more accurately explore a theory of development, in subsequent chapters, based on the fractal for progress. Subsequently, we will correlate modern day stock market movement with this fractal for progress and examine if this allows us a more penetrating understanding on why we have faced the recent global problems we have faced and, perhaps, gain insight into how to successfully navigate through these turbulent waters.

The fractal for progress and its underlying building blocks are critical in beginning to make sense of the stock market and, in fact, provide deeper insight into how current problems need to be better managed. The fractal for progress is embedded in the DNA of the circumstance, and complex organizations will tend to move in the direction indicated by the fractal for progress. Given this to be the case, it becomes important to understand where the stock market is currently. That is, in its own fractal journey, what phase(s) has it completed, and what phase does it seem to be currently in. Also, given that there is an existing body of stock market theory that has already been developed by academicians, the question then, is what phase in the fractal model does this theory actually refer to or apply to and has there been a misapplication of this theory because it is inherently out of sync with where the stock market actually is? I believe that understanding this will provide great insight into helping to redesign stock markets.

The Stock Market Journey from a Fractal for Progress Perspective

The stock market journey I refer to in this section is distinct from the historical journey that I will cover in the next chapter. Here I want to focus on an interpretation of the overall journey that will shed light on the phases from a fractal for progress perspective that the stock market has been through.

The following figures indicate the increase in volume of stock in major regions of the world. These figures follow stock market activity as indicated by various leading regional indices.

Figure 6.1 shows the increase in DJIA from 1928 to 2010 in the USA.

When examining this rise closely, one can see that from approximately 1930 to 1987 the DJIA (Dow Jones Industrial Average) increased by 2000. Then from 1987 to 1995, an eight-year period, it increased by the same amount as it did in close to 50 years. And then from 1995 to 2005, the DJIA increased by 10,000! This indicates the huge increase in volume in a few short years. This story is repeated in other major indices as we can see in the following figures.

Figure 6.1: Dow Jones Industrial Average Index Value

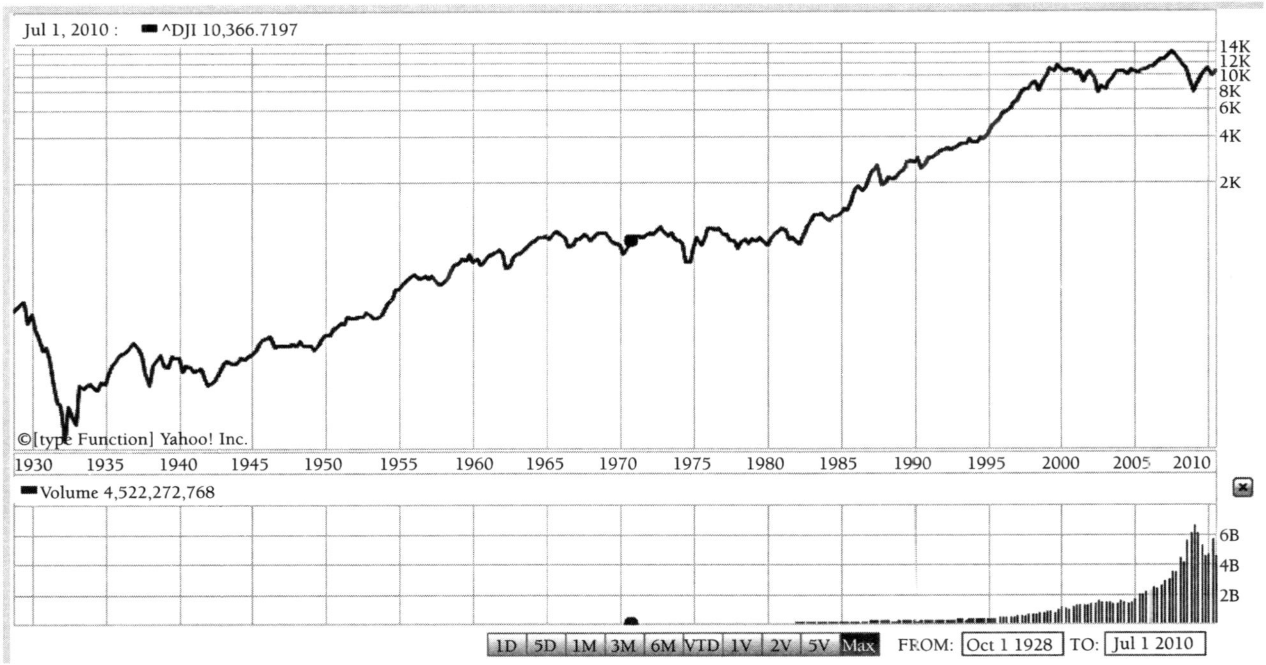

Source: Yahoo! Finance, 2010.

In the USA, from 1950 to 2007, the S&P 500 rose to 1,400 (Figure 6.2) Yet, from 1950 to 1985, the rise was only 200 points. From 1985 to 1992, it was another 200 points—doing in 7 years what had taken 35 years to do. And again from 1995 to 2000, there was an almost 1,000 point rise.

In the UK, FTSE100, rose from a base-level of 1,000 in 1984 to about 6,000 in 2010 (Figure 6.3). The steepest rise took place from 1990 to 2000, from 2,000 points to 6,000 points.

In Germany, the DAX was started in 1987 at a base rate of 1,000 (Figure 6.4). Its most rapid rise was from 1996 to about 2000, when it rose from approximately 2,000 points to about 8,000 points.

In Asia, the Hang Seng Index rose by close to 30,000 points from 1990 to 2007 (Figure 6.5).

By studying all these figures, one thing can be observed: it is approximately in the period 1985–1990 when the stock market volume the world over began to increase substantially. This can be thought of as the transition period from the physical to the vital. Further, it was in the period from 1995–2005 when there was a dramatic increase in activity. This indicates vital-level activity. While stock exchanges have been in existence in many parts of the world, for as much as a couple of centuries, the fact that many more stock indices have come into existence, is itself a signal of transition to the vital phase. For the indices are a symbol of organized though ill-directed energy, characteristic of the vital phase, and indicate the more rapid trading that takes place once these are in existence.

Further, even though there have been some crashes prior to 1985, these were few and far between and generally localized to regions of the world. From the period 1985 to 2010 though, the velocity of bubbles and crashes has increased and as Authers has pointed out, has become synchronized (Authers, 2010). These crashes include: Black Monday which affected global markets (October 19, 1987), the Japanese asset price bubble and crash spanning a couple of decades (1986–2008), Black Wednesday in the UK (September 16, 1992), the 1997 Asian Financial Crises, the October 27, 1997, mini-crash affecting global markets, the 1998 Russian financial crises, the 2000 dot-com bubble, the Global stock market downturn of 2002, the Chinese correction of 2007, the US bear market of 2007–2009, the Dubai debt crises of 2009, the 2010 Greece debt downgrade and European sovereign debt crises, and most recently, the Flash crash of May 6, 2010.

Figure 6.2: S&P 500 Index Value

Source: Yahoo! Finance, 2010.

Figure 6.3: FTSE100 Index Value

Source: Yahoo! Finance, 2010.

Figure 6.4: DAX Index Value

Source: Yahoo! Finance, 2010.

Figure 6.5: Hang Seng Index Value

Source: Yahoo! Finance, 2010.

Further, a look at the Tables 6.1 and 6.2 indicate the largest daily point losses and gains in the DJIA, which mostly all occur in the period 1997–2009 and also indicate the high volatility and again are a sign of the being in the vital level.

Just from the manifest signs of increase in the number of indices, the very rapid increase in index volume all over the world, the velocity of loss and gain in daily prices, and the number of crashes that have occurred, one can conclude that the texture of trading is very much at the vital level. And to put this in context again, the effects of vital-level trading are essentially irrational. Markets and economic theory are predicated on rational behavior. When behavior is irrational, then irrational things happen. When oil prices suddenly rise, the world goes into a recession. When food prices suddenly rise, huge and innocent populations all over the world are starved. When day-to-day prices fluctuate without control, national economies lose control over basic things like their cost of goods. When credit becomes easily available and then not, entire markets go from

Table 6.1: Largest Daily Point Losses

Rank	*Date (yyyy-mm-dd)*	*Close*	*Net Change*	*% of Change*
1	2008-09-29	10,365.45	-777.68	-6.98
2	2008-10-15	8,577.91	-733.08	-7.87
3	2001-09-17	8,920.70	-684.81	-7.13
4	2008-12-01	8,149.09	-679.95	-7.70
5	2008-10-09	8,579.19	-678.91	-7.33
6	2000-04-14	10,305.78	-617.77	-5.66
7	1997-10-27	7,161.14	-554.26	-7.18
8	2008-10-22	8,519.21	-514.45	-5.69
9	1998-08-31	7,539.06	-512.62	-6.37
10	2008-10-07	9,447.11	-508.39	-5.11
11	1987-10-19	1,738.74	-508.00	-22.61
12	2008-09-15	10,917.51	-504.48	-4.42
13	2008-11-05	9,139.27	-486.01	-5.05
14	2008-09-17	10,609.66	-449.36	-4.06
15	2008-11-20	7,552.29	-444.99	-5.56
16	2008-11-06	8,695.79	-443.48	-4.85
17	2001-03-12	10,208.25	-436.37	-4.10
18	2008-11-19	7,997.28	-427.47	-5.07
19	2007-02-27	12,216.24	-416.02	-3.29
20	2008-11-12	8,282.66	-411.30	-4.73

Source: *The Wall Street Journal*, "Historical Index Data: Dow Jones Industrial Average—All-Time Largest One Day Gains and Losses," http://online.wsj.com/mdc/public/page/2_3047-djia_alltime.html (downloaded on July 24, 2011).

Table 6.2: Largest Daily Point Gains

Rank	*Date (yyyy-mm-dd)*	*Close*	*Net Change*	*% OF Change*
1	2008-10-13	9,387.61	+936.42	+11.08
2	2008-10-28	9,065.12	+889.35	+10.88
3	2008-11-13	8,835.25	+552.59	+6.67
4	2000-03-16	10,630.60	+499.19	+4.93
5	2009-03-23	7,775.86	+497.48	+6.84
6	2008-11-21	8,046.42	+494.13	+6.54
7	2002-07-24	8,191.29	+488.95	+6.35
8	2008-09-30	10,850.66	+485.21	+4.68
9	2002-07-29	8,711.88	+447.49	+5.41
10	2008-03-18	12,392.66	+420.41	+3.51
11	2008-03-11	12,156.81	+416.66	+3.55
12	2008-10-20	9,265.43	+413.21	+4.67
13	2008-09-18	11,019.69	+410.03	+3.86
14	2010-05-10	10,785.14	+404.71	+3.90
15	2001-04-05	9,918.05	+402.63	+4.23
16	2008-10-16	8,979.26	+401.35	+4.68
17	2001-04-18	10,615.83	+399.10	+3.91
18	2008-11-24	8,443.39	+396.97	+4.93
19	2008-04-01	12,654.36	+391.47	+3.19
20	1998-09-08	8,020.78	+380.53	+4.98

Source: *The Wall Street Journal*, "Historical Index Data: Dow Jones Industrial Average—All-Time Largest One Day Gains and Losses," http://online.wsj.com/mdc/public/page/2_3047-djia_alltime.html (downloaded on July 24, 2011).

boom to bust. When foreign investments rush into a country, then inflation results and the sustainable foundation for global growth is severely compromised. Is there anything rational about avoidable loss of control, avoidable starvation, and avoidable compromise to national and global development? Absolutely not. So why do we allow that to exist? Essentially because we have become slaves to a machinery that is not rational. It is operating from the vital space.

So we know that the stock market is in the vital phase. Prior to 1985, it was in the physical phase. We also know that there is an implicit bias in complex organizations and markets, elaborated *Connecting Inner Power with Global Change* (Malik, 2009b), to move from the physical to the vital to the mental phase. This bias is actually a necessity and will happen in one way or another, no matter what the cost. If it is something that is architected consciously, the price will be low. If avoided, it will happen anyway but at a much higher cost to society. The point of this book is to help to lower the cost to society through redesigning stock markets to bring about the needed transition in the stock market from the vital to the mental phase.

We now need to turn our attention to existing theories and tools that drive trading activity today. Once we understand these, it will become easier to factor in corrections into the redesign of the stock market.

7

Theories and Tools to Manage Trading at the Vital Level

We now need to turn our attention to existing theories and tools that must drive trading activity today.

We have established that the stock market is in the vital phase. The vital phase is characterized by the principle guideline "reality as determined by assertiveness and the myriad play of energies." As stated earlier, the emphasis is on the assertion of energy. Organizations are absorbed in dynamic activity. In this dynamism, there is interaction of energies. Some energies overpower others. Some express themselves in harmony with others. All seek to grow in whatever way they can. It is hence, assertiveness and energy that dominates. This is Darwin's interpretation of evolution and the basis of much of today's interpretation of competitiveness. The energy of each seeks to assert itself, often at any cost. All seek to gather more energy by any means and to establish its rule over other forms. There is experimentation in this phase but it is not driven by order and thought. It is driven by the primal impulse to assert oneself and grow at any cost. Greed is the law. Fear ensures that greed can continue to live, if not today, then tomorrow. Hence, there is a devouring to devour and a conquering to conquer, and it is the strongest and longest-lasting energy that appears to triumph in the end.

There is no rationality in this phase. This is the phase of irrational gains and losses. This is the phase of irrational bubbles followed by irrational bursts. This is the phase of stock market rise and fall. This is the phase in which recessions are caused overnight, where governments lose control of their economies, where brainwashed people are sent to their death to secure resources that never belonged to them in the first place, where innocent people suffer starvation because of irrational speculation, and where accelerated destruction of everything we value and accelerated destruction of the body of the earth are the norm.

In Chapter 4, we looked at the manifest signs of the stock market vital phase. In Chapter 5, we looked at how the contextual transition was actually engineered, starting with the shift from the gold to the oil standard; the creation of market funds, index funds, and mortgage-backed bonds; and the easy availability of credit. But we have also stated that the root driver of all this loosening and shifting was greed itself and the expectation that the quick buck could be made by trading on the stock market. It was the force of greed-driven speculation that has unleashed all the consequent changes. And this force has come to be, in large measure, because of the existing theories and tools in place that have led from one wrong choice to the next.

At the vital level, what we really need is a set of tools that show clearly how greed is the prime driver of trading. No trader cares for the value proposition behind what is being traded. Reality is that all they care about is appropriating or, at the very least, skimming margin on a deal. Theories and tools must deal with this reality: greed–fear interaction, herd mentality, fractal effects, monopolization effects, and resulting stochastic variance. This is what needs to be in the portfolio of decision-makers. This is in stark contrast to what is actually driving decision-making: variations of efficient market hypotheses, portfolio theory, index modeling, and algorithmic trading. These latter tools belong to the mental phase of the stock market, and we are simply not there yet. These latter tools have also tended to drive decision-making in the physical phase. But this was the wrong choice and has strongly contributed to the global financial crises playing out today for the physical phase is driven by the guideline—"reality is determined by what the eye can see." This really did require another set of tools.

Theories Being Used to Propel the Vital Phase

But let us take a deeper look at the theories and tools that have driven the vital phase of stock market development.

Prime amongst these is the efficient market hypothesis (EMH) which asserts that financial markets are "informationally efficient." Simply stated, one cannot consistently achieve returns in excess of average market returns on a risk-adjusted basis, given the information publicly available at the time the investment is made (Wikipedia, 2010k). In other words, all information about companies and their actions, and the relative strength and weakness of corporations, is automatically embedded in stock prices, and stock prices change to reflect these conditions from moment to moment. I would even suggest the formulation of a Sustainable Market Hypotheses (SMH) that also factors in corporations' true impact on society and environments, the costs of externalization, and the consequent weakening of the very system on which all corporate activity depends to make the EMH more realistic.

EMH assumes a vastly and comprehensively intelligent system that is always correct, and therefore, to buy and sell stock in such a system will never allow gains beyond what the market is already offering. If a portfolio of stocks already provides you as an investor a certain return and if the prices to buy such stock already embed perfect information, then it is impossible to benefit in any way beyond this. So due diligence into companies, finding arbitrage opportunities, and seeking after inefficiencies in the market is futile. The risk behavior of such a market will be tightly Gaussian, that is, price–risk correlation will be a narrow normal distribution with the norm being that most prices will accurately reflect risk. Some will understate risk and some overstate it. But only very few.

Clearly, this is not the reality in the vital phase. Yet, this is the one most influential theory that has propelled stock market trading. Under the guideline that "the market is always right" and is in fact being guided by Adam Smith's invisible hand, there is in effect an equalization of meaning or deep value with stock market price. Trades will only take place that are most beneficial and most sustainable to the long-term health of humankind. This is clearly not the case; in fact the exact opposite is true. Trades are not being guided by the inherent meaning and value and their maximization but by a greed–fear guideline characteristic of the vital phase.

To not recognize this is to live an illusion. It is to give up the thought and reason and be led down a disastrous path such as one we see now with the advent of the global financial crises.

The birth of the index fund, which has popularized trading, with the implicit promise of making it richer, is what has resulted. For the very basis of the index fund is that there is no point competing against the market. Best just to follow it—create a portfolio that mimics companies already listed—and just go with the flow. Thus, the cost of managing such an instrument is driven down for the index fund manager, and consequently, the cost of being involved in a piece of the action is driven down for the individual investor. A vaster amount of money flows into these index funds, and the market goes more forcefully to where it is going anyway. Stupidity is followed by more stupidity and bubbles become bigger bubbles. Exxons, DOWs, Citibanks, Monsantos, Pfizers, Wal-Marts, and their clones all automatically receive more funding because of this. Thus, environmental and social degradation continue in force.

There are variations of the EMH. But we will come back to this soon.

The other major theory used that has also had disastrous effects is that of portfolio theory.

Modern portfolio theory (MPT) is a theory of investment which tries to maximize portfolio returns given an amount of portfolio risk or equivalently minimize risk for a given level of expected return by carefully choosing the proportions of various assets. MPT is widely used in practice in the financial industry and several of its creators won the Nobel Prize for the theory. It is a mathematical formulation of the concept of diversification in investing, with the aim of selecting a collection of investment assets that has collectively lower risk than any individual asset (Wikipedia, 2010o).

That this may be possible can be seen intuitively because different types of assets are supposed to often change in value in opposite ways. When prices in the stock market fall, then prices in the bond market are supposed to increase and vice versa. Corporation's funding needs in one part of the world are supposed to be independent of funding needs of corporations in other parts of the world. Development needs in emerging markets are supposed to require independent cycles of investment with respect of developed markets. Commodity markets are supposed to have independent cycles of growth and decline in investment, generally uncorrelated with other commodity cycles and markets. This is entirely true, were meaning and value prime differentiators in trading. In other words, if the stock market were in the mental phase, this would be true.

And where this is true the theory goes that a collection of different types of assets, with their independent risk behaviors, will tend to lower overall risk of a portfolio. Diversification is hence good for the investor, because given a certain level of investment, the returns will tend to be higher than in the absence of diversification.

But the reality is that the stock market is in the vital phase. Meaning and value have no play, and all that matters is that the few get rich at the irrational expense of the many. Accumulation of personal money has become the end rather than sustainable and rational development. As a result, as already mentioned, the flow of investment increases exponentially and that flow and the return from the object of the investment is what is important. This means that supposedly uncorrelated or independent risk behaviors of "diverse" assets, because they are in the same portfolio, become correlated. It does not matter anymore whether the investment needs are different in Japan and Uganda. If assets from both regions sit in the same portfolio, they receive the investment at the same time. They also stop receiving investment at the same time. Their independent needs, the result of unique development emanating from the essence of the nature of splendor, are tossed aside and in essence they get denominated in terms of their sole ability to generate returns. The portfolio functions as a time bomb.

As a result, investment has negated the safety of different risk behaviors clubbed together and the whole purpose of MPT comes undone. What should be unrelated bubbles become related and what results is a mega bubble. Yet, MPT is what drives much of investment activity today. It is wholly unsuited in any vital phase. It has more meaningful applicability in the mental phase, and even in the physical phase. As a framework for decision-making in the vital phase though, it is a recipe for disaster.

This combination of the use of EMH and MPT to drive decision-making and investment are perhaps the single biggest reason that the global financial crises has occurred. They have functioned as an irrational funnel to in effect destroy value and destroy the very system they aim to fortify.

The third tool that is prevalent in the stock market vital phase is that of algorithmic trading.

Algorithmic trading is the use of computer programs for entering trading orders with the computer algorithm deciding on aspects of the order such as the timing, price, or quantity of the order, or in many cases, initiating the order without human intervention. Algorithmic trading is about buying and selling quicker, faster, and better in order to leverage arbitrage opportunities. A third of all EU and US stock trades in 2006 were driven by automatic programs or algorithms (Wikipedia, 2010b). As of 2009, high frequency trading firms account for 73 percent of all the US equity trading volume (Iati, 2009). This pushes the aphorism "if you have a hammer in your hand then everything seems like a nail" (Maslow, 1966: 15) to a new level. To begin with, the misguided approaches of EMH and MPT are able to be used at a new level of comprehensiveness. Further, because algorithmic trading is used in a vital phase, any semblance of meaning and value are further obliterated and the profit motive, at any cost, becomes the abiding guideline.

Correction to Theories Driving Vital Phase

The reality is that it is more being recognized that the deadly cocktail of EMH, MPT, and algorithmic trading that have driven the stock market deeply into the irrationalities of the vital phase, are simply inadequate and other theories and frameworks have had to rise in their place. I will note that even these theories do not see the simplicity of the fractal for progress animating things from behind, and therefore, do not see the three phases of physical, vital, and mental. As a result, the corrections to the theories are precisely that—corrections. It really is a new framework that is needed to address the root causes.

One such framework is that of Behavioral Finance which seeks to highlight inefficiencies such as under overreaction to information as causes of market trends. Such reactions have been attributed to limited investor attention, overconfidence, overoptimism, herding instinct, and noise trading (Wikipedia, 2010c). This framework starts from EMH which is of course grounded in the notion of implicit efficiencies and seeks to highlight inefficiencies. What it really needs to do, however, is cut through the layers to realize that efficient markets are a function of a different order of perception where emotions such as fear and greed do not in any way even influence decision-making. Behavioral Finance as positioned is all about trying to understand the irrationalities of the vital phase. Therefore, it is by definition going to be an incomplete view unless it can grasp the underlying reality reflected in the physical, vital, and mental phases, and the implicit movement over time between one phase to the next in the physical–vital–mental sequence. That said, however, given that we are in the vital phase, and that some tools are required by decision-makers to begin to correct the deadly cocktail in existence, what Behavioral Finance comes up with will likely be useful at least to the academic and the trader who really cares about more sustainable progress. That notion, however, may be an oxymoron. If greed–fear behavior begins to be modeled and is embedded into decision-makers' heuristics and algorithmic trading heuristics, and if the active consciousness of such decision-makers and traders is still focused at making the quick buck, at any cost, all this will do is provide a more powerful tool to begin to make more profit with.

In addition there have been different versions of EMH that have come into being. Two of these include the Adaptive Market Hypotheses (AMH) and the Noisy Market Hypotheses (NMH), not to mention the "weak," "semi-strong," and "strong" versions of EMH.

AMH, as proposed by Andrew Lo (2004, 2005), is an attempt to reconcile theories that imply that the markets are efficient with behavioral alternatives by applying the principles of evolution—competition, adaptation, and natural selection—to financial interactions. He argues that much of what behavioralists cite as counterexamples to economic rationality—loss aversion, overconfidence, overreaction, and other behavioral biases—are, in fact, consistent with an evolutionary model of individuals adapting to a changing environment using simple heuristics. According to Lo (2004: 23), AMH can be viewed as a new version of the efficient market hypothesis, derived from evolutionary principles. "Prices reflect as much information as dictated by the combination of environmental conditions and the number and nature of 'species' in the economy." By species, he means distinct groups of market participants, each behaving in a common manner (that is, pension funds, retail investors, market makers, and hedge-fund managers, etc.). If multiple members of a single group are competing for scarce resources within a single market, that market is likely to be highly efficient, for example, the market for 10-Year US Treasury Notes, which reflects most relevant information very quickly indeed. If, on the other hand, a small number of species are competing for rather abundant resources in a given market, that market will be less efficient, for example, the market for oil paintings from the Italian Renaissance.

Market efficiency cannot be evaluated in a vacuum but is highly context-dependent and dynamic. Shortly stated, the degree of market efficiency is related to environmental factors characterizing market ecology such as the number of competitors in the market, the magnitude of profit opportunities available, and the adaptability of the market participants.

While this is an innovative adaptation of EMH, in that it does factor in some aspects of human behavior, there are two issues with it. First, it is still EMH and, therefore, simply unsuited to the vital phase. If it is to be considered, then it should be considered as an approach to be used at the mental phase. Remember, we are talking about massive, greed-driven flows that flood out any semblance of EMH type order and rationality at the vital phase in the first place. This is the abiding reality and all others are simply dwarfed by its power. The second factor, however, would suggest that the behavioral aspects be modified if it is to be used at the mental phase. And this is so, because at the mental level, it is true meaning, value, idea, development, sustainability—the higher ideals—that drive decision-making, and in such a scenario, the Darwinian notion of adaptation that Lo is suggesting, is simply less accurate. If AMH is to be considered as a tool, it will have to be modified to account for the large, irrational flows that dampen out any hint of EMH.

Noisy Market Hypothesis (NMH), framed by Jeremy Siegel (2006), contrasts the efficient market hypothesis in that it states that the prices of securities are not always the best estimate of the true underlying value of the firm. In the vital phase, as we have discussed, this is very true. Price of securities is determined by another heuristic altogether more tied to herd mentality and irrational speculation. NMH argues that prices can be influenced by speculators and momentum traders as well as by insiders and institutions that often buy and sell stocks for reasons unrelated to fundamental value, such as for diversification, liquidity and taxes. These temporary shocks referred to as "noise" can obscure the true value of securities and may result in mispricing of these securities for many years. NMH begins to get to an approach to transition out of the vital phase. At its core, NMH is suggesting that price-weighted indices such as at DJIA, and market-share weighted indices such as NASDAQ, S&P, and Hang Seng need to be replaced by fundamentally weighted indices in order for an investor to generally outperform the average investor.

Let us probe into this a little more. A price-weighted index is a stock market index where each constituent makes up a fraction of the index that is proportional to its price. For a stock market index, this implies that stocks are included in proportions based on their quoted prices. A stock that has a higher price will therefore have more of a weight in the portfolio. In such a case, there is a bias toward rewarding that which is already in demand. It is not necessarily fundamental underlying value that is attracting investment but herd mentality. Sooner or later, if what is receiving funds is actually destroying underlying value, then a bubble will burst and even more value will be indiscriminately destroyed. A price-weighted index would be more appropriate in the mental phase where price more truly does embed all available information. But again, we are not there yet.

A market-weighted index is an index whose components are weighted according to the total market value of their outstanding shares. That is, the total number of outstanding shares multiplied by the price of that share. This kind of index will really capture the herd mentality, and if investment decisions are driven off the movement of this index, it will even more forcefully than the price-weighted index reinforce the direction in which the market is headed. Irrationality will be followed by even more irrationality and bubbles will be created much faster. Market-based indexing will also cause bubbles to burst much faster and for value to be even more indiscriminately destroyed than in the case of price-weighted indexing. Again, this device is based on EMH and is best suited in the mental phase. Applied at the vital phase, it is going to create a lot more damage than good.

By contrast, a fundamentally weighted index is that in which stocks are weighted by one of many economic fundamental factors, especially accounting figures which are commonly used when performing corporate valuation. Such fundamental factors may be one or a composite of sales, earnings, dividends, cash flows, or book value. Using a composite of several fundamental factors has the added benefit of potentially averaging out other biases such as sector-specific or regional biases. This method, in contrast to others, tends to strip away the exaggerations created by herd mentality. In other words, it removes the "noise" that distorts how a company is actually doing. This approach to indexing will tend not to create bubbles and tend not to indiscriminately destroy built-up value, as do price-weighted and market-based indexing.

EMH itself has been "elongated" to apply to a larger range of circumstances. Hence, there are three major versions of the EMH. These are "weak," "semi-strong," and "strong" EMH. Weak EMH claims that prices on traded assets, whether stock, bonds, or other property, already reflect all past publicly available information. Weak EMH claims that it may be able to beat the market based on fundamental information about companies that is not currently known. There is no way, though, to profit based on past prices or trends because prices in effect follow a random walk and simply are not linked to the past. Semi-strong EMH claims both that prices reflect all publicly available information and that prices instantly change to reflect new public information. Semi-strong EMH claims that it is possible to beat the market only in the short term, until prices reflect all available information, which happens very quickly. Strong EMH additionally claims that prices instantly reflect even hidden or "insider" information. Strong EMH claims that it is not possible to beat the market because all information is instantly reflected in prices.

So it is just speed and comprehensiveness of information that vary. These versions can all be viewed as different shades of operating in a mental phase. Strong EMH acts most like a comprehensive, intelligent mind in that all prices always reflect completeness of a situation and therefore it is impossible to beat the market. Semi-strong EMH also gets to the comprehensiveness but not instantaneously. So it is like a "slower" mind that progressively gets to where strong EMH is. Weak EMH is like an even slower mind that requires more time to fold in all information. None of these versions, though, can be applied to a stock market at the vital phase because at this phase there are another set of dynamics, not related to comprehensiveness and thought at all, that are active.

Another theory that moves away from the rationality of EMH is that of Ralph Nelson Elliott's Wave Principle. The Elliott Wave Principle is a form of technical analysis that investors use to forecast trends in the financial markets by identifying extremes in investor psychology, highs and lows in prices, and other collective activities. Elliott developed the concept in the 1930s. He proposed that market prices unfold in specific patterns, which practitioners today call Elliott waves or simply waves. Elliott published his theory of market behavior in the book *The Wave Principle* (1938) in a series of articles in *Financial World Magazine* in 1939, and most fully in his final major work, *Nature's Laws: The Secret of the*

Universe (1946). Elliott said that "because man is subject to rhythmical procedure, calculations having to do with his activities can be projected far into the future with a justification and certainty heretofore unattainable (Wikipedia, 2010l)."

Elliott's waves actually depict fractal patterns in stock and other asset prices. At its root, these patterns illustrate a simple greed–fear dynamic that is played out again, and again, and again, regardless of market. Hence, greed feeds greed so that prices continue to rise as more investors jump on the bandwagon. At some point the greed turns to fear, and to protect investments, the trend reverses and there is a sell-off of assets to pocket as much margin as possible. When the reasons for fear have been placated then greed kicks in again, and the trend does another about turn. This continues again and again. While Elliott's work is a remarkable exploration into the psychology of the investor as applied to actual stock and other asset prices, I will contend that it is limited in its applicability in that it is true only so long as psychology is rooted at the vital level, which is all about asserting one's small possibility, regardless of cost to others—that is, so long as greed and fear are cornerstones of the psychology. The moment more idealistic thought enters into the situation greed and fear do take a back seat, and these kinds of Elliott waves will cease to exist. His notion of "man being subject to rhythmical procedure" may be so but we have hardly scratched the surface of what that may mean in the context of a more comprehensive psychology. Other fractal patterns will no doubt come into being once this vaster psychology is considered. Malik's *Connecting Inner Power with Global Change* (2009b) explores this. These patterns will no doubt affect stock market action. The physical–vital–mental fractal pattern we have been discussing here is an indication of how things will need to change.

What Needs to Be Used at the Vital Level

We have just discussed how EMH, MPT, and algorithmic trading have been the main frameworks and tools used in the vital phase. These have gotten us into the global financial crises. We have also discussed some corrections to these frameworks that comprise of Behavioral Finance, AMH, NMH, weak, semi-strong, and strong versions of EMH, and Elliott Waves.

Of these corrections, we also discussed that NMH and Elliott Waves are perhaps the most appropriate for the vital phase. We said this because what we really want is a set of tools that help us maneuver out of the mess we are in. NMH admits that there are dynamics that obscure true value. It suggests that fundamentally weighted indexing is a way to filter through the noise. Such filtering is no doubt much needed to help us to get to a stage where meaning and value, and therefore, more sustainable development becomes the focus. Elliott Waves is also useful because it shows how the greed–fear dynamic will shift prices of assets over time, so long as one is in the vital phase. It too can be used to help us maneuver out of the current situation by awakening us to the fact that so long as greed and fear are part of human psychology, we can and should expect trends in pricing that will be indicated by similar trends from the past.

But in addition, there are other frameworks that do suggest themselves. Gaussian-distribution is more suited to the mental phase where order and reason are primary drivers. In the absence of order and reason, it is greed and fear that drive, and it seems logical that a more stochastic type variance should abide. Mathematician Benoît Mandelbrot suggested as early as 1963 that the statistics prove this assumption (Mandelbrot, 2004) correct. Mandelbrot observed that large movements in prices (that is, crashes) are much more common than would be predicted in a normal distribution. Mandelbrot suggests that the nature of market moves is generally much better explained using non-linear analysis and concepts of chaos theory (Gammon, 2006).This has been expressed in non-mathematical terms by George Soros in his discussions of what he calls reflexivity of markets and their non-linear movement (Soros, 2003). Reflexivity is a concept in social theory that refers to the capacity of an individual to act against the influence of socialization. Mandelbrot also proposed that instead of following a strict random walk, stock price variations executed a Lévy flight. A Lévy flight is a random walk that is occasionally disrupted by large movements (Mandelbrot, 1963).

In addition to NMH, Elliott Waves, and Stochastic Modeling, I would also propose a couple of models to capture the destructive dynamics inherent at the vital level. These are the Value Loss Paradigm (VLP) and the Mushroom Factor (MF).

At its core, VLP positively correlates overall financial activity and flow of funds in global markets to a destruction in value of those markets.

This is because as the flow of funds increases, and as it increases in all directions, it is the flow itself that becomes important, and the objects that it is supposed to mobilize and develop, recede into the background. Benefiting from the flow, instead of the object, becomes the focus. The markets may be countries, industries, companies—these all get simplified and rather than express the inherent and built-up value created over decades or centuries, instead these begin to express value in terms of some short-term cash equivalent. For example, in this scenario it does not matter if some artist has spent years to carve a figure in gold, say. What is more important is the weight of the gold and not what the figure expresses. Countries and companies are not expressions of uniqueness but the cash-equivalent of their broken up parts. Just as one would melt the golden figure to create blocks of gold, which is the medium of value, so too a company would be broken up and the value of its balance-sheet assets would become the most important measure of value. In VLP, the more the number of indiscriminate financial actors and the more the flow of funds, the more the inherent value of everything is reduced to become a bare-bones asset understood in crude tradable terms only. VLP brings into focus a truth of the vital level—value is reduced to a crass, single dimension of its possibility rather than the rich multidimensions that lie inherent within it.

The MF is related to the notion of a mushroom as a parasite. It crops up everywhere and lives off other species. It is not able to create anything of value on its own. The more mushrooms we have, the more our notion of value gets distorted and destroyed. Financial players and financial products can be thought of as mushrooms. They do not really create any value of their own. They suck on some basic product or infrastructure and give the illusion of activity. Getting lost in the illusion gives everyone the sense that value is being created.

Part III

Lessons from the History of Stock Market Crashes

8

Stock Market Seed

So far we have looked at what we want from business, what we have from business, and the role the stock market has played in today's rendering of business. The key question, of course, is how could stock markets help create more of what we ideally want than what we have. In looking at the role that stock markets have played in today's rendering of business, we actually considered the micro and macro effects of stock market dynamics. We also considered the fractal for progress, a significant dynamic of the contextual system we exist in, to understand where in this fractal, stock markets actually are. We unequivocally established that stock markets are in the vital phase. We then stepped back and considered the active financial theories that have driven stock market activity over the last few decades. These theories have been created for a financial reality at the mental level, and quite simply, are completely unsuited for financial reality at the vital level. Continued misapplication of these approaches has played a key role in the creation of the global financial crises. We also considered what tools and theories should come into effect to begin to steer us into the mental phase and we will come back to this later in the book.

In this chapter we want to briefly look at the history of the birth of the stock market to determine the very seed that has caused the continuing fractal effect of stagnated stock market behavior. Understanding how the seed came into being is important because unless the nature of the seed is shifted, the frequency of crashes is going to increase rather than decrease, given that we are securely in the vital phase.

The Birth of the Stock Market

In his book, *The Ascent of Money*, Niall Ferguson (2008) makes a strong case about the benefits of financial innovation. He models his approach much like Jacob Bronowski's classic, *The Ascent of Man* (1976), in which Bronowski correlates man's ascent to breakthroughs in science that then had massive societal and cultural impacts. Ferguson traces the history of financial innovation and in his introduction states that "behind each great historical phenomenon there lies a financial secret." So as in Bronowski's advance in science, it is Ferguson's advance in finance that has allowed man and society to progress. He illustrates:

> The Renaissance created such a boom in the market for art and architecture because Italian bankers like the Medici made fortunes by applying Oriental mathematics to money. The Dutch Republic prevailed over the Hasburg Empire because having the world's first modern stock market was financially preferable to having the world's biggest silver mine. The problems of the French monarchy could not be resolved without a revolution because a convicted Scots murderer had wrecked the French financial system by unleashing the first stock market bubble and burst. It was Nathan Rothschild as much as the Duke of Wellington who defeated Napoleon at Waterloo. It was financial folly, a destructive cycle of defaults and devaluations, that turned Argentina from the world's sixth-richest country in the 1880s into the inflation-ridden basket case of the 1980s. (Ferguson, 2008: 4–5)

While there is no doubt that finances are necessary for action in the current scheme of things, it is my opinion that Ferguson is putting the cart before the horse. The real secret behind great historical phenomenon lies in nature's implicit urge to continue along the fractal for progress from physical to vital to mental (Malik, 2009b), and finances in its various forms are a secondary means to assist this urge to be completed.

Ferguson looks at the key components of the modern financial system—money and credit, the bond market, the stock market, insurance, real estate, international finance—and relates how each has been a remarkable financial innovation that has allowed remarkable things to happen. In his chapter on the stock market, he relates how when looking at the Andes, it is hard to imagine how any human organization could overcome such a vast natural barrier. "But for one American company, their jagged peaks were no more daunting than the dense Amazonian rainforests that lie to the east of them." That company set out to construct the longest gas pipeline in the world—from the tip of Patagonia to the Argentine capital of Buenos Aires. He goes on to say that such grand schemes, exemplifying the vaulting ambition of modern capitalism, were made possible by the invention of the joint-stock company where the company's capital was jointly owned by multiple investors (Ferguson, 2008: 120–21).

Yes, if we all operated at the mental phase where stockholders would keep companies in check through being objectively vigilant, such big investments may be a good thing. But if we have to rip apart the rainforests, cut through numerous communities, cause innumerable environmental and social problems, and all that to appropriate the balance of natural flows and repositories in the earth that we do not fully understand, when instead we could have used all that money to harness local energy sources, including solar, in new and innovative ways, whether that is really a good or a bad thing is a question of perspective.

It is all a question of which level in the fractal model we operate from. But going back to the recorded beginnings, 12th-century France saw the rise of the first brokers who were concerned with managing and regulating the debts of agricultural communities on behalf of the banks and also traded with debts (Wikipedia, 2010s). In the 13th century, the family Van der Beurze had a building in Antwerp where merchants met to trade. The idea quickly spread around neighboring counties and "Beurzen" soon opened in Amsterdam. Further, in the middle of the 13th century, Venetian bankers began to trade in government securities. In 1351, the Venetian government outlawed spreading rumors intended to lower the price of government funds. Bankers in Pisa, Verona, Genoa, and Florence also began trading in government securities during the 14th century. The Dutch later started joint-stock companies, which let shareholders invest in business ventures and get a share of their profits or losses. In 1602, the Dutch East India Company issued the first share on the Amsterdam Stock Exchange. It was the first company to issue stocks and bonds. The Amsterdam Stock Exchange (or Amsterdam Beurs) is also said to have been the first stock exchange to introduce continuous trade in the early 17th century. The Dutch "pioneered short selling, option trading, debt-equity swaps, merchant banking, unit trusts and other speculative instruments, much as we know them" (Wikipedia, 2010s). There are now stock markets in virtually every developed and most developing economies with the world's biggest markets being in the US, the UK, Japan, India, China, Canada, Germany, France, South Korea, and the Netherlands.

Ferguson sheds insight into the origins of the stock market at the beginning of the 1600s. Dutch traders wanted more control over the sea trade routes than their Portuguese and Spanish competitors. Six existing East India companies set up to get spices and other goods from the East Indies and operating out of the major Dutch ports had to be combined in order to build up permanent bases and fortifications to supplant the Portuguese and Spanish. The single entity was chartered in 1602 to enjoy a monopoly on all Dutch trade east of the Cape of Good Hope and west of the Straits of Magellan. Like its predecessors, this entity was supposed to exist for a fixed period after which the investors were entitled to withdraw their money. Further, subscription to the company's capital was open to all residents and there was no upper limit of how much might be raised. Many residents rushed to acquire shares and the capital raised—6.45 million guilders—made the company the largest corporation of the era. The capital of the company was divided between six regional areas of Holland. Seventy directors from these areas appointed 17 lords to be the board of the company. With the initial capital trade networks were set up, ships were built, and factories were built to make garments. Garments were used to trade for spices. The Dutch fleet had to war with the Spanish fleet in order to gain control of trade routes. In fact, the company made more money from captured enemy vessels than from trade. When a few major investors protested against the company's warlike conduct and sought their money back after the initial 10-year contract, publication of the accounts and repayment of the capital were both postponed. Instead, the 17 Lords agreed to pay shareholders a dividend. It was also announced that the company would not be liquidated as originally planned. This meant that any shareholders who wanted their cash back had no alternative but to sell their shares to another investor. This was in 1612 and marked the real beginning activity in this stock market. The Amsterdam Stock Exchange had already been set up in 1602 by the Dutch East India Company for dealing with its printed stocks and bonds. Apparently turnover in the company shares was high and within a few years one third of the stock had been transferred from the original owners. Further, because the company did not open its books often, a forward market in company shares soon developed, which allowed sales for future delivery. This period also saw the birth of the Amsterdam Exchange Bank, since a stock market cannot function without an effective monetary system. Once bankers began to accept company shares as collateral for loans, the link between the stock market and the supply of credit began to be forged. Company, bourse, and bank, thus, provided the foundation for a new kind of economy (Ferguson, 2008: 128–33).

In looking at the effective birth of the stock market, we see first, that it was an outcome of a reneged deal in the charter of the company in which the 17 Lords had in effect wrested rights from other shareholders to continue what must have been very attractive in terms of maintaining personal power. Even the vehicle used to make most money—conducting war—shed insight into the nature of this arrangement. It was therefore, even 400 years ago, decidedly vital in its start. In *Connecting Inner Power with Global Change* (Malik, 2009b), I talk about the nature of seeds, the base fractal pattern that then by virtue of creativity reinforces its own seed pattern on every subsequent level it comes into contact with. If the initial people were in it to primarily assert their own and their collective possibility at the expense of all others whom they came into contact with, then that is the nature of the seed that multiplies its raison d'être.

Thoughtful schemes—a mental capacity—were used to prolong and fortify the rule and power of the few as opposed to the many. If this is still being done today, it should be no surprise that it happened as much as 400 years ago. In fact, at that time, where as a race we were probably less thoughtful than we are now, the vital must have naturally overpowered any other capacity to easily take the lead. The seed that existed in the few, became the seed of the East India Company. This also became the seed in the stock exchange that was erected. This became the seed that animated investor activity and speculation with the high return possibility was sown. This became the seed in the bank that was created. And then as we shall see soon, this seed spread. John Law, whom we will talk about soon as we consider a subsequent stock market crash, took this seed and applied it to a whole unsuspecting country—France.

Yet, it is remarkable to note, that this very first Amsterdam Stock Exchange, erected 400 years ago, did not suffer a crash. This amplifies the fact that even though financial activity was high, it was still contained and affected the relatively few—it was still very much in the physical phase.

But also, the creation of the seed was preceded by some fortunate elements that benefited the local populations. There was the fact that once the Dutch East India Company had raised the enormous sum of money that it had, there was deliberation of its use at the level of parliament that necessarily meant that more voices and points of view were considered in subsequent decisions. It was decided that funds raised would be distributed amongst all regional provinces to minimize hostility between one region and the next. Further, the initial public issue itself was subscribed to by all layers of society. Not only did noblemen and merchants subscribe but so too did artisans and servants. The wealth, therefore, relatively speaking, filtered not only horizontally across the local regions but vertically as well, through various layers of society. Because many segments of society in a sense organically contributed to and benefited from the development of the Dutch East India Company, there were no wild investments from widespread people wanting a piece of the action. The subsequent dynamics of the Amsterdam Stock Exchange was therefore more ordered and contained—more at the physical level. The fewer number of financial products and financial players—both sellers and buyers—meant that the dynamics of the VLP could not really kick in.

If we are talking about a sequence, then the fact that a birth is followed by the physical, then the vital, and then the mental phases makes sense. Note, that the seed still remains vital. But it still journeys through the three phases which are the nature of progress. Further, every phase has its sub-phases and sub-sub-phases, the fractals within fractals, which in the end, are borne out to be the pathways by which progress happens. This initial fractal pattern has now multiplied across the earth. Companies, stock exchanges, banks exist to feed the initial pattern and the question is, what will it really take to alter what is essentially vital in its birth and very being? Is this even possible? Could the initial setup of the company, stock market, and bank—the natures of this new economy—have proceeded any differently? If what had preceded the development of the seed—the notion of all segments of society somehow organically benefiting—had been contained in the seed, then likely things would be different. If somehow that level of thinking and societal pragmatism was embedded into the running of the stock market itself, then likely the development and dynamics of subsequent stock market action would have tended to proceed differently. However, as John Law was to reinforce in his experiments in France, this was not to be the case. For Law felt that what had happened in Amsterdam was still too conservative.

Law's vision was that a supreme monarch, such as existed in France, would effectively

> ... delegate his credit to a trading company into which all the materials of trade in the kingdom fall successively and are amassed into one...For the absolute prince who knows how to govern can extend his credit further and find needed funds at a lower interest rate than a prince who is limited in his authority ... The whole nation would become a body of traders, who have for cash the royal bank, in which by consequence all the commerce, money, and merchandise re-unite. (Wasserman, 1934: 653)

John Law sought to change the nature of the seed to remove any kind of social component to it, to in fact make it entirely capitalist. Further, as evidenced by his becoming the Controller General of France with control over collection of all indirect taxes, the French national debt, 26 French mints, the colony of Louisiana, the Mississippi Company, amongst numerous other personal holdings (Ferguson, 2008: 147–49), he sought to benefit his own power and reach. That is he wanted to make the essential seed completely vital.

This also pushes us into the notion that each of these devises were themselves functions of embedded perception and ways of being at the individual level at the time. If the seed consciousness was vital, it is very difficult for any creations of the vital consciousness to be anything but vital. It was greed and fear that propelled transaction, then the greed and fear had to continue to create the outcome of such unholy matrimony.

9

Lessons from 20th Century Stock Market Crashes

In this chapter, we will look at the Crash of 1929, which has parallels to the contemporary financial crisis, the Bear Market of 1973–1974, which was really the result of moving decisively into the vital phase—the Crash of 1987 which was the first synchronized global crash, the Japanese Asset Bubble which unleashed significant vital-level flows that further undermined the notion of true value on a global scale, the subsequent Asian Financial Crises, and the 1998 Russian Financial Crisis, which while triggered by the Asian Financial Crises, pointed to a fundamental physical-level instability. We will gain important insights into how financial markets and the stock market need to be redesigned to avoid similar situations.

Crash of 1929

The Crash of 1929 was estimated to be amongst the worst stock market crashes in history. The DJIA lost about 90 percent of its value (Wikipedia, 2010g), and the Crash was the start of what is now termed as the Great Depression. There were many similarities to today's global financial crises. The Crash was preceded by breakthroughs in technology, by an array of financial innovation, and by irrational exuberance on the part of the investor. The Crash resulted in an important piece of legislation in the *Glass–Steagall Act* of 1932 that sought to bring about a separation between commercial and investment banks. Such separation is essential so long as we are in the vital phase because it is too difficult for any profit-seeking entity to overcome conflict of interest in its various forms. To begin with, depository institutions possess enormous financial power by virtue of their control of other people's money. The extent of this power must be limited to ensure soundness in the market for funds. Conflicts of interest brought about by granting of credit and use of credit by the same entity have to be controlled. For a depository institution to be able to participate in inherently high-risk security activities such as mortgage-backed securities, to thereby threaten the integrity of deposits is unacceptable. The aura of being a depository institution in fact heightens the problem because its investment vehicles are easily given an AAA rating. This rating is illusory and does not lessen the riskiness of the investment being made. Yet, this is precisely the situation that existed before the crash of 1929, and unfortunately, the situation that existed in the current buildup to the global financial crises that started in 2008, when the Glass–Steagall Act was finally repealed in 1999. The separation of depository and investment institutions, and the tighter regulation over both kinds of institutions is an imperative going forward, so long as we continue in the vital phase. The control of size of banks so that they do not become too big to fail is also an imperative. There is no reason why inefficient and plundering entities that exist to embody the VLP should be given carte blanche to continue such activities. These are some changes that will need to be made going forward. Another change that took place following the Crash of 1929 was that of temporarily suspending trading in the event of rapid declines. This too is a necessity so that the long built-up value is not lost in a few hours of ultimately meaningless trading. This also calls for a deeper change—that of making trading more meaningful.

The Bear Market of 1973–1974

The Bear Market of 1973–1974 is incredibly important when considering lessons for the future. This Bear Market affected all the major stock markets in the world. Major stock markets lost as much as 40 percent of their value (Wikipedia, 2010a). This period is especially important because of the many fundamentals shifting at the same time. The Gold Standard and the global currency peg to the US dollar was removed. Global order was therefore undone overnight. Consequently, not having to follow strict rules to keep currency values within bands, exchange rates began to float with all their attendant changes in loss and gain of value at country and corporate levels. Further, there was a loosening of the money supply that essentially ushered in a shift from the physical to the vital phase of stock market activity. As though this was not enough, OPEC announced an oil embargo that in effect led to the Gold Standard being replaced by an Oil Standard. In the uncertainty and the immediate shifts that followed, there was a slowdown in global stock activity. That this should happen is not unexpected. In contrast, the recent global financial crisis that began in 2008 is almost the result of these shifts that happened in the early 1970s. There has been a further loosening of the money supply, and as described, many shifts, whereby the market has taken over the functions that should be performed by a bank. The phase 1973–1974 is important to consider, because in effect, if some of the changes made then are not reversed, then the current phase where we appear to be climbing back up in terms of stock market activity will be highly illusory and will result in a scenario characterized by multiple dips of increasing complexity. The impulse after a slowdown in activity is to increase activity almost exponentially. If the fundamentals are not shifted though and if money supply is not bought back under a rational control, the effects will be devastating on many fronts. All bear markets are not the same. In their recent book *Crises Economics*, Roubini and Mihm (2010) argue that all financial crises have the same fundamentals underlying them. In fact, I will argue differently that crises are fundamentally different, and in fact, need to be handled differently. The essential variability must be perceived against the backdrop of where in the physical–vital–mental progression or landscape, the crash or the bear market is occurring and how in fact it is contributing to that universal pattern. In effect, the money supply needs to be bought back in control. There are many ways to do this. Further, the oil standard, which has already been argued is only temporary, needs to give way to a more long-lasting standard that is a source of wealth for global citizens as opposed to the global elite. Having been the doorway into the vital phase, the question at hand now, is how can what we do be the doorway to a mental phase. Only if that is not possible, and perhaps it is too soon for that, should we be talking about how to control the vital phase so that a greater degree of rationality is apparent.

The Crash of October 1987

The Crash of October 1987, when stock markets around the world crashed shedding a huge value in a short time, is also an interesting phenomenon. The year 1987 was about the time when stock market activity began to enter an accelerated phase. This Crash stands out because it is the first time that a synchronized crash affecting global markets occurred. A synchronized crash implies that true or deeper value has now been replaced by another notion of value. It is a sure sign that the stock markets were now deeply in the vital phase. It also marked the day of greatest stock market decline, and therefore, of irrational loss of value. It is clear that such irrationality has to be rooted out. For this to happen though forced decoupling has to occur. Blanket index investment instruments and portfolio investing has to be regulated. Algorithmic trading has to be altered to include different conditions for buying and selling stock. The very use of program trading will need to be regulated until such a point as we are securely in the mental phase.

The Japanese Asset Bubble

The Japanese Asset Bubble boom and bust that boomed between 1986 and 1991 and busted from 1991 all the way to the present day is also very instructive. There are some really important lessons to be gained from this. First, following World War II, the Japanese government implemented policies that encouraged people to save their income. Having exited form the devastation of the War, there was a different set of energies active, and Japanese companies and people worked in unison to recreate the country. Because of this solid, grounded approach, capital was more readily available, and having just exited from the pain, there was a hunger to build value. This continued for a few decades and by many estimates Japan became a wealthy country.

However, the global shifts that had begun in 1971 under Nixon's reign in USA, had their effect on all countries, including Japan. Caught up in the fever of speculation, the Tokyo Stock Exchange and real estate markets became hot-beds of investment. Banks became increasingly lax and granted riskier loans. The notion of value shifted from true creation to one of vital creation. That is, the notion of true value and worth were lost, and this inevitably caused a massive asset bubble that fed further speculation and became the source for laxer credit release. Bubbled assets at the heart of the boom became surrogates for cash, and the notion of real value was further bastardized. Of course this was bound to burst. A couple of points: First, all that money should have continued to be invested in things that really matter. Just as recreation of the country really mattered for the Japanese following the War, there are a number of things that really matter now. The balance of the world's development depends on this. To maintain the value of money it needs to be invested in such things that matter.

To facilitate this, other kinds of "stock markets" that encourage critical areas of global development need to be created. The notion of what is critical spans a spectrum. At one end are the obvious global issues of a social and environmental nature that seriously need to be addressed. At the other end of the spectrum, development of arts, knowledge, and service need to be encouraged. For it is only in the uncoupled development of these other pursuits that the spirit of humanity can continue to advance and a truer era of global sustainability be brought to bear.

Further, incentives and returns on investment should be denominated in kind rather than in cash—a free course or degree to the person of your choice, a supply of fresh water, carbon credits, and so on. Thus, first-tier markets would not only include investments for business reasons and in existing corporations which of course have other filters already discussed to monitor and regulate these investments, but also markets to make investments for environmental, social, knowledge, and artistic pursuits that would be regulated by another non-business reason altogether. Further, there would be second-tier or secondary markets where some of the goods and return of investments in kind could be allotted. It would require direct involvement on the part of the allotter though, so that it does not become a loophole to feed further inconsequential vital fires.

Second, when the bubble burst, then all that money had to go elsewhere in the absence of true areas to invest it in. More of the same in other countries continued, and this money began to fuel bubbles in other parts of the world. Clearly a mechanism to reverse this, needs to be put in place. Rating agencies need to step up to the plate to assess the true risk and capability of a country to absorb these massive flows of investment. Markets that truly require investment should be fed instead.

In the absence of operating at the mental level, this will likely not happen. Therefore regulation is necessary unless the bases of money creation are democratized, in which case, different constituencies around the world would create money and local means of development based on the promise of true and local development.

Third, because Japan has a lot going for it in terms of companies whose products are valued globally, it could become a sustainable source for carry trade. In essence, the carry trade allows citizens of a country to incrementally sell off their country through devaluing their own currency and asset base. Japanese yens are exchanged for bets on other currencies. Because of the short-term higher return due to other country bonds paying higher interest, the longer-term repercussions are thrown aside. Instead of continuing to invest in what really matters in the country, the money is funneled elsewhere for purely vital reasons.

The carry trade itself funds other irrational bubbles the world over. Further, when relied on it, it can cause havoc overnight if relative exchange rates change. This was the situation in Iceland where residents had borrowed money in Euro denominated loans. When the Euro rose, Icelanders were unable to repay loans. This caused the Icelandic financial crises of 2008–2009. Further, the reverse appreciation can take place, and this can cause major financial crises if other loans are denominated in the appreciating currency. Arbitrage is of course a fact of financial activity. Still, there has to be regulation so that countries do not go bankrupt from relying on arbitrage as a source of value. Real value must be the result of real activity. Going forward we need to ensure that all these limiting possibilities do not continue to exist.

The Asian Financial Crises

The Asian Financial Crises was by many estimates caused because of the massive inflows of speculative money that needed a new home for quick returns. In part, this was due to the higher interest rates offered by countries such as Thailand, Malaysia, and Indonesia, which were at the epicenter of the crisis. Further, given that the Japanese Asset Bubble had just burst, there was a huge amount of money that had previously been invested there that needed a new home. All this money rushed about, driven by the lure of vital value of making that quick buck, regardless of true creation or destruction of value.

Naturally with large inflows of capital, asset prices began to rise. Corporations and individuals alike experienced a rise in their vital-level wealth—whether wealth was really increasing can only be judged by anchoring on the mental level where it is truer development that is the focus. This perception that all were richer because some asset—whether real estate or stocks—at the center of the bubble continued to rise in escalated vital-level value, caused heightened irrationality and risk-taking on the part of all constituents, including banks that began issuing loans based on the perceived vital-level wealth. When it was realized however, that underlying development had not really taken place and that many individuals and corporations were naturally beginning to default on loan payments, then there was a massive retraction of capital and the Asian Financial Crisis came into being.

Foreign investors flooded the exchange market with respective country currency, and as a result, the value of these currencies began to depreciate. This put even more burden on international loan payments and heightened the default rates on loans thereby causing more bankruptcies and even more pulling out of investments. To try and prop up the currency rate, respective governments increased interest rates, which made further loan origination in the country even more difficult. Thus, there was a senseless and destructive cycle put into place that naturally exceeded the boundaries of the vital-level notion of wealth to destroy truer mental-level wealth in the bargain.

What this teaches us again, is that it is necessary to maintain focus on true underlying development. To use mass-scale vital-level euphoria manifesting in a vastly increased demand relative to supply, is in fact a highly misleading measure of value. We need metrics that peel these illusionary layers away to focus on what actually is being done with the money, how it is actually being used, and further, how that development is in fact development of a true, sustainable, mental-level order. Anything else is going to cause massive turmoil and destroy the hard work and livelihoods of many innocent people. I say again, that even, and in fact necessarily, at the level of the stock market, it is not the fluctuations of stock price that should determine whether to buy or sell a stock but the underlying value as determined by broad standards of sustainability that should drive buy and sell decisions. This is especially true at the vital level where we have already determined that the notion of EMH and of price automatically reflecting all market information is quite simply inaccurate and baseless.

For EMH and such pricing to work, at the very least, massive and irrational vital-level flows driven by a desire or greed–fear based decision-making paradigm has to be permanently removed. Such phenomena as carry trade investments, massive speculation, hot money inflows, massive government intervention, especially of the type being experienced in the aftermath of the 2008 global financial crises will need to be regulated out so that the noise factor is removed. Then there is the chance that the market and supply and demand will begin to approach an EMH type reality. It has to be recognized that this is the case, and it has to be recognized that the real challenge we face today is maneuvering away from a vital-level market reality to a mental-level market reality. That is an imperative if the global economic scenario is to proceed on a surer and more sustainable footing.

The 1998 Russian Financial Crisis

There are valuable lessons to learn from the 1998 Russian Financial Crisis. This crisis was triggered by the Asian Financial Crisis. Russia was a net exporter to Asia providing many commodities required to fuel the Asian Bubble. Such commodities included petroleum, natural gas, timber, and metals. With a sudden drop in revenues generated from these exports, the government was not able to fund its debt payments thereby heralding the start of the crisis.

The Russian government was unable to institute market reforms to alter its balance of payments, and investor confidence was further eroded with a run on Russian assets and a pulling out of foreign investments. Russia had to inject billions of US dollars to buy Ruble and artificially hold it up. Subsequently its stock, bond, and currency markets collapsed and the only thing that reversed this situation was the sudden increase in global demand for petroleum. This caused a massive trade surplus in 1999–2000 which ended the crisis.

The Russian Financial Crisis sheds insight into what is deemed to be a financial crisis. It is essentially about being able to meet international debt payments. This however, is a narrow view of crisis, and again, is rooted in dynamics representative of the vital level. The fact is that the economy was already in a reality of deep crisis. The price of fundamentals such as food rose as much as 100 percent; basic wages of workers could not be paid; several major banks were closed down. The primary constituent of wealth was commodity based: the country obviously had not done much to push levels of creativity and build on inherent value in its land. Its bases of wealth were therefore at the physical level—commodities which could be touched and seen.

The ubiquitous fractal for progress demands that development continue to proceed along the physical–vital–mental trajectory. If there is stagnation, then crisis must occur to allow the journey to continue. In that, all and any kind of crisis is useful whether it is defined at the physical, vital, or mental level. But were the perception or interpretation of crisis to change to the mental level, then the reality that the crisis has existed for a while would more effectively come into relief and would not result in irrational short-term fluctuations that in the final analysis do more damage than good.

At the physical level, crisis does not really exist so long as commodities exist. Perception of this nature will in fact cause major long-term crises in that the bases of sustainability will most likely be compromised in the one-pointed pursuit of extraction of commodities, regardless of impact on environment. At the vital level, crises exist only when there is default on payments. The wrong levers of wealth are therefore being focused on. It is only when the focus is on the reason and more holistic development that truer wealth can manifest and that the compromising of this wealth can more effectively be managed. Risk can be called out in advance, and subsequently, the right developments and investments made. But this can only be if the mental-level metrics replaces physical-level metrics such as estimated availability of raw materials, and vital-level metrics such as real estate and stock prices. Mental-level metrics, such as true development, true citizen happiness, true state of the environment from a sustainability perspective, true level of creativity, have to become the focus of attention and the levers by which decision to invest or not are made. These have to become front and center at the level of stock markets, and in fact, in all other markets. If the focus is here, rather than solely at the physical or vital level, then even the reality of crisis as we perceive and understand it today will change so that crises in general becomes less of a reality.

The claim that the Russian crisis was short in length is in fact a paradox. The longer-term effect on global sustainability of high levels of perhaps even irrational extraction, driven by vital-level dynamics, will be disastrous. Wealth of the world will be reduced as a result of trying to maintain the semblance of vital-level health and wealth. The fact that Russia was not at the time heavily integrated with the global financial environment, in contrast to the South East Asian economies for instance, created the perception that its crisis is of a shorter duration. At the vital level, this is no doubt true, and its very physical-level focus buffered it from having to go through the fate of some South East Asian countries. But these narrow perceptions representative of the physical and vital levels are misleading and can easily cover up the seriousness of a situation gelling in the background. On the positive side, its crisis is no doubt pushing it to move more to the vital level where more energy comes alive on a larger scale. Indigenous industry and creativity gets a kick start. The dangers of this phase are of course huge. Hopefully, Russia can learn from the lessons of the rest of the world though, to temper the negative effects of the vital phase through more mature regulation.

10

Lessons from 21st Century Stock Market Crashes

In this chapter, we contrast the essentially valuable Dot-Com Crisis with the essentially valueless US Housing Crises; we look at the Chinese Stock Bubble of 2007 which shows us how a reasonable mental-level maneuver by the government is interpreted and acted on by a meaningless vital-level response; we look at the US Bear Market of 2007–2009 which brings into question the very indexes used to monitor stock market activity; we look at the 2009 Dubai World Crisis which reinforces the notion of taking with a grain of salt all vital-level activity; and we look at the Greek Debt Crisis of 2010 which brings up fundamental questions of national sovereignty, which will likely become more and more prevalent so long as we continue at the vital level.

The Dot-Com Crises of 2000 and the US Housing Crises of 2004

The Dot-Com crisis of 2000 brings into view another set of lessons. The massive inflow of money in fact was highly beneficial in this environment because the Dot-Com phenomenon was fundamentally about moving away from many of the irrationalities of vital-level monopoly toward the possibilities of a more diverse individual-level creativity. Plays such Amazon, eBay, Yahoo, Google, and more recently, Facebook, and Twitter upset the balance of vital-level dynamics to bring another set of possibilities to bear. Of course, there was a lot of wasted money and vital-level euphoria that caused a boom and a bust. But the net-net has been huge. Innovation of this kind that is grounded in how activity, work, process of socialization are fundamentally altered, and in real greater freedom for the individual and different scales of collectivity, is of a real kind. People, communities, posterity benefits as a result of such risk and such flows of wealth. This must be contrasted to what has been termed as innovation in the financial field though. Innovation in the financial field is not based on real tangible development.

The recent US-based housing crises is a perfect example. Sub-prime type mortgages were securitized. Traditionally a mortgage was a one-to-one transaction. That is, a bank gave a loan to an individual to buy a house after significant due diligence and the buyer of the loan then made principal and interest payments to the bank until the loan had been paid off. The bank owned the reward and the risk. With mortgage-backed securities, however, an investment bank created a Special Purpose Vehicle to pool mortgages together that it then sold to generate additional revenues. Thus, the originating lender of debt was first rewarded for issuing the mortgage. There was no risk they took on and therefore the level of due diligence and risk monitoring was completely removed. That mortgage was then pooled with many other such mortgages and marketed as a robust investment opportunity.

After all, according to portfolio theory, which anyway is more applicable at the mental as opposed to the vital level and therefore quite inapplicable in current times, pooling assets will minimize overall risk and therefore in theory there is no more need to conduct due diligence—just keep adding in assets of different types, even if they are different types of mortgages and all will be well. Securities were created and these securities were sold to investors around the world. Obviously the value of money gets inflated as a result. The buyers of the securities now in effect get paid a monthly payment by the would-be homeowner. The buyers of the securities can further sell financially manufactured products based on that same tangible asset, and the value of money is further inflated. At the end of the day, if creation of money is not backed by an equal creation of tangible value, then the world suffers in the bargain. But all recent financial innovation has been of this kind. A whole breed of mushroom-type activity is set up, and all the while, everyone thinks everyone is getting richer. Financial returns of these mushroom companies increase. This draws more funds and more of the same irrational type cycles are initiated. A mega bubble is created that ties everyone to illusory assets. When this one bursts, then real trouble results.

The 2008 global financial crisis was the result of over dependence on toxic assets of this nature. They were toxic because they were not based on any real tangible value. There is one level of toxicity when adequate due diligence has not been performed. This, of course, was the case. There is another level of toxicity when the very same tangible product, the house, is used to inflate the flow of money in the economy. Creation of securitized mortgage and other products assured that. There is a third level of toxicity when highly leveraged funds such as hedge funds now focus their resources on the securitized products thereby in effect severing all links with reality. For now, the game is focused on the illusory bubble and the asset at the center of this, the toxic securitized products, becomes collateral and a starting point for a whole array of additional financial innovation. The fourth level of toxicity is that such assets are viewed as assets rather than liabilities in the first place. This points to the toxicity of the financial system itself which allows such meaningless valuations to drive, what is at the end of the day, highly destructive activity negatively affecting the lives of millions of people.

Clearly, when these two bubbles are contrasted, the dot-com bubble and the bubbles that followed it, discrimination as to where to invest has to come to bear. If all we focus on is the claim of organizations that they are generating huge profit, because they happen to be at the center of a financial innovation type bubble, at the end of the day that is like spreading a cancer through society because destructive wealth diminishing type activity has overtaken productive activity. Claims by companies and fluctuations of stock prices can hardly be taken at face value. A deeper penetration, a deeper, more meaningful array of metrics that indicate the truer ground-level value needs to be front and center and become the arbiter of whether or not to invest in a particular stock. This will require corporations to become truly more accountable to society.

Initiatives such as the Global Reporting Initiative are huge steps in this direction. For now through a process of self-disclosure, corporations list out environmental and social implications of their activities that will be of concern to various independent stakeholder groups around the world. Business corporations cannot act in isolation, creating their own rules for life. They are an intricate part of a single global system and must act as so. Stock markets need to be redesigned to help this to happen. As they exist currently they are irrationally funneling money into areas that are at the end of the day oftentimes highly destructive to the fabric of life. But this kind of holism can only happen if stocks are traded on a more holistic set of parameters in the first place. Stock price is clearly not that, because as already stated, we are clearly not in a reality of an efficient market. In the case of the Dot-Com, we know we are at a boundary state—breaking from the vital to the mental. In the case of supposed financial innovation, all we are doing is driving deeper into the irrationalities of the vital phase. The former investment needs to be encouraged. The latter forestalled. This perspective of progress, following what has been identified as the universal fractal for progress, has also to become part of the holistic set of parameters that drives investment decision.

The Chinese Stock Bubble of 2007

The Chinese Stock Bubble of 2007 has some ironic lessons to it. It refers to the stock market plunge on February 27, 2007, that wiped of hundreds of billions US dollars in market value globally in a single day. The trigger was actually a very logical response to the heating stock markets in China by the government. Rumor had it that the government wanted to raise interest rates to curb inflation, and further, wanted to put a clamp on speculative trading using borrowed money. In fact, such announcements, if analyzed from the long term, should have yielded a rise in stock market value because it takes off unnecessary and irrational pressure to grow in the short term, recognizing that slower growth is of the more sustainable kind. Instead, the stock markets took a 10 percent hit that day and this rippled over into stock markers globally.

After the Chinese market drop, the DJIA in the US dropped 416 points or 3.29 percent from 12,632 to 12,216 amid fears for growth prospects, then the biggest one-day slide since the September 11, 2001, terrorist attacks. The S&P 500 saw a comparable 3.45 percent slide. Sell orders were made so fast that a second analysis computer had to be used, causing an instantaneous 200 point drop at one point in the Dow Industrials (Associated Press, 2007).

The response reinforces how entrenched we really are at the vital level. It also points to how macro-level indicators need to become part of a range of parameters that drive investment in stock markets. Buy and sell decisions cannot be made solely on stock price until such time as we have securely moved into the mental level. So long as we continue at the vital level, parameters that cause a break in trading without penalizing stock price have to be instituted. Such parameters may include the reality of global overshoot, where demand is greater that what the earth can possibly supply, or increase in GHG emissions, or destruction on ecosystem services, or truer happiness at the individual level, or simple overheating of an economy as in the case of China, amongst others.

The US Bear Market of 2007–2009

The US Bear Market of 2007–2009 was declared in June 2008 when the DJIA had fallen 20 percent from its October 11, 2007, high (Wikipedia, 2010u). The underlying reasons for the Bear Market are of course related to the underlying levels of toxicity already described and elaborated by the many shortfalls already pointed out in previous chapters.

It is useful to note though, that the DJIA is a price-weighted average of 30 large companies on the New York Stock Exchange. A price-weighted index is where the relative price drives the weight of the company in the index. That is, stocks are included in proportion to their quoted price. Amongst these companies are those we pointed out in Chapter 4 as being leaders in creating an unsustainable world. Controversial industries included are food processing, oil and gas, pharmaceuticals, banking, and retail. Many of the companies represented are, quite frankly, yesterday's as opposed to tomorrow's companies. From this point of view, since we are operating at the vital level, there is going to be a bias to support companies that are perceived as hot in terms of returns. In other words, we will be funding the continued acceleration of hot-spots. Money will go where money is and will not necessarily be driven by the truer underlying value of a company that will tend to be better captured by following a fundamentally weighted index.

Capitalization-weighted indexes tend to be more like price-weighted indexing but vary in that it is the market value of the company as calculated by number of shares outstanding that gives it its relative weight in an index. From this point of view, capitalization-weighted indices will also be biased toward the vital consciousness. If something is attracting a lot of money, it will attract more, regardless of truer underlying value. Underlying value may be there or it may not, but that tends to get obscured in this perception. Note that if we were in a reality of efficient market, truly operating at the mental level, then both price and capitalization-weighted indices would likely be a superior approach to fundamentally weighted index since the wisdom of many different stakeholder groups would influence demand for a stock.

In research conducted by Arnott, Hsu, and Moore (2005), 40 years of back-tested indexes weighted by any of several fundamental factors including sales, ebit, earnings, cash flow, book value, or dividends in US markets outperformed the S&P 500 by approximately 2 percent per annum with volatility similar to the S&P 500. In non-US markets, fundamentally based indexes outperformed capitalization-weighted indexes by approximately 2.5 percent with slightly less volatility and outperformed in all 23 MSCI EAFE (Europe, Australasia, and the Far East) countries (Research Affiliates, 2007). [The MSCI EAFE Index is a stock market index that is designed to measure the equity market performance of developed markets outside of the US and Canada. The EAFE acronym stands for Europe, Australasia, and Far East. The index is market capitalization weighted.]

Even the fundamental indexation though, from a sustainability perspective, is narrow, and more sustainability oriented indexes that get to the true drivers of long-term wealth creation need to become the arbiters of whether we are truly in a bear market or not. The point is, we may declare a bear market but that is hardly the case because we are just looking at the wrong metrics of development. What the decline of the common indexes may really be telling us is that an old vitally driven world is drawing to an end. But we still do not have adequate metrics in place to see the dawn of a newer mentally driven world. Stock markets need to be driven by these newer mentally driven indexes so that we may hone in on and rightly invest in tomorrow's world.

There has also been some significant legislation in the US that has exasperated the global financial crises, increased volatility in markets, and further obscured sense in the stock market. Significantly, the *Gramm–Leach–Bliley Act*, also known as the Financial Services Modernization Act of 1999 (Wikipedia, 2010n), repealed part of the *Glass–Steagall Act* of 1933, opening up the market among banking companies, securities companies, and insurance companies. The *Glass–Steagall Act* prohibited any one institution from acting as any combination of an investment bank, a commercial bank, and an insurance company. The *Gramm–Leach–Bliley Act*, by contrast, allowed commercial banks, investment banks, securities firms, and insurance companies to consolidate. It also allowed traditional investment brokers to create and sell high-risk investment products to traditionally low-risk commercial banks.

Considering the sub-prime mortgage crisis just discussed, what this means is that through the action of investment banks, the toxic assets were now widely distributed and in effect became an intricate part of the global financial landscape. It was inevitable that much of the edifice would have to crash, given that it was being rebuilt on such a flimsy foundation.

The *Sarbanes–Oxley Act* of 2002, also known as the *Public Company Accounting Reform and Investor Protection Act* and *Corporate and Auditing Accountability and Responsibility Act*, is a US federal law enacted on July 30, 2002, which set new or enhanced standards for all US (Wikipedia, 2010r) public company boards, management, and public accounting firms. The bill was enacted as a reaction to a number of major corporate and accounting scandals including those affecting Enron, Tyco International, Adelphia, Peregrine Systems, and WorldCom. These scandals, which cost investors billions of dollars when the share prices of affected companies collapsed, shook public confidence in the nation's securities markets. The act contains several sections, ranging from additional corporate board responsibilities to criminal penalties and requires the Securities and Exchange Commission (SEC) to implement rulings on requirements to comply with the new law. The SEC adopted dozens of rules to implement the *Sarbanes–Oxley Act*. It created a new, quasi-public agency, the Public Company Accounting Oversight Board which was charged with overseeing, regulating, inspecting, and disciplining accounting firms in their roles as auditors of public companies. The Act also covered issues such as auditor independence, corporate governance, internal control assessment, and enhanced financial disclosure.

Several have denounced this Act stating that it has caused capital flight from the US because of the additional onus on companies to comply to this. This is a typical vital-level response, and in the scheme of things, so long as we continue at the vital level, is absolutely necessary to help keep sanity and further disastrous breakdown typical at the vital level. Frameworks and acts of this nature are critical, and in a subsequent chapter we will take a step back to put together a framework that should similarly be passed as an act and moderate how global business is conducted. We may focus on the US but quite clearly such a framework and acts have to exist across the world.

The Dubai World Crisis of 2009

There are lessons to be learned from the Dubai World Crises of 2009. Dubai World is an investment company that manages and supervises a portfolio of businesses and projects for the Dubai government across a wide range of industry segments and projects that promote Dubai as a hub for commerce and trading. It is the Emirate's flag bearer in global investments and has a central role in the direction of Dubai's economy. On July 2, 2006, it was launched as a holding company with more than 50,000 employees in over 100 cities around the globe (Wikipedia, 2010i). If ever there was a big-bang start to a company, then this was it. Big-bang starts are of course movements typical of the vital level, and when that is recognized, then judgment and action should be commensurate with managing such dynamics.

The group now has extensive real estate investments in the US, the UK, and South Africa. Dubai World threatened to take the fund's money out of Europe shortly after the EU attempted to lay out "a set of principles for transparency, predictability and accountability" for sovereign wealth funds (O'Grady, 2008). But such principles are exactly what needs to be in place to minimize collateral damage from big investments of a vital type. Threats need to be called and managed so that future damage that is entirely probable in any vital-level play is minimized. The vital level, after all, is where stochastic variance rather than the Gaussian bell-curve is the norm.

Needless to say, in November 2009, Dubai World proposed to delay repayment of its debt (MEED, 2009), which raised the risk of the largest government default since the Argentine debt restructuring in 2001. The extent of the debt rattled many markets causing many indices and oil prices to drop.

In the midst of frenzied vital-level activity, any corporation that grows so rapidly, coming in so apparently strong, must be taken with a grain of salt. Especially given that much of the global financial landscape had begun to synchronize and independence is not a reality at the vital level where monopolistic forces come into being much more fully. It is not that Dubai World was investing in new and future-oriented technologies. Rather, a significant portion of its investments were clearly focused on the property and real-estate segments that were already deviously riddled with toxic assets and the attendant difficulty of being unable to separate the true from the false. Further, if anything, what this reinforces is that all that glitters is not gold. Rapid growth is always going to come with a price. Hence, the rate of additional funds coming into a hot-spot has to be controlled once it has been identified that indeed what is being funded is a hot-spot. Algorithms to slow down trading have to be put in place. Not doing so destroys a lot more wealth over the longterm.

The Greek Debt Crisis of 2010

The Greek Debt Crisis of 2010 brings up some very fundamental questions. Issues of national sovereignty, and therefore, centuries-old wealth as established by deep cultural and spiritual values made evident in the uniqueness of a nation versus adherence to stability measures at the regional collectivity level of the EU come face-to-face in such a crisis. So too does the notion of wealth itself. Is wealth the one-dimensional trait as captured by modern-day currency or is wealth multidimensional, transcending today's notion of it? Answers to these questions need to determine the limits and rules with respect to investment and speculation. This is true of financial markets in general and also may suggest how stock markets are to be redesigned.

Is all of life tradable? Or should limits be placed on what can be speculated on and what cannot. If an institution opens itself to seeking for loans, how far should the consequences of default go? Like the story of Shylock, the money-lender, in Shakespeare's *The Merchant of Venice*, what does a pound of flesh mean? Is it okay to reduce the soul or spirit of a country to nothing? Are austerity measures sending many into a state of poverty and compromising deeper spirit, the blood in Shylock's pound of flesh, and therefore, off limits in trading or speculative relationships? What is the responsibility of a country to its people? It is almost as though the very basis of money creation has to change. A rich, cultural community should have the bases of creating money based on its richness. It is the failure of a government if this cannot be done. If natural talents and indigenous ability of a country cannot be mobilized to mobilize creativity, then the government needs to pay for that in some way. This may be through social rebellion, as in the riots that plagued Greece following announcement of austerity measures.

The US government's handling of the financial crisis that has hit USA over the last two years is a case in point. The government has set new standards of intervention that seem to be being progressively adopted by other central banks around the world. Its primary goal has been the facilitation of the flow of money in the economy to counter any possibility of deflation. Hence, not only has the Federal Reserve been a lender-of-last-resort to established commercial banks, thereby extending them an unprovisional line of credit to minimize the possibility of bank-runs, but it has also become the lender-of-last-resort to nondepository financial enterprises. Even those financial enterprises that were at the center of causing the crises in the first place were in effect "forgiven." Given the goal to assure flow of money and business transaction, and given the extent of which the financial world is in a sense a monopoly, a domino effect that may hit innocent business could not be allowed to occur. The Federal Reserve in effect bought all the toxic assets on the balance sheets of US-based financial institutions (Roubini and Mihm, 2010). Because the US is a leader in the world by contemporary standards, the US dollar still commands respect and has proven to be a currency of investment amidst the global uncertainty spawned by the global crisis. This is so even though it lay at the center and was the starting point of the global crisis. Through these actions, the US has preserved its infrastructure and asset base, and at a deeper level, its current culture that very well could have become the target of internationally led takeovers. In fact, the Federal

Reserve has also extended swap lines so that central banks in troubled countries have been able to exchange their currencies, whether it be Swiss Francs or Japanese Yen or British Pounds for the US dollar, thereby in effect forgiving US dollar-denominated loans in respective countries while further strengthening the place of the US in the world. While this is admirable, at the same time the viability of money created to back toxic assets is clearly questionable. Such a deal has to have its negative effect sooner or later. Let us hope that something is quickly done to allow more "positive" money to be created.

When we think about the Greek debt crises, the question is, does Greece too not have a right to preserve its infrastructure and asset base and deeper culture? Because commercial enterprise is prized in today's world, and the institution of business is generally placed on a pedestal, we recognize and acknowledge the power held by USA. But every country has its strength and uniqueness, even though it may not be commercial. Why shouldn't then, their cultures be held intact and upheld? Greek people, as have the people of Mexico, South America, South East Asia, Russia—wherever recent financial crises have struck—have been subjected to austerity measures and many have been permanently displaced as a result of bankruptcies. Arguably, the social and environmental capitals of these countries have been permanently negatively affected in the bargain. Does this mean that a country has to be commercially dominant to guarantee its place in the world? Because of its inherent commercial strength, the USA was able to preserve its way of being pretty much untouched. If countries such as Greece have from the outset established a different social contract with their people and have followed deficit spending as a result, it too should be able to wipe the sleight clean and "forgive" its accumulated errors, whether through innovative monetary or fiscal policy, as has the USA, or simply as an application of what is to me an inherent principle of existence, whether for a person or for a country. And it should be able to do this on the promise of its unique wealth it brings to the world—not commercial wealth which frankly is incredibly one-dimensional—but on the bases of increasing the multidimensional wealth and therefore longer-term sustainability of the world.

If a country is to use fiscal policy to solve its ills, then the choice of where it invests money is critical. Road projects are well and good. But there are many environmental and social issues that need to be urgently addressed, whether of building up environmental capital through the replenishing of ecosystem services or of building social capital through the creation of robust communities, for example. If the government is going to pull money out of thin air, such acts should be quickly grounded to create real benefit and a source of future wealth, at the very least, for the country. Deficit spending that is going to yield substantial positive returns even if they are 5, 10, or 20 years in the future should hardly be penalized. In the vaster scheme of things, such social and environmental investments increase the wealth of the world. For, is not every single resource we utilize in every single enterprise of any kind a part of the earth, and even of the splendor behind things? To therefore reinvest in it, as opposed to groundless financially based securitization, Ponzi and other financial-innovation type schemes is money well spent.

To this effect, stock markets that increase multidimensional as opposed to single-dimensional type wealth have to be encouraged. This may be through the mechanism of different types of stock markets or through a current type stock market that has environmental and social investment filters embedded in its very running. Sustainability-type indices that funnel money into stock markets from the outside are one thing but what we are suggesting here is a step beyond so that the very algorithms that facilitate the act of trading itself be hard coded with social and environmental screens and filters.

Greece as part of the EU is unable to freely exercise monetary policy. This is part of the deal of becoming a part of the EU. Slapping on austerity measures in exchange for better borrowing rates from the EU originated loans means in effect that even Greece's freedom to exercise fiscal policy is being curtailed. As a country, when one compares a government's range of responses to crises between the USA and Greece, for example then, it is clear then that Greece is fast losing control over its country and its people. It is being subsumed into a global financial protocol and machinery that recognizes bottom line financial return only, and under this trajectory, Greece will not be Greece for much longer but just another clone in a senseless monopoly seeking for a headless and irrational world-dominion. If this is not a tragedy then what is? Clearly this has to be stopped in its tracks.

Niall Ferguson, the author of *Ascent of Money*, in a *Financial Times* piece (Ferguson, 2010) reflected that it is poignant that the financial crisis of the West has started in Greece, the birthplace of Western civilization, and is spreading from there, just as Western civilization spread from there. Let us hope that this crisis is viewed as more than a spreading financial crisis, to get to what it really is—a failure to perceive and align with the deeper and truer meaning of wealth. Stock markets have to be redesigned to facilitate the emergence of such wealth.

Concerns over a European Sovereign Debt Crisis also arose with respect to Spain, Portugal, and Ireland, in addition to Greece. As one steps back from this, the question is what is the EU about? A union must be based on more than economic convenience. It is the shortfall of our times that economy is placed above the possibilities of the human spirit. No doubt, excellence with respect to economic matters is desirable. But let us make sure that the economic is such that such excellence is based on something enduring. If a country has to sacrifice part of itself, and lead many of its people toward displacement, then the Union is likely not integral enough. For countries to come together in a sustainable way, all aspects of wealth have to be developed. Investments should recognize this, and creation of money should be based on such a holistic generation of wealth. Likely the Intent of the EU needs to be expanded and deepened. Financial and stock market action that supports such an expanded and deepened purpose behind the EU is what should be focused on.

Part IV

External Changes Affecting the Stock Market

11

Current External Changes Affecting Stock Markets

As discussed in Chapter 8, the seed of the stock market is vital in nature. Even though the birth of the stock market may have had some balancing mental influence in its early days in Amsterdam, John Lock worked his power to firmly alter the seed so that it became decidedly vital in its structure. This of course, reflected his selfish ambition, and the unrefined vital ambition of all around, who through their continued speculative actions endorsed it. This root-pattern has since then played its undulating havoc with financial markets. The stock market, more than any other market, has been like the tremendous singularity pointed to by physicists that has bent financial space and possibility to create the dysfunctions we experience in global markets today.

A fractal is of course a pattern that repeats itself on different scales. These scales can be thought of as bond markets, real estate markets, foreign exchange markets, commodities markets, futures markets, derivatives markets, and so on, that through the seductive influence of that root-pattern at the base of the global financial fractal has indelibly imprinted its way of being on them. The root at the root is human consciousness itself and its stagnation around the vital level. It is almost as though a tremendous markets-fractal, business-fractal, world-fractal emanate from this root at the root and cause the dysfunctions we concretely experience, so that the root at the root confronted with the resultant ugliness, finally has no option but to change its own functioning—that is, to shift to the mental level.

In its play across the world though, and as it imprints its way of being on more and more areas of life, deeper identity replete with different possibility, emerges in different areas and the vital way is challenged. Challenges of this sort are today happening more and more, and their drift or trend seems to point to the very need to change that initial seed that has been reinforced through the centuries. Socially Responsible Investing (SRI), Global Reporting Initiative (GRI), Dow Jones Sustainability Index (DJSI), Principles of Responsible Investing (PRI), frameworks such as Registration, Evaluation, Authorization and Restriction of Chemical substances (REACH), and global movements such as Hawken's Blessed Unrest are significant examples of such challenges, and in this chapter we will discuss these in more detail. The reason we do this is to understand what has naturally emerged from the play of life in its intersection with financial and stock market activity.

It is clear that in any redesign of stock markets, it is such significant movements that arise naturally that have to be considered, to do justice to the natural progression of life and to the on-going viability of stock markets themselves.

Socially Responsible Investing (SRI)

SRI has been active for perhaps as long as the institution of business has been active. It is like the first visceral cry of rebellion that has emerged as the child of those more socially conscious. In relatively modern times, this cry has perhaps naturally arisen from the more religiously minded. In John Wesley's 18th century sermon on the *Use of Money*, for example, he outlines basic tenets of responsible investing (Wesley, 1872). His formula, "We ought to gain all we can gain but this it is certain we ought not to do—we ought not to gain money at the expense of life, nor at the expense of our health," and again, "Having, first, gained all you can, and, secondly saved all you can, then give all you can" caused the more conscious then to avoid investing in industries that would harm oneself or others. Such industries included those where toxic chemicals were abundantly used, or those that employed slaves, or that dealt in the sin-industries. Through the decades the portfolio of socially responsible investing has gradually increased to include equality for women, civil rights, labor-management issues, apartheid, and environmental threats that have social repercussion.

As the Social Investment Forum, a membership association for professionals and organizations engaged in socially responsible and sustainable investing reports, today SRI is a broad-based approach to investing that recognizes that corporate responsibility and societal concerns are valid parts of investment decisions (SIF, 2010a). SRI now encompasses an estimated US$3.07 trillion out of US$25.2 trillion in the US investment marketplace today (SIF, 2010d). SRI spans a wide range of financial products and investments, from stocks and bonds to savings, checking, and other banking accounts, to venture capital. Socially responsible investors seek a competitive financial return on their investments, and the evidence is that it is possible to consistently achieve this. A growing number of academic studies have demonstrated that SRI mutual funds, for example, perform competitively with non-SRI funds over time (Center of Responsible Business, 2010).

On their website, the Social Investment Forum further reports,

> ... another indication of the competitive performance of SRI funds is the performance of SRI indexes. These indexes are designed to be benchmarked to non-SRI indexes, such as the S&P 500. The longest-running SRI index, the FTSE KLD 400, was started in 1990. Since that time, it has continued to perform competitively—the FTSE KLD 400 with returns of 9.51 percent from inception through December 31, 2009, compared with 8.66 percent for the S&P 500 over the same period. Further, the rapid growth of SRI in recent years is the best evidence that socially responsible investing yields competitive returns. Over the past 20 years, the total dollars invested in SRI has grown exponentially, as has the number of institutional, professional, and individual investors involved in the field. Between 1995 and 2007, total dollars under professional management in SRI grew from $639 billion to $2.71 trillion, outpacing the overall market. SRI investing has become part of the mainstream, and as a result, a number of conventional companies now offer SRI products to their clients. The bottom line is that more and more investors adopt and use SRI strategies not only because such investments allow a focus beyond the bottom line, but also because returns are comparable to those of more conventional investments. Ample evidence of the competitiveness of SRI is also found in the increasing investment in SRI by state pension funds, university endowments, and foundations. These fiduciaries are obligated by law to seek competitive returns for the portfolios they manage. The fact that a growing number of major US fiduciaries

> are either screening their portfolios, engaging in shareholder advocacy, or directing assets to community investing, demonstrates that these three SRI strategies do not impede financial returns. (SIF, 2010c)

The three SRI vehicles include screening, shareholder advocacy, and community investment. As the Social Investment Forum reports,

> ... screening includes both positive and negative screens, and is the practice of evaluating investment portfolios or mutual funds based on social, environmental and good corporate governance criteria. Screening may involve including strong corporate social responsibility performers, avoiding poor performers, or otherwise incorporating CSR factors into the process of investment analysis and management. Generally, social investors seek to own profitable companies that make positive contributions to society. Conversely, many social investors avoid investing in companies whose products and business practices are harmful to individuals, communities, or the environment. It is a common mistake to assume that SRI screening is simply exclusionary, or only involves negative screens. In reality, SRI screens are being used more and more frequently to invest in companies that are leaders in adopting clean technologies and exceptional social and governance practices. (SIF, 2010c)

Shareholder advocacy involves socially responsible investors who take an active role as the owners of corporations (SIF, 2010c). These efforts include talking with companies on issues of social, environmental, or governance concerns. Shareholder advocacy also frequently involves filing and co-filing shareholder resolutions on such topics as corporate governance, climate change, political contributions, gender/racial discrimination, pollution, problem labor practices, and a host of other issues. Shareholder resolutions are then presented for a vote to all owners of a corporation. The process of dialogue and filing shareholder resolutions generates investor pressure on company management, often garners media attention, and educates the public on social, environmental and labor issues. Such resolutions filed by SRI investors are aimed at improving company policies and practices, encouraging management to exercise good corporate citizenship, and promoting long-term shareholder value and financial performance. In 2007 and 2008, members and allies of the Social Investment Forum filed approximately 300 shareholder resolutions annually on social and environmental issues for consideration at the US companies' annual meetings (SIF, 2010b). Included in this group were resolutions asking firms for better disclosure and oversight of their political contributions and activities. Other recent social and environmental resolutions have addressed equal employment opportunity, climate change, global labor standards, and environmental management and reporting. Many of the sponsors were religious investors, mutual funds, and investment managers focused on environmental, social, and corporate governance (ESG) investing, state and city pension funds, trade union funds, foundations, and non-profit organizations.

Community investing directs capital from investors and lenders to communities that are underserved by traditional financial services institutions (SIF, 2010c). Community investing provides access to credit, equity, capital, and basic banking products that these communities would otherwise lack. In the US and around the world, community investing makes it possible for local organizations to provide financial services to low-income individuals and to supply capital for small businesses and vital community services such as affordable housing, child care, and healthcare. Community investing is the fastest growing area of SRI. In the last three, years it has grown 60 percent from US$25 billion to US$41.7 billion in assets (SIF, 2010c).

Global Reporting Initiative (GRI)

If SRI started off as a visceral cry that progressively shaped the investment strategies of more and more investors, GRI has been the systematic framing of all the positive and negative screens employed by such investors, and more. In fact, GRI is now referred to in the shaping of positive and negative screens.

As reported by GRI, it is a network-based organization that has pioneered the development of the world's most widely used sustainability reporting framework and is committed to its continuous improvement and application worldwide (www.globalreporting.org). The network-based organization is a large multi-stakeholder network of thousands of experts, in dozens of countries worldwide, who participate in GRI's working groups and governance bodies, use the GRI to report, access information in GRI-based reports, or contribute to develop the reporting framework in other ways—both formally and informally. The network-based organization ensures the highest degree of technical quality, credibility, and relevance. Having multiple stakeholders ensures that multiple needs and all stakeholders are considered. This contrasts to what might happen if, for example, just business representatives or just NGO representatives created the guidelines. It is also beneficial as it helps to increase the chances that all relevant sustainability issues are included and the accompanying best measures are developed.

This framework sets out the principles and indicators that organizations can use to measure and report their economic, environmental, and social performance. The cornerstone of the framework is the Sustainability Reporting Guidelines. The third version of the guidelines—known as the G3 Guidelines—was published in 2006. The guidelines outline core content for reporting and are relevant to all organizations regardless of size, sector, or location. They are the foundation upon which all other GRI reporting guidance is based. The G3 Guidelines outline a disclosure framework that organizations can voluntarily, flexibly, and incrementally adopt. The G3 Guidelines outline principles to define report content—materiality, stakeholder inclusiveness, sustainability context, and completeness. Outlining of such principles is important given that it is easy to talk about doing stuff in CSR (Corporate Social Responsibility) without it being meaningful.

Hence, materiality means that the information in a report should cover topics and indicators that reflect the organization's significant economic, environmental, and social impacts or that which would substantively influence the assessments and decisions of stakeholders. Stakeholder inclusiveness implies that the reporting organization should identify its stakeholders and explain in the report how it has responded to their reasonable expectations and interests. Sustainability context implies that information on performance should be placed in context. The underlying question of sustainability reporting is how an organization contributes or aims to contribute in the future to the improvement or deterioration of economic, environmental, and social conditions, developments, and trends at the local, regional, or global level. Completeness implies that coverage of the material topics and indicators and definition of the report boundary should be sufficient to reflect significant economic, environmental, and social impacts and enable stakeholders to assess the reporting organization's performance in the reporting period (GRI, 2010a).

Reporting on sustainability performance is an important way for organizations to manage their impact on sustainable development. The challenges of sustainable development are many, and organizations have not only a responsibility but also a great ability to exert positive change on the state of the world's economy, and environmental and social conditions. Reporting leads to improved sustainable development outcomes because it allows organizations to measure, track, and improve their performance on specific issues. Organizations are much more likely to effectively manage an issue that they can measure. As well as helping organizations manage their impacts, sustainability reporting promotes transparency and accountability. This is because an organization discloses information in the public domain. In doing so, stakeholders can track an organization's performance on broad themes—such as environmental performance—or a particular issue—such as labor conditions in factories. Performance can be monitored year on year or can be compared to other similar organizations.

GRI Guidelines are regarded to be widely used. As of January 2009, more than 1,500 organizations from 60 countries use the guidelines to produce their sustainability reports (GRI, 2010b). GRI Guidelines apply to corporate businesses, public agencies, smaller enterprises, NGOs, industry groups, and others.

Dow Jones Sustainability Index (DJSI)

As reported on the DJSI website, the DJSI was launched in 1999 and tracks the financial performance of the leading sustainability-driven companies worldwide (DJSI, 2010c). While SRI is a movement involving conscious investors and GRI is the development of a forward-looking and balanced assessment of broader corporate impact, the development of DJSI takes these dual inspirations and by creating an investment vehicle, begins to get closer to the heart of the stock market trading itself. The DJSI family currently comprises global, European, Eurozone, North American, US, Asia Pacific, and Korean benchmarks. There is currently over US$8 billion in DJSI-based investment vehicles.

DJSI utilizes an integrated assessment of economic, environmental, and social criteria with a focus on long-term shareholder value in order to invite companies to be part of the index. Once a company is listed on the DJSI, it is monitored daily for any critical arising issues, which can lead to the exclusion of the company if deemed critical enough. Examples of events that would lead to exclusion include: commercial practices, human rights abuses, layoffs or worker disputes, or catastrophic disasters. These companies are monitored through publicly accessible information including media and company contact. If one of these critical events happens, the situation is analyzed for the scope which it reaches. If large enough, the event will be analyzed further based on severity, media coverage, and crisis management. Analysts decide from here whether the company will be excluded from the DJSI (2010b). An assurance report is completed by the global accounting firm, Deloitte, to ensure the validity of the company's information.

In 2009, 1,200 companies were assessed for their corporate sustainability practices. This represented an 8 percent increase from the previous year. At the onset of DJSI's assessment criteria, the focus was primarily on government compliance and regulations. This has evolved to embrace a broader set of criteria including corporate citizenship/philanthropy, social reporting, labor practice indicators, talent attraction and retention, codes of conduct/compliance/anti-corruption and bribery, human capital development, environmental reporting, risk and crisis management, and corporate governance (DJSI, 2010a). The total number of invited companies is now 2,617.

In addition to an increase in the number of companies being assessed for inclusion on the set of indexes, and an increase in the range of criteria being used to rate and rank these companies, the number of indexes Dow Jones has spawned, has also increased. Thus,

- The Dow Jones Sustainability World Index (DJSI World) covered the top 10 percent of the biggest 2,500 companies in the Dow Jones Global Total Stock Market Index in terms of economic, environmental, and social criteria. This index was first published on September 8, 1999.
- The Dow Jones Sustainability North America Index (DJSI North America) covers the leading 20 percent in terms of sustainability of the 600 biggest North American companies in the Dow Jones Global Total Stock Market Index. This was introduced on September 23, 2005.

- The Dow Jones Sustainability Asia Pacific Index (DJSI Asia Pacific) captures the leading 20 percent in terms of sustainability out of the largest 600 companies in the developed Asia Pacific markets in the Dow Jones Global Total Stock Market Index. The Dow Jones Sustainability Asia Pacific 40 Index (DJSI Asia Pacific 40) is a subset of the DJSI Asia Pacific which tracks the largest 40 sustainability leaders in Asia Pacific. These indexes were launched on January 16, 2009.
- The Dow Jones Sustainability Korea Index (DJSI Korea) tracks the leading 30 percent of the largest 200 South Korean companies listed in the Dow Jones Global Total Stock Market Index. The Dow Jones Sustainability Korea 20 Index is a subset of the DJSI Korea and comprises the largest 20 companies of this index. This set of indexes was launched on October 20, 2009.
- As a benchmark for European sustainability investments, the Dow Jones Sustainability Europe Index (DJSI Europe) covers the leading 20 percent in terms of sustainability of the largest 600 European companies in the Dow Jones Global Total Stock Market Index. This index was launched on August 4, 2010.

Principles for Responsible Investing (PRI)

PRI represents the further mainstreaming of what is represented by SRI, GRI, and DJSI. As reported on the United Nations-backed Principles for Responsible Investment Initiative (PRI) website (UNPRI, 2010), in 2005 the United Nations Secretary General invited a group of the world's largest institutional investors to join a process in developing the Principles for Responsible Investment. Individuals representing 20 institutional investors from 12 countries agreed to participate in the investor group. The group accepted ownership of the principles and had the freedom to develop them as they saw fit. The group was supported by a 70-persons multi-stakeholder group of experts from the investment industry, intergovernmental and governmental organizations, civil society, and academia. The process, conducted between April 2005 and January 2006, involved deliberations in a series of all-day long discussions and debate. The Principles for Responsible Investment emerged as a result of these meetings.

The process was coordinated by the United Nations Environment Programme Finance Initiative and the UN Global Compact. Following the launch of the Principles, the PRI Secretariat was created to help coordinate the adoption of the Principles by additional investors, provide comprehensive resources to assist investors in implementing the Principles, and to facilitate collaboration among signatories. As of October 2010, over 800 investment institutions from 45 countries have become signatories.

These Principles are as follows:

> As institutional investors, we have a duty to act in the best long-term interests of our beneficiaries. In this fiduciary role, we believe that environmental, social, and corporate governance (ESG) issues can affect the performance of investment portfolios (to varying degrees across companies, sectors, regions, asset classes and through time). We also recognise that applying these Principles may better align investors with broader objectives of society. Therefore, where consistent with our fiduciary responsibilities, we commit to the following:
>
> 1. We will incorporate ESG issues into investment analysis and decision-making processes.
> 2. We will be active owners and incorporate ESG issues into our ownership policies and practices.
> 3. We will seek appropriate disclosure on ESG issues by the entities in which we invest.
> 4. We will promote acceptance and implementation of the Principles within the investment industry.
> 5. We will work together to enhance our effectiveness in implementing the Principles.
> 6. We will each report on our activities and progress towards implementing the Principles. (UNPRI, 2010)

The Principles reflect the view that ESG issues can affect the performance of investment portfolios and therefore must be given appropriate consideration by investors if they are to fulfill their fiduciary duty. The principles provide a voluntary framework by which all investors can incorporate ESG issues into their decision-making and ownership practices and so better align their objectives with those of society at large.

REACH

The question is how pervasive are the challenges to a vital way of being, and generally speaking, from what quarters are they arising? We see that SRI is a movement from the more conscious investor community—perhaps those investors who are already at the boundary from a vital to a mental way of being or who have already made the transition to a more mental level of operation. GRI is a major stakeholder movement potentially affecting the operation of every corporation, and therefore progressively, a corporate movement itself. DJSI and PRI are key instruments affecting the mainstream investment community. Ideally we would also like to see concrete sustainable financial type top-down movement from the realm of policymakers and regulators. This book will make some concrete suggestions for this important category of stakeholders. In the meanwhile, frameworks such as REACH, are important to consider since they affect the very operations of business entities.

As reported by the REACH website,

> REACH is a new European Community Regulation on chemicals and their safe use (EC 1907/2006). It deals with the Registration, Evaluation, Authorisation and Restriction of Chemical substances. The new law entered into force on 1 June 2007. The aim of REACH is to improve the protection of human health and the environment through the better and earlier identification of the intrinsic properties of chemical substances. At the same time, innovative capability and competitiveness of the EU chemicals industry should be enhanced. The benefits of the REACH system will come gradually, as more and more substances are phased into REACH.
>
> The REACH Regulation gives greater responsibility to industry to manage the risks from chemicals and to provide safety information on the substances. Manufacturers and importers will be required to gather information on the properties of their chemical substances, which will allow their safe handling, and to register the information in a central database run by the European Chemicals Agency (ECHA) in Helsinki. The Agency will act as the central point in the REACH system: it will manage the databases necessary to operate the system, co-ordinate the in-depth evaluation of suspicious chemicals and run a public database in which consumers and professionals can find hazard information.
>
> The Regulation also calls for the progressive substitution of the most dangerous chemicals when suitable alternatives have been identified. One of

> the main reasons for developing and adopting the REACH Regulation was that a large number of substances have been manufactured and placed on the market in Europe for many years, sometimes in very high amounts, and yet there is insufficient information on the hazards that they pose to human health and the environment. There is a need to fill these information gaps to ensure that industry is able to assess hazards and risks of the substances, and to identify and implement the risk management measures to protect humans and the environment. REACH provisions will be phased-in over 11 years. (European Commission Environment, 2010)

Such regulations coming from the top-down signal the inevitability of the changing times toward sustainability. The seriousness of the issues being addressed needs to be taken to heart and adopted by organizations to positively reinforce the tides of the time so that there is even more incentive to make the changes needed. Imagine if similar principles or regulation was enforced on the stock market so that companies had immediate incentive to make such changes. We will explore how this may be made possible soon.

Blessed Unrest

Blessed Unrest is a term coined by Paul Hawken, describing the world's largest movement that no one saw coming. He is the author of a book by the same name. In the book, Hawken describes how over the past 15 years, he has given nearly 1,000 talks on the environment, and in the process, came into contact with thousands of people around the world typically working on the most salient issues of our day—climate change, poverty, deforestation, peace, water, hunger, conservation, and human rights. They came from civil society and as he says, they "looked after rivers and bays, educated consumers about sustainable agriculture, retrofitted houses with solar panels, lobbied state legislatures about pollution, fought against corporate-weighted trade policies, worked to green inner cities, and taught children about the environment" (Hawken, 2007: 1).

In time Hawken began to wonder how many groups and organizations were actually involved in progressive causes. After some investigation into government records for different countries, he finally arrived at an estimate of perhaps one to two million organizations working toward ecological sustainability and social justice worldwide! As he goes on to say,

> By any conventional definition, this vast collection of committed individuals does not constitute a movement. Movements have leaders and ideologies. People join movements, study their tracts, and identify themselves with a group. They read the biography of the founders(s) or listen to them perorate on tape or in person. Movements, in short, have followers. This movement, however, doesn't fit the standard model. It is dispersed, inchoate, and fiercely independent. It has no manifesto or doctrine, no overriding authority to check in with. It is taking shape in schoolrooms, farms, jungles, villages, companies, deserts, fisheries, slums—and yes, even fancy New York hotels. One of the distinctive features is that it is tentatively emerging as a global humanitarian movement arising from the bottom up. Historically social movements have arisen primarily in response to injustice, inequities, and corruption. Those woes still remain legion, joined by a new condition that has no precedent: the planet has a life-threatening disease, marked by massive ecological degradation and rapid climate change. As I counted the vast number of organizations it crossed my mind that perhaps I was witnessing the growth of something organic, not biologic. Rather than a movement in the conventional sense, could it be an instinctive, collective response to threat? Is it atomized for reasons that are innate to its purpose? How does it function? How fast is it growing? How is it connected? Why is it largely ignored? Does it have a history? Can it successfully address the issues that governments are failing to do: energy, jobs, conservation, poverty, and global warming? Will it become centralized, or will it continue to be disbursed and cede its power to ideologies and fundamentalism? (Hawken, 2007: 2–3)

Hawken's ending questions reinforce the notion of emergence of identity through battle between the fractal for progress and numerous contrary-fractals. This global movement involving over a million organizations is a bottom-up movement, perhaps the most important one, and reinforces the need for the stock market to be redesigned to take heed of what is fast coming.

12

Principles of Sustainability

At its heart, redesigning the stock market is an imperative in moving the world along a trajectory of sustainable development. All the work that is currently being done in the field of sustainability will come to naught unless this primary engine of business dynamism is redesigned to embody deep and true principles of sustainability. The impulse of greed is deeply rooted in the human psyche, and why would not it be given that we live as vital beings, primarily. Even when we rise on flights of idealism, these journeys are short-lived and we easily return to a choppy level marked by the vicissitudes of ego. Greed and fear remain our primary drivers and to get to a level of sustainability that is enduring this very notion of existing for our small selves has to be overcome at its core. In other words, we have to at the very least become mental beings driven by thought, reasoning, imagination, and the deeper possibility that only the mental powers enduringly applied can lead us to.

We see that there is a spontaneous movement that has arisen organically to counter the deep-seated irrationalities, the deep-seated greed and fear that drives business activity today. SRI, GRI, REACH, Sustainability Indices, Stakeholder Resolutions, Blessed Unrest, which we have discussed in previous chapters, are all manifestations of this. Various consulting organizations have also arisen in the last couple of decades to work with corporations and set them on a path of at least partial sustainability. Any forward looking peoples should consider these as inevitable signs of the future, and proactively begin to redesign or design new forms of stock markets that capture these flutings from the future. It is fine, and obviously the reality of today that such pressures and signals come in from the outside to try to harmonize to some extent the activity on the stock markets and we need to look at what the stock markets would look like were these arising principles to be embedded into the design of stock markets. But even further, we need to examine these principles and ask whether they are in themselves all that is required for truer sustainability to manifest?

Hence, the path of redesign seems like it can proceed in stages. Stage 1, which is obviously what the mind of humanity is more opening to, is to embrace the rising principles captured by the spontaneous movements to cause business to proceed more sustainably as captured by the movements summarized in Chapter 11. Stage 2 is the result of deeper questioning of what would it really take for sustainability to become a reality, and how if at all, stock markets could be redesigned to embody even these requirements? We will address these considerations in the next chapter. To prepare for that though, let us turn our attention to the field of sustainability itself to understand the existing and future drivers that must be embodied in any engine that at the end of the day is responsible for global business activity and must therefore also be a key part for sustainable global business activity.

A Deeper Dive into Sustainability

Around the 1950s–1960s, as the business paradigm began to get universalized and commonly accepted as the context for living, it was naturally found that all was not well. Social costs and externalities had already been alive for as long as the institution of business has been around. But now major environmental costs and externalities were also rapidly coming into focus. At one end, the hard facts were captured in significant works such as Rachel Carson's *Silent Spring* (1962) that documented detrimental effects of pesticides on the environment. At the other end, new systemic frameworks that suggested a different interpretation for the concept of environment and captured in works, such as James Lovelock's *Gaia Hypothesis* (1972), began to appear at the same time in the 1960s and early 1970s. These seminal works heralded the start of the modern-day environmental movement.

But this has to be the case since business has proceeded along an artificially created trajectory that does not sync with the reality of life. In life everything is integrated. In business, under the aegis of the vital orientation, there are artificial boundaries set up, which define rules of business. The primary rule is profit-maximization, regardless of total cost. Such a construction cannot but run into increasing problems as the trajectory continues. Markets, being the playing field of business, are also therefore artificial constructions and cannot but create huge problems as they continue to "develop." These are the huge unconsidered bubbles of modern-day life. We have paid attention to bubbles of the financial kind. The bursting of these has created a lot of heartache. But these are only bubbles within bubbles. Their bursting gives us a small taste of pain. This is nothing compared to the heartache that will be unleashed if we do not quickly address the larger, contextual, systemic bubbles that we live in now.

The business bubble has cut itself off from the deep realities, and it is developments such as SRI, GRI, PRI, and DJSI that are like projectiles being thrown from these bubbles to reality to help ground the bubbles and ease their decompression. Some of these deeper principles that these projectiles seem to be aiming at are at the very least seeking to reverse harm done to natural Ecosystem Services and are captured in frameworks such as the Earth Charter Principles, Cradle to Cradle Principles, Natural Step Principles, and so on. We will briefly review some of these frameworks since these principles appear to be more consonant with an integrated view of life. In our larger interest of true sustainability, we must factor them in, in some way, into the redesign of stock markets.

But further yet, and deeper still, we need to explore the other systemic bubbles we are entrapped in for it is only with the bursting of these that we will more truly be able to get to the deepest principles of sustainability that must be considered in our attempt to meaningfully integrate any future business development with reality. We have referred to one such bubble we continually live in, the vital bubble, which seems to define much of who we are, and through fractal-pressure, the nature of many common institutions of our lives. In *Connecting Inner Power with Global Change:The Fractal Ladder* (2009b), I make the case that being animated by the physical–vital–mental fractal so that is the mental-orientation that leads, is what is critical to step onto the Fractal Ladder, and correspondingly, into a reality of sustainable sustainability—this is what is required to burst the bubbles. Getting stuck in what I refer to as "stagnated fractals" is what creates the bubbles we escape from reality in.

Therefore, some Fractal Ladder Principles will also be reviewed with the view of also integrating these into the design of stock markets.

Ecosystem Services

A manifest and increasingly acknowledged sign of living in bubbles is that real, ground-level developments and services get marginalized, even reversed, and at their extreme destroyed. Practically speaking there is no more valuable service that gets destroyed and which our lives and all activity are dependent upon, be it business of otherwise, than that of Ecosystem Services (Wikipedia, 2010j). Humankind benefits from a multitude of resources and processes that are supplied by natural ecosystems. Collectively, these benefits are known as ecosystem services and include products like clean drinking water and processes such as the decomposition of wastes. While scientists and environmentalists have discussed ecosystem services for decades, these services were popularized and their definitions formalized by the United Nations 2004 Millennium Ecosystem Assessment, a four-year study involving more than 1,300 scientists worldwide (MEA, 2005).

The assessment grouped ecosystem services into four broad categories (MEA, 2006):

1. Provisioning services, which include:
   - Food (including seafood and game), crops, wild foods, and spices
   - Water
   - Pharmaceuticals, biochemicals, and industrial products
   - Energy (hydropower, biomass fuels)
2. Regulating services, which include:
   - Carbon sequestration and climate regulation
   - Waste decomposition and detoxification
   - Purification of water and air
   - Crop pollination
   - Pest and disease control

3. Supporting services, which include:
   - Nutrient dispersal and cycling
   - Seed dispersal
   - Primary production
4. Cultural services, which include:
   - Cultural, intellectual, and spiritual inspiration
   - Recreational experiences (including ecotourism)
   - Scientific discovery

Living in bubbles means that we have lost sight of these fundamentals and are chasing financially created castles in the air instead. As a result, there has been real and continued destruction of the life-giving ecosystem services.

The following are some of the real changes observed by the MEA:

- Over the past 50 years, humans have changed ecosystems more rapidly and extensively than in any comparable period of time in history. This has resulted in substantial and largely irreversible loss in the diversity of life.
- Cultivated systems cover 25 percent of earth's terrestrial surface. More land has been converted into croplands since 1950s than in any comparable period before. This signifies an unprecedented change in global ecosystems.
- Further, 20 percent of the world's coral reef was lost and 20 percent degraded in the last several decades and 35 percent of mangrove areas have been lost in the last several decades.
- Amount of water in reservoirs has quadrupled since the 1960s, largely due to intercepted continental runoff. Further, withdrawals from rivers and lakes have doubled since the 1960s.
- Five to ten percent of the area of five biomes was converted between 1950 and 1990. (Biomes are climatically and geographically defined as similar climatic conditions on the earth, such as communities of plants, animals, and soil organisms.)
- More than two-thirds of the area of two biomes and more than half of the area of four others had been converted by the 1990s. (A team of biologists convened by the World Wide Fund for Nature

developed an ecological land classification system that identified 14 biomes globally (Olson, 2001).)

- Since the 1960s, the flows of biogeochemical cycles have radically altered— a biogeochemical cycle is a pathway by which a chemical element or molecule moves through the biosphere, lithosphere, atmosphere, and hydrosphere compartments of earth. Biologically available nitrogen in terrestrial ecosystems has doubled. Flows of phosphorous have tripled. Sixty percent of the increase in atmospheric CO_2 since 1750 has taken place since 1959.
- There have been significant and largely irreversible changes to species diversity. Humans have increased the species extinction rate by as much as 1,000 times over background rates typical over the planet's history. Further, 10–30 percent of mammal, bird, and amphibian species are currently threatened with extinction.
- Approximately 60 percent (15 out of 24) of the ecosystem services in the MEA are being degraded or used unsustainably.
- With respect to provisioning services, while ability to provide crops, livestock, and aquaculture have increased, ability to provide capture fisheries, wild foods, wood fuel, genetic resources, biochemicals, medicines, and freshwater has decreased.
- With respect to regulating services, air quality regulation, climate regulation at the regional and local levels, erosion regulation, water purification and waste treatment, pest regulation, pollination, natural hazard regulation, have decreased.

Costs associated with these irreversible destructions is huge. As a sample of these costs, consider some of the examples also pointed to be the same MEA Study:

- The 1992 collapse of the Newfoundland cod fishery costs approximately US$2 billion in income support and retraining.
- The "external" cost of agriculture in the UK in 1996 (damage to water, soil, biodiversity) was US$2.6 billion or 9 percent of yearly gross farm receipts.
- The frequency and impact of floods and fires has increased significantly in the past 50 years, in part due to ecosystem changes. Annual losses from extreme events totaled approximately US$70 billion in 2003.

- Further, loss of wealth due to ecosystem degradation is not reflected in economic accounts. Ecosystem services, as well as resources such as mineral deposits, soil nutrients, and fossil fuels are capital assets. A country could cut its forests and deplete its fisheries, and this would show only as a positive gain in GDP without registering the corresponding decline in assets.

Further, the degradation of ecosystem services exacerbates increase of poverty for the poor:

- Around 1.1 billion people are surviving on less that US$1 per day. Seventy percent of these people are in rural areas where they are highly dependent on ecosystem services.
- Inequality has increased over the last decade. During the 1990s, 21 countries experienced declines in their rankings in the Human Development Index. The Human Development Index is a composite statistic composed from data on life expectancy, education, and per-capita GDP, used to rank countries by level of human development.
- An estimated 852 million people were undernourished in 2000–2002, up 37 million people from the period 1997–1999.
- Some 1.1 billion people still lack access to improved water supply, and more than 2.6 billion lack access to improved sanitation. Water scarcity affects roughly one to two billion people worldwide. Half the urban population in Africa, Asia, Latin America, and the Caribbean suffers from one or more diseases associated with inadequate water and sanitation.

Increase of poverty creates social instability and erodes the very foundation of progressive civilization.

Therefore, in the redesign of stock markets it is imperative that some filters be created and attention placed on the degree to which these ecosystem services may be being compromised on one side, and certainly benefited on the other. As suggested, rather than have money being channeled to companies that are addressing these serious issues from the outside, through some index fund or other external mechanism, these parameters have to be integrally ingrained in the act of trading itself.

Earth Charter Principles

The Earth Charter represents a human aspiration for a more sustainable life and is a useful framework to consider. It has involved millions in its design and has taken seven years to craft. It is frameworks such as this that have arisen organically, that are needed to counter the incredible damage to ecosystem services the world over. The preamble of the Earth Charter recognizes the difficult situation we are currently in—"We stand at a critical moment in Earth's history, a time when humanity must choose its future. As the world becomes increasingly interdependent and fragile, the future at once holds great peril and great promise" (Earth Charter Initiative, 2010). Further, it asks us to recognize our integrated bases of life—"To move forward we must recognize that in the midst of a magnificent diversity of cultures and life forms we are one human family and one Earth community with a common destiny" and calls us to meaningful action—"We must join together to bring forth a sustainable global society founded on respect for nature, universal human rights, economic justice, and a culture of peace. Towards this end, it is imperative that we, the peoples of Earth, declare our responsibility to one another, to the greater community of life, and to future generations."

In other words, the preamble has recognized the danger of the bubble that we are in, asked us to ground ourselves, and to take action to deflate the bubble. The nature of the call to action is captured by its 16 principles, organized under four overarching pillars:

I. Respect and Care for the Community of Life

1. Respect Earth and life in all its diversity.
2. Care for the community of life with understanding, compassion and love.
3. Build democratic societies that are just, participatory, sustainable and peaceful.
4. Secure Earth's bounty and beauty for present and future generations.

II. Ecological Integrity

5. Protect and restore the integrity of Earth's ecological systems, with special concern for biological diversity and the natural processes that sustain life.

6. Prevent harm as the best method of environmental protection and, when knowledge is limited, apply a precautionary approach.
7. Adopt patterns of production, consumption and reproduction that safeguard Earth's regenerative capacities, human rights and community well-being.
8. Advance the study of ecological sustainability and promote the open exchange and wide application of the knowledge acquired.

III. Social and Economic Justice

9. Eradicate poverty as an ethical, social and environmental imperative.
10. Ensure that economic activities and institutions at all levels promote human development in an equitable and sustainable manner.

    a. Promote the equitable distribution of wealth within nations and among nations.
    b. Enhance the intellectual, financial, technical, and social resources of developing nations, and relieve them of onerous international debt.
    c. Ensure that all trade supports sustainable resource use, environmental protection, and progressive labor standards.
    d. Require multinational corporations and international financial organizations to act transparently in the public good, and hold them accountable for the consequences of their activities.

11. Affirm gender equality and equity as prerequisites to sustainable development and ensure universal access to education, health care and economic opportunity.
12. Uphold the right of all, without discrimination, to a natural and social environment supportive of human dignity, bodily health and spiritual well-being, with special attention to the rights of indigenous peoples and minorities.

IV. Democracy, Nonviolence, and Peace

13. Strengthen democratic institutions at all levels, and provide transparency and accountability in governance, inclusive participation in decision-making, and access to justice.
14. Integrate into formal education and lifelong learning the knowledge, values and skills needed for a sustainable way of life.
15. Treat all living beings with respect and consideration.
16. Promote a culture of tolerance, nonviolence and peace. (Earth Charter Initiative, 2010)

As such, each of the pillars has implications for how business is to be run and not run in order that it may more seamlessly emerge from the dangerous bubble it is currently in. Beyond GRI, which is already a huge step forward, business needs to be held accountable to principles of this nature that call out pillars that must be upheld for life to develop sustainably. While the GRI has been pragmatically designed so that its metrics are measurable, the measure of non-measurability should hardly be a condition to exclude other important parameters of decision-making and action. At the very least, each business should agree to the principles pointed to in something like the Earth Charter. That is then the starting point for a new level of accountability that they can then be held to. A filter in stock markets can simply be something to the effect if corporations have agreed to the Earth Charter principles. If not, the stock cannot be traded.

Biomimicry Principles

Biomimicry or biomimetics is the examination of nature, its models, systems, processes, and elements to emulate or take inspiration from in order to solve human problems (Wikipedia, 2010d). Such an approach goes a long way in integrating day-to-day business innovation with the cradle-of-life we have all emerged from and will work to burst some of the business bubbles we are currently afloat in. As such it is also an important perspective to have in considering what really are the deeper principles that will lead to sustainability and needs to be factored in to any business evaluation system, especially if the business is focused on the design of product.

A useful and popular example of biomimicry is embodied in Cradle to Cradle Design Principles (Wikipedia, 2010f). It is useful to consider because at its base is the belief that it is the application of biological methods and systems found in nature that must be applied to the study and design of engineering systems and modern technology. Further, engineered systems and modern technology must seamlessly integrate with nature as though it were a natural extension of nature.

Cradle to Cradle Design suggests that industry must protect and enrich ecosystems and nature's biological metabolism while also maintaining safe, productive technical metabolism for the high-quality use and circulation of organic and synthetic materials. Put simply, it is a holistic economic, industrial, and social framework that seeks to create systems that are not just efficient but essentially waste free. Some of the key Cradle to Cradle Design principles are the following (Wikipedia, 2010f):

- All materials used in industrial or commercial processes are either technical nutrients or biological nutrients.
- Technical nutrients are basically inorganic or synthetic materials manufactured by humans—such as plastics and metals—that can be used many times over without any loss in quality, staying in a continuous cycle. Technical nutrients are strictly limited to non-toxic, non-harmful synthetic materials that have no negative effects on the natural environment; they can be used in continuous cycles as the same product without losing their integrity or quality.
- Biological nutrients and materials are organic materials that can decompose into the natural environment, soil, water, etc., without affecting it in a negative way, providing food for bacteria and microbiological life.
- Downcycling refers to the "downcycling" of materials into lesser products. A plastic computer housing becomes a plastic cup, which then becomes a park bench, eventually becoming waste.
- Waste = Food is a basic concept of organic waste materials becoming food for bugs, insects, and other small forms of life who can feed

on it, decompose it, and return it to the natural environment which we then indirectly use for food ourselves.

The work of Karl-Henrik Robèrt is also relevant in this regard (Wikipedia, 2010t). Based on the laws of thermodynamics, he derived the following principles of sustainability:

- To become a sustainable society, we must eliminate our contribution to the progressive buildup of substances extracted from the Earth's crust (for example, heavy metals and fossil fuels).
- To become a sustainable society we must eliminate our contribution to the progressive buildup of chemicals and compounds produced by society (for example, dioxins, PCBs, and DDT).
- To become a sustainable society, we must eliminate our contribution to the progressive physical degradation and destruction of nature and natural processes (for example, over-harvesting forests and paving over critical wildlife habitat).

Fractal Ladder Principles

Fractal Ladder Principles (Malik, 2010) are based on observation of sustainable, progressive systems, regardless of organizational scale. Thus, they are true of organizations that range from an idea to a whole market, for example. These principles provide an important perspective on sustainability in terms or orientations held by actors or organizations and are included to also be considered as part of the deeper principles that are important in a study of sustainability.

- There are common building blocks that animate each level of organization. These building blocks can be physical, vital, or mental in nature.
- Organization refers to an idea, a theory, a habit, an event, a circumstance, a person, a team, a corporation, a collectivity, a market, an economy, our world; basically anything whose structure, processes, meaning is defined by the common physical, vital, and mental building blocks.

- Dynamics of a particular organization are entirely determined by which of these building blocks are active at that level of organization.
- Like DNA, the stringing together of building blocks in a particular sequence or with particular dominance, determines that active dynamics of that level of organization.
- There is only one particular sequence of stringing together building blocks that allows an organization to progress sustainably—that is the physical–vital–mental sequence with the mental orientation leading.
- This particular sequence exists in all progressive organizations, regardless of level of complexity, and forms the seed pattern of which the Fractal Ladder is the fractal.
- When organizations embrace sequences other than that of the progressive fractal, they become a part of a general fractal vortex that animates ordinary or "as usual" as opposed to progressive life.
- These unprogressive or contrary-fractals are the bases of bubbles because at its heart it is something other than the requirement of the time or space that is being artificially "developed."
- The requirement of the time or the space can be connected to only by connecting to the fractal for progress.
- All sequences tend to repeat their raison d'être and way of being not only at their own levels but by influence, at other levels also. This is what reinforces fractal reality.
- When a fractal for progress inevitably encounters contrary-fractals, a rite of passage is created by which deeper identity can emerge.
- The Fractal Ladder is a zone of possibility that causes the world-system to progress in the most sustainable way possible.
- The Fractal Ladder is the signature of a progressive, conscious, and fully integrated world system.

The Fractal Ladder Principles ground development concretely because it always connects to the bias or direction of the system behind the apparent system. In this regard, there is a natural instinct to break all bubbles and for development to proceed most sustainably. Assessments of where corporations and markets are, in terms of their physical, vital, mental realities and the fractals that drive them, have to be used as a backdrop or context for most intelligent investing. A market in the midst of the vital level requires a different treatment of investment from an organization—be it a corporation or market—at the boundary, say between the vital and the mental. This kind of intelligence would benefit us all if it were to be automatically incorporated into the functioning of stock exchanges. Perhaps this could be done by the creation of a general physical–vital–mental map that also helped plan or adjust investment decisions in real-time. As may be apparent, the analysis in this book and the basis for redesign of the stock market are based on the Fractal Ladder Principles.

Part V

Redesigning the Stock Market

13

Current Sustainability in Stock Exchanges

In "Sustainable Stock Exchanges", a discussion paper prepared by Responsible Research (2010) as a starting point for the Sustainable Stock Exchanges 2010 Global Dialogue, the landscape of current stock exchanges with respect to sustainability is clearly laid out. The ongoing dialogue, co-hosted by the United Nations Conference on Trade and Development (UNCTAD), the United Nations Global Compact, and PRI, brings together institutional investors and CEOs from stock exchanges to explore how the world's exchanges could work together with investors, regulators and business to encourage responsible long-term approaches to investment.

The premise is interesting—that stock exchanges can themselves be major change agents in a way of business being that they are themselves fully an active part of. This is so by virtue of the way that major stock exchanges around the world are set up today. This is as for-profit institutions that compete against other stock exchanges to become the vehicle by which public corporations can raise equity-based funds. This setup means that stock exchanges have a bias to maximize profit since they are accountable to shareholders, just as any other business enterprise is. This setup creates an implicit conflict of interest, in that stock exchanges would be driven to increase trading volume, regardless of the nature of trades taking place through the stock exchange. Therefore, there will be a bias to list as many companies as possible, often regardless of what the company is actually engaged in or the company's stance toward sustainability and Corporate Social Responsibility (CSR).

The broader issue we are concerned with is the sustainability of society and the world. Businesses as primary actors in this landscape have a key role to play to ensure this. But given the vital-orientation business will naturally be anchored in for them to act at the mental level, requires constant intervention. The proof of this is of course the significant global problems we are currently enmeshed in of which Climate Change and the ongoing Global Financial Crises are the consummate symbols, and as acknowledged, the result of continued short-sighted, selfish desire-based, vital-level decision-making. Arguably both these devastating issues have been expedited because of the massive amount of funds public corporations have received through the stock market. Solution to these issues requires another way of being altogether, one that is more rooted at the mental level where orientation is more naturally biased toward the bigger picture and one's unique and ongoing positive contribution toward the creation of a sustainable world. This shift to the mental level is critical, and the question is, what is required at the societal level in order to expedite this? It is against this twin backdrop—the urgency required to navigate toward a safer, more sustainable world and the critical role that stock exchanges play in giving continued life to public corporations—that the question must be explored.

For stock exchanges themselves to be change agents in such a scenario is highly unlikely. The issue is one of the nature of the larger financial playing field in which stock exchanges have undoubtedly played a critical role because of the attraction of becoming rich quick, looked at from various different angles—from the corporate perspective, the investor perspective, the broker perspective, the stock exchange perspective. The creation of the stock market has been a powerful singularity of sorts, which in a manner of seeing, is the fractal-reflection and manifest imprint of a deeply ingrained vital-level urge for wealth and power, which makes it all the more powerful, and as has been argued in this book all along, has "bent financial space" or created the nature of all financial markets replete with their many levels of dysfunction, that we see all around us today.

Therefore, practically speaking, it is likely the policymaker and the regulator of financial markets who will have to play the primary role for now.

This is backed up by the research that Responsible Research conducted (2010) in which it was evident that stock exchanges prefer that voluntary, as opposed to mandatory, ESG requirements be placed on listed companies. In a world driven by business competition such a preference is natural. It is only the exceptional stock exchange that would dare to turn away business to uphold longer-term sustainability-based principles. However, this is the place to enforce requirements. It is the place where the public, the business, the investor, and the regulator practically meet. This is where the rubber hits the road and where conditions can be placed on corporations in order that they are able to receive ongoing funds from the public. It is the place, where like it or not, policy can be translated into practice and small steps toward longer-term societal sustainability-based outcomes can be managed day-to-day. Even if there is reluctance today, it has to become the avenue by which large societal goals are managed. If stock exchanges are themselves reluctant to play this role, then it has to be mandated on them.

The Slow Route Forward

In the Responsible Research (2010) discussion paper, there are a number of recommendations made on how to integrate sustainability at stock exchanges. These recommendations obviously reflect what is deemed possible given the current orientation toward sustainability from a stock exchange perspective. The orientation is itself captured by the report in a series of questions that explore this.

Thus, in a question that asks if stock exchanges have a responsibility to encourage greater corporate responsibility on sustainability issues, on a scale of 1 to 5, with 1 being strongly disagree and 5 being strongly agree, the average response was that stock exchanges agreed (3.9/5.0). So at least conceptually, there appears to be a positive orientation toward this critical area. In a question that asks if having very strong sustainability requirements of listed companies makes good business sense for a stock exchange, the response was more or less neutral (3.3/5.0). This points to the short-term orientation of the stock exchanges themselves. The fact is that over the longer term, this makes incredibly good business sense because absent such pressure, crippling realities as pointed to by Climate Change and the Global Financial Crises will only worsen, and then even the resource-base of business will be too compromised for any business to exist as a business. In a question that asks if regulators should not compel stock exchanges to make listed companies disclose their sustainability practices, the response was more toward agreement (3.5/5.0). This shows a bias in stock exchanges away from immediately handling the problem, which is a problem, given the gravity of the issues and the immediacy with which these need to be addressed.

Given this orientation, there is a suggestion to create a sustainability committee at each stock exchange, which perhaps is aimed at making the stock exchange itself more aware through self-exploration of the gravity of the issues surrounding business-as-usual activity. The sustainability committee would thus be concerned with listing requirements, ESG data and reporting standards, and stakeholder engagement. Highlights of the listing requirements actions would involve defining the minimum expectations for sustainability reporting by sector for new listings and enhancing ESG due-diligence capacity in the pre-IPO ecosystem.

Sustainability reporting itself can mean different things, and a couple of key issues that must be covered are first, that companies report on issues that are material as opposed to existing loosely in the CSR space, and second, that the reporting be fully integrated with the financially based annual report which implies that sustainability is itself fully integrated into company operations. What the discussion paper really indicates is the nascency of sustainability issues within the realm of stock exchanges. On the positive side, what this implies is that there is a real opportunity to influence how stock exchanges think about sustainability and what they do to make it a living force in their operations and impact. On the negative side it implies that little has been done so far in an area that is clearly critical, even when looked at from the narrower window of the future viability of stock exchanges themselves.

With respect to the action around enhancing ESG due-diligence in the pre-IPO system, while well intentioned and again useful so that the stock exchange itself awakens to ESG issues, as we discover amply time and time again, it is power that corrupts and absolute power that corrupts absolutely. The point is, it is the IPO itself and then the following capital injections that come into being through the stock market itself that cause the company to easily gravitate toward the vital level if it is not already operating from that space. As a result, and in the pressure to show continual profit in the short term, many ESG issues will inevitably be compromised. The solution to address this problem is quite simply to change the mechanism for stock trading itself so that breaching of ESG filters will cause a slowdown or allowing of stock to move in one direction only, so long as the ESG criteria that have been breached are not corrected. Stock exchanges will clearly be very reluctant to do this because corporations will not want to be penalized in this way. Further, if ESG criteria have been breached but if the public or investors really want to invest in a particular company, then resulting gains can be placed in escrow and disbursed as and when the company actually fulfills on a pre-specified ESG correction schedule.

It is therefore imperative that two things happen—first, that such mechanism for stock trading be mandated by regulators. Second, that all regulators all over the world comply so that the playing field is leveled and reoriented toward the longer term, and by increasing estimates, even the shorter term health of the world.

The discussion paper has a number of recommendations for stock exchanges in the ESG Data and Reporting Standards space. These have to do with educating companies on the difference between qualitative and quantitative sectorally material ESG reporting and CSR at one end to introducing a watch list for companies not reporting on ESG or lacking clarity in their reports at the other. This is all well and good if time is on our side and is respectfully cognizant of the reality that stock exchanges are currently in. However, time is not on our side and more needs to be done than the creation of watch lists. More radical action needs to be taken now rather than tomorrow, and the onus for this action has to be placed on companies themselves. The carrot and stick principle of clear rewards and punishment will need to be made alive, and for many companies stock markets is the best avenue by which this can happen. Stock exchanges will therefore need to be redesigned to allow this to happen.

Current Leading Practices

In survey responses by stock exchanges in this very same report, there are a number of leading practices that come to light. Any redesign of stock markets will need to factor in the existing leading edge. Some of these leading actions and practices include:

On the subject of stock exchange providing sustainability guidance for listing companies—

- Bursa Malaysia introduced a CSR Framework in 2006, evaluated the quality of CSR reporting in Malaysia, and published a detailed report on companies' progress in 2008.
- The Stock Exchange of Thailand established the "Principles of Good Corporate Governance for Listed Companies" which are in line with those recommended by OECD.

On the subject of stock exchange considering altering listing requirements to oblige companies to be more proactive with respect to ESG—

- In Taiwan, the regulator has asked all public companies to disclose the state of the company's CSR performance in the annual report and prospectus. Although this is not articulated in the stock exchange's listing criteria, companies are still obliged to do so in order to be listed on their exchange.
- In 2010, the Johannesburg Stock Exchange became the first exchange in the world to require listed companies to move towards integrated reporting.

On the subject of enacting policies to allow shareholders to comment on the quality of the ESG reporting and approve the sustainability strategy proposal of the board of directors—

- The Taiwan Stock Exchange promulgated CSR best practice principles in 2010. It is considering revising these principles to recommend listed companies allow shareholders to comment and approve CSR reporting and proposal.

On the subject of requiring that listed company meet ESG criteria—

- The BM&FBOVESPA does not require ESG criteria for all listed companies. Instead it has three listing segments that companies can voluntarily adhere to with different standards of corporate governance. Though the adhesion is voluntary, once listed in a particular segment, adopting the standards is mandatory and enforced by the Exchange.

On the subject of offering sustainability-related investment indices—

- The following exchanges already have one or more sustainability-related indices—BME, BM&FBOVESPA, Deutsche Borse, Hong-Kong Stock Exchange, Indonesia Stock Exchange, Johannesburg Stock Exchange, Korea Exchange, London Stock Exchange Group, NASDAQ OMX, National Stock Exchange of India, NYSE Euronext, Shanghai Stock Exchange, Shenzhen Stock Exchange, and Tokyo Stock Exchange. (World Federation of Exchanges, 2010)

On the subject of supporting the trading or development of carbon markets—

- The NYSE launched Bluenext jointly with the Caisse des Depots et Consignation in 2007. This exchange aims to be the world's largest exchange for carbon and environment-related products.
- Deutsche Borse Group, through its cooperation with European Energy Exchange and Eurex, is already active in offering a trading platform to utilities and financial markets for trading of European Emission Allowances under the European Emissions Trading Scheme as well as international CER under the Kyoto Protocol.

On the subject of mechanisms for community development—

- The Istanbul Stock Exchange adopted an eight-year compulsory primary education project in Turkey in 1997, which it continues to finance through the ISE Education Fund. As of September 2009, the program constructed 376 schools serving approximately 200,000 students.

14

Summary of Stock Market Redesign Suggestions

In the last 50 years, the stock market has played a major role in accelerating business activity. The very raison d'être of society have come to mean business activity and stock markets because they have been at the center of a powerful cycle between companies seeking funds, individual investors seeking profit, and numerous intermediaries who get rich either way, have played a key role in making this happen. Decades ago, banks were the disbursers of funds. There was a higher degree of due diligence that went with decisions to provide funds or not. With this function being appropriated by the market, that due diligence disappeared, and as a result, things have quite simply gone out of control. The stock market has ushered in a global casino mentality. True value on several fronts is continually being destroyed on both an environmental and a social front and numerous spontaneous developments have arisen to try to put things back into control.

These developments are still too distant from the center of the contemporary business engine for immediate results to be felt. Reporting by companies, stakeholder activism, shareholder resolutions, region-wide regulations, guiding principles, sustainability market indexes, are all good and necessary. But for immediate impact, trading at the very center, on the stock market itself, has to change so that sustainable global development becomes a reality. For this to be, the very nature of the functioning of the stock market needs to change. In this chapter, we will review some of the suggestions to change the very functioning of the stock market. The next chapter will systematize these suggested changes.

Some Suggestions from Chapter 1: Utopian Patterns

A macro-level suggestion for bringing about global sustainability was the notion that all life and all organizations, regardless of type and scale, are a projection from an underlying reality of splendor and have unique paths of development. Given this, to believe that business activity and development as defined today is the be-all of development is shortsighted. True sustainability is a result of harmonizing a broad set of development drivers. Hence, *stock market activity should support developmental efforts of other fundamental drivers*—be they of knowledge, service, adventure, and harmony, amongst others, in contrast to its current one-pointed support of perceived profit. Social enterprise, academic enterprise, enterprise of true adventure with breaking of boundaries on all fronts, enterprise of art, must equally receive the stimulus of funding because it is only in such unrestricted development that global sustainability can be assured. To continually develop that which does not yield short-term profit only, is what will ensure profit from generation to generation because in this manner true creativity is stoked. But for this to be, obviously the incentive system, the system by which investors are currently rewarded, will need to go through a major change. *At least in part, monetary reward needs to be replaced by reward in kind.* For investing in an institute of knowledge, the investor can now partake of the development of that knowledge in himself or in chosen others. For investing in a social enterprise, the investor can participate in the social activity or again chose another who will in some way participate in that activity, and so on.

Some Suggestions from Chapter 2: The Power of Patterns

In moving from the vital to the mental level, the notion of movement away from a unipolar or bipolar world toward the development of a more elaborate multipolar world, is necessary. That means that money should not continually be invested in one region or in one company or in one industry but truly become more universal in its method of disbursement. Current practices *of following the market through mutual fund investing or stock market-based indexing will simply have to give way to another* way of investing. Further, it means that *sensible investment limits* must be placed on companies, industries, regions if it is known that the organization does in fact harbor or indulge in questionable environmental, social, or economic practices.

There must be a conscious shift away from the vital way of being toward the more mental way of being. That is, there must be a conscious consideration of the reason, the dream, the intention behind a practical system or its assessment of value. To value trade in terms of commoditized monetary value, because that is simply more convenient, destroys long-term value and the bases of sustainability. Somehow the *act of trading has to consider this more intrinsic value and set limits* to the amount it may lose within a given window of time. In other words, there has to be an intelligent layering of value, another system of filtering beyond the crude buy-sell dynamic that animates stock trading today. Price of a stock, according to EMH, is supposed to capture all the elements and be adjusted almost as though by an "invisible hand." The fact of the matter is that at the vital level of operation, this does not happen, and *therefore, the mechanics of trading will have to change* to make this a reality.

Some Suggestions from Chapter 3: Pandorian Business

The notion that in today's vital world, money and profit are central and are the bases of power are reinforced. Pursuit of this principle will push us to the absolute limits of this lopsided perception and destroy whatever remaining bases of sustainability exist. Ecosystem services will all but be irreversibly depleted, and we will have subjected the human race to a sure end. This foundational basis of stock market action has, therefore, to be utterly reversed. *Stock market purpose must be recast* so that: sought after *funds may become intelligently available wherever there is the possibility of true development*; concerned investors who want to play in the sustainable development of the world contribute with the *expectation of rational as opposed to windfall returns* knowing that their investment will benefit generations to come; *parasitical financial players who create no real value* but profit from arbitrage and the irrational greed and fear of others are marginalized or even removed from the system. The removal of these non-value adding entities further moderates the functioning of the financial system so that as a whole it begins to operate far more rationally.

Further, the *true purpose of industry has to become a factor in how funds are disbursed*. Again, this implies that a filter of purpose be embedded into actual stock market trading. This is especially so at the vital level where deeper purpose is by definition missing from consideration. To illustrate, *the map of what the world really needs in terms of each industry has to be created*, and when trades occur, if they do not fill some required need that benefits the whole, there will be a disincentive to discourage that particular trade. Hence, there will be a map created for the agricultural industry, the pharmaceuticals industry, the chemicals industry, the automobile industry, and so on, that must factor in the dynamics of the actual trading. This means that beyond buying and selling stock in a company, *the stock market will have to be redesigned to invest in stock of a particular kind of project, or in a particular industry, or in a particular region,* and so on. The parameters of trading will, therefore, have to be changed so that trading in general becomes more specific than buying or selling a stock or a block of stocks in a company. This also means that an *investor will need to do more than follow the flock and pursue a higher level of due diligence before making a trade*. In other words, the act of investing becomes more intelligent, as opposed to more desire-oriented. As suggested before, the reward too, may be commensurate with the trade. It is not that reward is dictated solely by price. Rather, it may be dictated by kind. This will also ensure that a would-be investor has more appreciation for the intrinsic value behind the trade.

Some Suggestions from Chapter 4: Stock Market Role

In the chapter, many questionable practices across leading global, public companies across industry were surfaced. Each of these companies had received a huge boost in funding from the stock market, and as a result, have become reliant on funding from the stock markets. They hence play a game to ensure short-term profits, destroying much true and sustainable value in the process. These issues are summarized here so that the reader can see the breadth and seriousness of what funds received from stock markets end up supporting: sabotage of efforts to deal with environmental issues such as climate change; fraudulent manipulation of peer-reviewed scientific studies; misleading and lying to civilians, government officials, and global community; destruction of fisheries, ecology, ecosystems, through major pollution and chemical leaks; illegal trade, bribery, and corruption to win deals; kickbacks and tax evasion; assisting in human rights violations including torture, rape, and murder by providing material support to military forces; manipulation of the legal system; discrimination based on sexual orientation; price-fixing; overcharges as a result of price-fixing passed through to consumer; subsidization of products through exercising government influence; influence to change national industry policies through excessive lobbying and exercise of influence with government; trafficking of children into forced labor situations; destruction of natural ecosystems through other developmental activities; creation of superfund sites; strong arming of suppliers and customers in the business-to-business arena; inducing unnatural growth through artificial means such as hormones; creating conditions for obesity through unhealthy products; aggressive advertising targeted at children; excessive use of non-biodegradable packaging; major environmental catastrophes due to explosions, etc.; ill-treatment of workers; illegal marketing of drugs; death of trial users of drugs; defective health devices causing death; off-label promotional practices causing consumer harm; using "too big to fail" argument in compromising other stakeholders; unapproved human testing; promoting conspicuous consumerism; replacement of idealism by crasser motives; mass rise of externalities; converting communities into supply chains; suppression of freedom; becoming too big to fail; money laundering; conflict of interest on investment research; exaggerated research reports to promote own client base; supporting questionable customers; theft from customer accounts; and inappropriate use of bailout funds.

From 1987, as the availability of funds have become less of an issue, many of these violations have increased. Many of the issues are related to the size of companies and the unnatural influence they then have with decision-makers and those in power to therefore act with impunity. Absent the huge inflows of capital from the stock markets, these companies that often act as though the world was their bedroom, would not be able to make acquisitions that then make them "too big to fail" and "too powerful to ignore." *What needs to happen at the level of the stock market is an inbuilt check, a focused circuit-breaker of sorts that stops stock buying activity for a company if it is in violation of issues of the sort listed above.* In this manner, only companies that operate ethically on all counts can receive funding through stock markets. Conversely, if a company is completely clean in that it has not a single violation of the type listed above, *then a reverse circuit-breaker should go into effect that would stop irrational selling activity of its stock,* and therefore, destruction of its value.

Some Suggestions from Chapter 5: Evolution of the Macro-environment

In Chapter 5, we looked at the macro-environment that created the shift from the physical to the devastating vital way of operating and gave financial transaction its easily surfacing destructive power. Many suggestions for reversing the destructive effects of uncontrolled vital action emerge. Most of these are macro-level suggestions that must be considered in any redesign of stock markets that is to be sustainable and far-reaching. This is especially so because the stock market has created an attitude of investing that has in fact created a value–destruction monopoly in its wake. That is, destruction is used to make money, rather than money being used to build creation, and that too in a monopolistic way. The irrational connections implicit in this monopoly have to be reversed so that the scope of potential destruction is increasingly minimized. Many of the suggestions are focused on doing this:

- Increase deposit insurance for commercial banks: The value of money is different for different people. To equate money at one level of society with another is a problem, and this is what happens when commercial banks, which are value–repositories for the common man, are allowed to use these types of funds to invest irrationally. To protect society, commercial banks must be made to have a higher level of deposit insurance. This will in turn temper their forays into irrational markets, temper the level of investment in hot-spots, and help to control the heat generated during an irrational vital phase of financial activity. It will also help to control destruction of value since dollar for dollar, the common man's wealth has been created through harder labor than wealth at more affluent strata of society.

- Separate commercial banks from investment banks: Investment banks are involved in a high-risk, high-reward environment with much less regulation than commercial banks in general. For commercial banks to take on the level of risk that investments banks do, is to put into the high-risk pool a lot of hard-earned money that once lost will easily create havoc for large sections of society. Hence, the arenas should be separated out, or at the very least, restrictions placed on commercial banks stipulating the amount of funds that can be invested in high-risk areas, with conditions that must accompany such speculation.
- Create more skin in the game for middle-men: Before the stock market entered the vital phase, investment was dominated by those investing their own money. With the birth of various funds, where a manager was responsible for increasing the pool of investor money and then investing it to try and maximize returns, the level of risk-taking was increased since none of the money invested was the manager's own, and they were typically incentivized by size of fund being managed rather than returns. Hence, reward system for fund managers needs to be changed.
- Specialized investors for different asset classes: In the vital phase, the difference between different asset classes effectively does not count. What does count is making a profit regardless of what is involved. This is to use creation to make money rather than use money to create. With different asset classes being managed by specialized investors who most likely actually understand how true value as opposed to investment value can be built up as a result of investment, the perversity of a monopolistic flow of investment will be reversed.
- Higher degree of regulation: Macro-level metrics and reality checks need to be put into place to ensure that economic, sustainable,

financial development is happening in a positive way. When these metrics begin to turn in an opposite direction than desired, then regulation needs to kick-in to reverse this. This is essential while the economy and financial activity is at the vital level. Self-regulation only makes sense in an economy that is truly operating at the mental level.

- Reverse handing over of bank transactions away from the free-market back to specialists: A free-market is beneficial only when it is sustainable and driven by ideals that transcend the unrefined profit–motive. That is, only when it is at the mental level of operation. The reality is that today's market is securely at the vital level. Being so, to hand over basic financial and commercial transaction that drives the operations of society is foolhardy. Institutes that have objective due diligence processes, that care for the development of society, segments, communities, or that have operating principles that they follow to promote this, are those that should be the stewards of basic financial transaction. Such institutes were at one time commercial banks. Perhaps this can become the case again. In less developed countries that have not yet fully entered into the vital phase, this tends already to be true.
- Automatic stop in trading when bubble is being created—circuit-breaker: When an area becomes too hot, then break the trading to let a cool off happen.
- More sensible long-term ranking of funds by independent ranking organizations: Credit rating organizations such as Moody's need to get into the business of ranking organizations on their long potential rather than the short term return on investment.
- Increased regulation for money market funds: While money market funds take over functions of commercial banks, they do not require deposit insurance. This reduces their cost of operation and they can further take over a commercial banks core business at a lower cost. This marginalizes the better practices of commercial banks such as that of conducting due diligence prior to issuance of loans. If money market funds are taking over the role of the bank, they need to be regulated as such.
- Limited use of index funds as vehicle for investments: Index funds are driven by the theory that it is impossible to beat the market.

As a result, they easily become the hot-beds to attract funds. This is not ideal in the vital phase and, therefore, there needs to be a limit on the use of index funds as an investment vehicle. Perhaps this could be setting a limit of the size of the fund.

- Breaking of increasing correlations between different asset classes: The increasing correlation of investment in asset classes needs to be broken. Such correlation is typical of the vital phase. In the absence of operating at the mental phase, manual interventions need to be made to halt irrational activity such as correlating different asset classes that in fact have a completely different reason for existing.
- Much greater due diligence on mortgage-backed bonds: Bonds by their very nature are supposed to be instruments of lower risk. It is a contradiction in terms though when bonds are backed by a highly risky asset. This needs to be reversed so that stable assets are the basis for instruments such as bonds.
- Stopping of irrational market creation through financial instruments such as junk bonds: A more detailed look at claims by research that when smaller, riskier companies are pooled together they provide a better investment return than well-established large companies obviously needs to be balanced by common sense. In the vital phase, the filter for decision-making is potential of return. Only at the mental level would common sense kick in. Hence, when flow of investments is fast and furious, as in the vital stage, then grand proposals and theories need to be taken with a grain of salt.
- Control of carry-trade investments: Using "cheaper" money from one country to finance investments in another is also taking the profit view as opposed to the value view. This needs to be regulated for two reasons. First, the practice of citizens weakening their own country's currency by selling it for the promise of higher returns denominated in other currencies is questionable. Secondly, investments made using carry trade are inherently risky in that relative currency value can change overnight. There needs to be control over the amount of investments made in such a manner. Thirdly, carry trade is used to finance bubbles. This needs to be regulated.
- Solar or equivalent standard of money creation: The bases of money creation need to be changed to remove artificial scarcity and the

in-built bias of Central Bank money creation to create an unsustainable economic playing field. Cost of money creation has to become zero and based on creativity at the community level.

- Parasitical value needs to be controlled. The finance industry that creates instruments that have no innate bases of creativity but simply rely on other assets needs to be controlled. This is a huge impetus to inflation and the one-directional destruction of value. Every new and ungrounded instrument created must be backed by the creators own assets.

Some Suggestions from Chapter 6: Where in the Fractal Journey Is the Stock Market?

In Chapter 6, we established that the stock market was indeed in the vital phase. We determined this from the rapid increase in number of stock indexes, the astronomical increase in trading volume, the velocity of loss and gain of stock prices on a daily bases, and the number of stock market and related crashes. The fact is that the stock market has been the primary device by which all the different markets have begun to synchronize. Stock markets provide an easy approach for investing, reinvesting, diverting funds, and have heightened the reality of irrationality. The existence of the stock market makes shifting fund allocation and investments easy from geography to geography and from asset class to asset class. As such, there is an easy bastardization of value.

The primary recommendation to create a more sustainable world is to *change the access and reward system associated with stock markets*. It has to become *less easy to invest in stock markets* or rather there should be more due diligence associated with making investments. Perhaps would-be investors, rather than blindly investing cash, would go through an approach where they *specify their value-based as opposed to return-based investment goals*. This may be of the type: I want to invest in "x" part of the world and want to help the telecom sector there, etc. Further, the reward system could be altered so that there is payment in kind rather than in cash or that there is now part payment or reward in kind with greater investment for receiving in kind as opposed to cash. If someone invests in P&G and if the stock price goes up and the investor wants to "cash out," then they should receive the cash equivalent of the products produced by P&G. This will bring home to the investor what they are actually investing in. It is likely that *secondary markets will be created to funnel these products and services*—that is fine: it will still be less easy for an investor to make immediate returns. With the velocity of funding there is entry into another field and investors lose touch with what their money is actually being used for. Changing the access and reward systems will help investors be more grounded in what they are actually investing in.

Some Suggestions from Chapter 7: Theories and Tools to Manage Trading at the Vital Level

In Chapter 7, we looked at theories and tools used to manage trading. As suggested, most tools and theories used are more relevant if the stock market were operating at the mental level. These tools include EMH, Portfolio Theory, Index Modeling, and Algorithmic Trading. In reality, we are in the vital phase and a *different set of tools needs to be used to manage investment* at this stage. Such tools should focus on the reality of the greed–fear cycle and the resultant fractals that create exorbitant costs to humanity. Tools should also bring into focus the obscuration of value or the reflexivity causing feature as George Soros calls it of herd mentality. They should also focus on the effects of monopolization of flow and fund and on stochastic variance as opposed to Gaussian distribution.

If these sets of tools were in the portfolio of all fund managers, central banks, investment banks, then the destruction of long-term value would become more apparent. In fact, these tools need to relate short-term decisions with the destruction of long-term value. *Macro policy needs to awaken to the reality of vital versus mental, and misapplication of the tool set needs to be penalized by regulatory agency*. The basic, underlying problem is that value at the vital level is not value as described at the mental level. This difference has not been adequately called out. Value at Vital (vital value) is something entirely different from Value at Mental (mental value). Tools need to call out the destruction of deeper, underlying, sustainable value (mental value) that is caused by increasing vital value. *It is mental value that really needs to be managed*. It is that which is going to lead to longer-term prosperity. Vital value and its waves of destruction need to be fully understood so that abandonment to such a notion of value does not occur again.

Policy, regulation, principles of financial activity, corporate operation need to all become more enlightened to ensure that we make a sustainable shift to the mental level and to actively managing mental value so that sustainability can become real. Vital value has an effect of "monopolizing" funds and flows of financial resources—that is, because the real value represented by an asset, its mental value—is drowned out in a standardizing flow of vital value. The true value of all assets suffers this fate, and as a result, there is just one large, monopolized flow that comes to exist. Such flow ultimately causes serious destruction, and the work of years and centuries is reversed in a few hours. If decoupling of assets and categories of assets begins to occur, so that pricing and buying and selling activity does not occur in lock step with each other, it likely means that a different notion of value from the vital value is beginning to surface. This differentiation has to be encouraged. Reportedly it is only such decoupling that have been exercised by countries such as India and China that have allowed the world to continue on a path of global development. If India and China gave in to the whims and demands of western investors and financiers, then the destruction would have been much more prevalent. Therefore, *tools also need to indicate when decoupling is occurring and encourage more of such decoupling.*

Some Suggestions from Chapter 8: Stock Market Seed

Chapter 8 focused on the creation of the stock market seed. The seed was transfigured from the vital with its mental undertones to one with absolute vital undertones through the efforts of John Locke. The seed has had its fractal pressure and created a whole way of being that has rippled out from it in the centuries that have followed it. With increase in activity, the perversities associated with it stand out far more. It is this seed that now needs to change. *The seed has to be re-created through the activation of mental-level principals that lead, vital-level activity that follows, and physical-level activity that grounds.* In its essence, this is what this book is about—about creating a new seed with which to change stock market related activities for the benefit of posterity. It has been too long, and little has been done to change the nature of trade. We have reached a point now where such lassitude can no longer be ignored. As activity based on the current seed increased, the element of grounding was all but missing. Many small investors the world over, not to mention the larger investors, have been oblivious to the true effects of stock market related activity. All this must change going forward.

Some Suggestions from Chapter 9: Lessons from 20th Century Stock Market Crashes

There is a lot of richness in Chapter 9 in terms of potential suggestions for stock market related redesign, only because the chapter highlights a number of 20th century stock market crashes, with potential lessons learned from each of them. Key suggestions are listed:

- Bring back into effect some equivalent of the Glass–Steagall Act to separate depository from investment institutions and have stronger regulation of both kinds of entities, so long as we continue in the vital phase. Also place limits on the size of a bank so that it does not become "too big to fail."
- Encourage money to be created and monitored at the community level, and further, be legitimately exchanged for national currencies.
- Regulate blanket index and portfolio-based investment instruments that cause unnecessary coupling to occur.
- Alter algorithmic trading to sell and buy stock based in part on inherent conditions that promote environmental and social sustainability and good corporate governance practices.
- Trade on fundamental value being created by corporations rather than on stock price.
- Build a new breed of stock markets that encourage needed development—social, environmental, artistic, knowledge based, service focused—the world over.
- Denominate returns in kind rather than in cash.

- Rating agencies need to assess the true capacity of a country to intelligently absorb funds without risk of overheating.
- Regulate carry trade so that only an insignificant percentage of national currency can be traded. Need metrics at front and center of currency trading that remind us of how money is actually being used and what real value is being created and destroyed.
- Facilitate development of commodity-based wealth to more mature forms of wealth at the national level. Set limits on extent of commodities that can be extracted on an annual basis.

Some Suggestions from Chapter 10: Lessons from 21st Century Stock Market Crashes

Chapter 10 highlights a number of 21st century stock market crashes, with potential lessons learned from each of them. Key suggestions are listed as follows:

- Reinterpret value based on physical–vital–mental fractal for progress and use this to decide whether to invest in an area or not. Where transition between one phase and another is being facilitated, invest there. If frenzied activity within a phase, do not invest there.
- Tie investment to grounded basics. Do not invest in seeming assets at the center of a bubble. Development of grounded set of value metrics to guide investment activity.
- Temper stock market irrationality with sustainability oriented macro-level indicators such as overheating of an economy, reality of global overshoot and local and national contribution to it, destruction of local and national ecosystem services, increase in local and national GHG emissions.
- Less reliance on price-weighted and capitalization-weighted indexing and more on fundamentally-weighted indexing to better capture underlying value.
- Use of sustainability-type indexes to decide whether we are truly in a bear market or not.

- Creation of a code of principles for sovereign wealth funds.
- Regulation of funds coming into an established hot-spot.
- Creation of different types of stock markets and sustainability-filters embedded into existing stock markets.
- Clear calling out of toxic assets that have no real underlying value backing them. Regulation so that money and wealth cannot be created on the back of toxic assets.

Some Suggestions from Chapter 11: Current External Changes Affecting Stock Markets

Chapter 11 points to some organic changes that have been occurring to counter the effects of vitally driven trading. These changes will continue to have a growing effect over financial and stock markets over time and give us a sure indication of how the very act of trading may alter to become more holistic in the future. If we wanted to expedite the development of sustainable stock exchanges, then we could take some of the suggestions that are currently being practiced on the periphery of trading and embed them into that actual act of stock trading. This possibility is taken up in the final chapter. Summarizing though, it is possible to integrate the following into the functioning of stock markets:

- Use the various SRI screens and SRI backed shareholder resolutions to change the heuristics at the heart of trading in the way the stock market itself functions.
- Similarly embed elements of GRI, DJSI, and PRI into stock trading heuristics itself.

Some Suggestions from Chapter 12: Principles of Sustainability

Chapter 12 similarly also points to the inevitable direction in which stock markets will move. This is not just a matter of choice but of necessity. We live in a finite-resource world, which has laws that need to be followed if we wish to survive as a species. Our frenzy of activity characterized by the massive and prolonged vital phase we have been in has obscured this reality. But limits have now been exceeded, and natural principles and limits will need to be adhered to for us to emerge intact. Many of these laws and principles have been captured in frameworks, such as Earth Charter Principles, Biomimicry Principles, Fractal Ladder Principles, and can also be embedded into the way stocks are traded. At the very least, a simple flag can be set if aspects of these sets of principles are countered. *This flag can then slow down or even stop trading activity based on the severity of the flag.*

15

From the Vital to the Mental Level

Stock markets and the financial arena are in the throes of the vital phase. There is a great amount of irrationality that marks this—quite the opposite of EMH. What has to be done is that the irrationalities of the vital phase have to be immediately handled. The vital phase is replete with ups and downs. When things look good, they look really good. When things look bad, they look really bad. This of course is because the filter of perception and, therefore, even of action is more often than not the irrationality of feeling-based thought as opposed to more holistic, far-seeing thought. Therefore, selfishness, egoism, aggressiveness, short-sightedness are the de facto operating principles. These principles reflect the nature of the seed, and definitely it is the nature of the seed that must be changed.

Changing the nature of the seed has to become part of the solution—the world's sustainable development depends on it. Naturally this is a longer-term solution. However, this can be facilitated by building a bridge between the vital phase and the mental phase. Fractal principles suggest that the only way to do this is for players to enter into the mental consciousness. This will happen in its own time, no doubt, helped by an increasing number of contrary-fractals that challenge the egoistic life. However, in making rationality and guiding principles more alive and referred to, and the thought as opposed to desire increasingly the arbiter of decision-making, this shift in consciousness and the change in the nature of the seed can be facilitated.

Governments and Central Bank action the world over, following the financial crises of 2008–2010, has obviously been focused on the short term. But let us look at the nature of their short-term interventions. They have done much to allow the flow of money to continue as per vital-level growth models. Therefore, they have sucked up junk assets, lowered interest rates, and forgiven parasitic corporations. This intervention is perhaps warranted because in the absence of this, the world as we know it, would have changed too rapidly and social unrest risen meteorically. Rebellion, *à la* the French Revolution, would have become the norm and Bastille Days the common nature of day. This may still happen if a longer-term mental-level outlook is not quickly worked out. That is why the seed has to change.

But also, the danger of the extreme moods of the vital has to be managed in the short term. The fundamental problem has been that value has been equated with vital level as opposed to mental-level value. This is a form of Nazism. It is a bastardization of all that is sacred in which standards of excellence are equated to contours on the surface or on the face of things, as opposed to the uniqueness inherent in development and culture and civilization. When value of assets sync up, so that investment in India and investment in Brazil are not related anymore to the unique need in India and the unique need in Brazil, but simply to an investors overall level of fear or greed, then we know that this bastardization has become the way of life. It is imperative that this be reversed in its tracks. The financial system as a whole has to be overhauled for this to happen.

The nature of the financial system is reflected in the seed that engendered the stock market. By changing this, now, the entire financial system will begin to change as well.

In their book, *Crisis Economics* (2010), Roubini and Mihm argue that all crises are essentially the same. While I agree that there is a common pattern that marks the unveiling and play out of a crisis, crises have to be viewed from the point of view of where in the physical–vital–mental arc they are occurring to truly understand them. A crisis in the physical phase is fundamentally different from one at the transition between the physical and vital stages, and so on.

Our current global crisis is unique. It has never happened before in recorded history. This is evident from some simple observations. First, the very playing field of all business is uniquely challenged by the phenomenon of climate change—it is not negative local effects from local action any more but negative global effects from local action now—a dangerous situation. Ecosystems get destroyed as temperatures rise, and the very resource base of any modern-day business is permanently crippled. The perception that it is an exploitable resource base is flawed at its root, and it is the fundamental perception that has to change to right this. This base-fractal, decidedly vital in nature, creates many contrary or stagnated fractals in its wake. Climate change is the ultimate macro wake-up call pointing to the absolute urgency of shifting the base-fractal at its very root. Figure 15.1 from *Connecting Inner Power with Global Change* (Malik, 2009b) reproduced here, illustrates this.

Consumer action, business action, regulatory practices are all marked by the unrefined vital stamp. This bubble has to burst so that more integrated thought and perception become the norm. Nor will climate change be the last wake-up call even if we successfully regulate it away, simply because other macro effects will arise from the same micro causes. It is the shift in micro causes that needs to occur. This too is reflected in Figure 15.1.

If we are at the boundary between the vital and mental way of being, then that has to become the context of truly addressing the current crises.

Figure 15.1: Arrestation of Global System Fractal at Vital Level Requires Global Wake-up Call

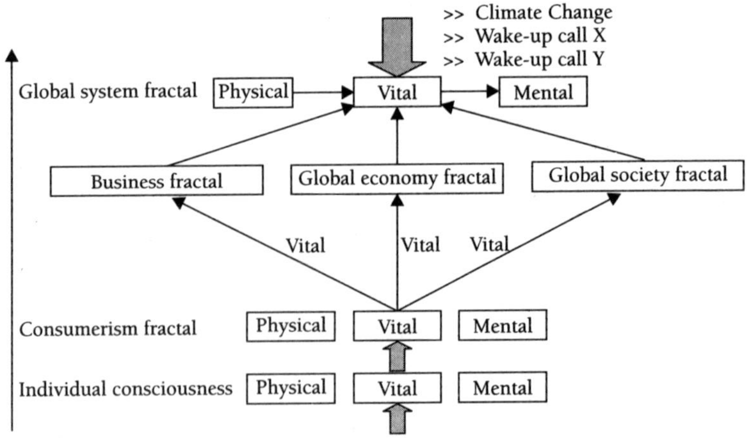

Source: Malik (2009b).

This is not a one-time crisis. We have been living in this overarching vital-level arc since at least the birth of the Amsterdam Stock Exchange, if not even before that. Crises have occurred because of the bubbles that keep bursting. And this will continue until we make the needed shift into the mental way of operating. We have discussed many crashes in this book. In some sense, they were all opportunities to shift away from dysfunction. Instead as a result of the crises, we have quickly always tried to put things back to the way they were. The Crash of 1929, preceding the Great Depression, has been likened as being similar to today's global crisis. Some important measures were taken then to reverse the bastardization of value. But little was done to democratize markets to really move to the creativity, uniqueness, and sustainability which are more inherent at the mental level.

This is at the crux. We need to democratize markets so that truer local and sustainable innovation is unleashed. Instead, we began a much longer arc that integrated more and more of the world into the unstable equation of bubbled business and markets. The integration and synchronization and bastardization have reached the limit of its playing field. We are at the inevitable end of a dysfunctional way of being. In some respects, if we assume that we live in a purposeful world, then we can see that such an integration may have its purpose in that it ensures that there can be no havens that will not finally want to change. The chances that the change we need will take place universally, is much higher as a result of the decades-long integration we have now gone through. We either proactively pay a price and make the changes to become more functional now or we pay a much higher price to become functional later. This book is about intelligently making that change now.

The following suggestions must be placed in this context.

Creating stability is fine but only if the stability can become a bridge to the more needed longer-term changes. Some have argued that crisis is a terrible thing to waste. The fact that central banks all over the world have acted to create immediate stability, albeit vital-level stability, has in a sense stalled the crisis. Some would consider this a grace. But then we should act as though it really is a grace and make the changes we need to in order to avoid impending and serious instability. To create ongoing stability, the larger context and direction as pointed to by fractal insights, need to be considered. These are captured by the following overarching guidelines which have been gleaned by the many challenges through the course of the materials in the book:

- The overarching physical–vital–mental arc must be the context of financial understanding and decision-making.
- There is an inbuilt need of the contextual system to move from the essentially physical to the vital to the mental level.
- It is necessary to understand the nature of a financial crisis by understanding where in the physical–vital–mental arc a crisis is occurring.
- A crisis can be physical, vital, or mental in nature. It can also be of a transitional type, transitioning from physical to vital or from vital to mental. Depending on the type, addressing it will differ.
- If a crisis is marked by the extremities or vicissitudes of the vital, then as a first step it will need to be stabilized or bought to a balanced vital level. This is a common type of crisis we have been experiencing recently.
- If a crisis is transitional from the vital to mental, then all must be done to help that transition to take place.
- Getting to the mental level means de-monopolizing power so all markets are democratized.
- Democratization of markets also means that the deeper drivers of progress responsible for formation of uniqueness are mobilized. The essence of these drivers is the urge for knowledge, the urge for adventure, the urge for harmony, and the urge for service.
- Many contrary-fractals will be created as the focus gets on moving to the mental. For success in the transition, these contrary-fractals must be recognized and countered as such.

Since we are at the limits of the vital, as indicated as such in global conditions like the climate change, our real path forward is to transition into the mental. This could be achieved by just cutting straight across into the mental—plunging into the waters and learning to swim or sink—so as to speak or by first stabilizing the vital excesses and then meaningfully moving into the mental—learning to swim and then plunging into the waters. Central Bank and government intervention the world over, as already discussed, has in our current crisis aimed at least to allow people to continue to act the way they like to act. This has forestalled panic and allowed the market not to take a likely, stochastic-type plunge into the abyss. But a lot more must quickly be done to truly stabilize the vital and to learn to swim.

Assuming that the moderate path—of stabilization followed by movement into the mental—as opposed to a forced short cut, is wisest, then a barrage of macro-environmental changes need to be made. The following are focused on controlling the vicissitudes of the vital, to allow us to reasonably remain afloat. Many of these have been discussed in previous chapters and are summarized here:

- Increase deposit insurance for commercial banks and non-commercial banks.
- Separate commercial banks from investment banks.
- Create more skin in the game for middlemen.
- Revised compensation schemes for financial intermediaries.
- Specialized investors for different asset classes.
- Higher degree of regulation on non-bank financial institutions.
- Higher degree of regulation on innovated financial products.
- Automatic stop in trading when bubble is being created.
- More sensible long-term raking of countries, companies, and funds by independent ranking organizations.
- Increased regulation for money market funds.
- Limited use of index funds as vehicle for investment.
- Breaking of increasing correlations between different asset classes.
- Much greater due diligence on mortgage-backed bonds.
- Stopping of irrational market creation through financial instruments such as junk bonds.
- Control of carry-trade investments.
- Greater control of parasitical value generated in financial activity.
- Allowing more big players to fail, protecting smaller targets instead.
- More reliance on fundamentally weighted indexing.
- Increased control of funding focused on hot-spots.
- Macro policy needs to awaken to the reality of vital versus mental, and misapplication of the tool set needs to be penalized by regulatory agency.

While such changes will stop the macro-level bastardization of value, stock exchange changes aimed at the same result must also be made. This will further reinforce the stepping back to view value through the right lens. Some tactical changes already discussed previously include:

- Rewards also in kind as opposed solely through price.
- Ability of investor to specify their value-based as opposed to return-based investment goals and for trades to take place based on that.
- Reduction in investing in hot-spots through mutual funds, market-based indexing.
- Placing of investment limits by industry, region, and company. Further, the ability to invest in stock of a particular kind of project or in a particular industry or in a particular region and so on.
- An intelligent layering of value, another system of filtering, beyond the crude buy–sell dynamic that animates stock trading today by incorporating filters for purpose in stock market trading.
- An inbuilt check that puts an environmental/social circuit-breaker into effect that stops buying of a company's stock if it is in violation of sustainability/CSR issues.
- A reverse circuit-breaker that would stop irrational selling of a stock if it was completely clean on sustainability/CSR issues.
- Algorithmic trading altered to include different conditions for buying and selling of stock.
- Manipulate stock price based on environmental and social metrics.
- Establish moratorium on sale of stocks unless fundamental sustainability/CSR conditions are fulfilled.

New tools to help transition from the vital to the mental will also need to be created:

- Escrow accounts be set up for disbursement of funds—conditions of sustainability have to be fulfilled.
- Global and industry maps of investment/development need to be developed as a five-year plan that is followed and subscribed to by stock exchanges, even becoming part of the overall metrics for stock exchange performance.

- Day-to-day tools made more meaningful by focusing on:
  - reality of greed–fear cycle;
  - fractal effects of trades;
  - herd mentality;
  - large, monopolized-type flows;
  - stochastic variance;
  - management of mental as opposed to vital value, with regulatory implications;
  - tools to notice decoupling, other results of correctly managing mental value; and
  - meaningful array of metrics that keep focus on ground-level activity.
- Need for macro-level indicators to temper stock market irrationality: overheating of an economy, reality of global overshoot, increase in GHG emissions, destruction of ecosystem services.

Further, to facilitate the emergence of the mental level, new structures will need to be created:

- Creation of secondary markets to trade in kind if need be.
- Creation of different types of stock markets.
- Democratized bases of money creation.
- In addition, the following structures to be discussed in the next chapter will also need to be put in place—
  - leveraging technology—nano, networking, security, telecommunications—to change nature of environmental and social measurement so that it can be instantaneously recorded and siphoned to stock exchanges around the world;
  - fund measurement ability from stock activity; and
  - governed by citizens, accountable to citizens.

Finally, the following guidelines to change the very nature of the stock market seed need to be put in place:

- Disbursement of money is more universal, going to where it is needed most. This is facilitated by support of broader range of fundamental drivers of sustainability. It is also facilitated by having different types of stock markets in place—a stock market focused on knowledge creation, on arts, and so on.

- Notion of physical, vital, and mental value ingrained into investment type. Recognition that physical–vital–mental fractal needs to be completed for sustainable wealth to manifest.
- Mechanics of trading needs to change to reflect more of EMH-type reality. This can be done by considering a deeper and broader set of values.
- Notion of value as reinforced by stock market dynamics/trading has to be reversed: sought after funds must become intelligently available whenever there is the possibility of true development; expectations change so that there is rational as opposed to windfall returns for investor and company alike.
- True purpose of industry becomes a factor in how funds are disbursed.
- Stock market redesigned to invest in stock of particular kind of project or in particular industry or in particular region. Parameters for trading changed so that such macro options are available.
- Reward system changed to disburse gains partly in type.
- Need for macro-level indicators to temper stock market irrationality.

16

The Path Forward

The creation of the stock market was a powerful singularity which has bent financial space so that many of its implicit dysfunctions became explicit ways in which the financial world came to operate. The seed of this singularity resonated with a deep need in the human psyche to fulfill its egoistic vital-level urges and desires. Hence, formidable and unsustainable barriers came to exist, and today these must be reversed if humanity is to proceed along a forward and sustainable path. Overcoming these barriers will mean that the stock market as a whole will begin to function more at the mental level as opposed to its current operation at the vital level.

Many of these barriers are being increasingly called out through voices gathering force and are subtly or overtly demanding change to how stock markets function. Many of these voices have arisen from the religiously minded and those who are socially aware or who have been advocating another way to invest money. At its core, these proponents have seen life more completely than business juggernauts. For them, there tends to be a larger wholeness in which aspects of life meet in practicalities. For the business world, the opposite has been true—generally speaking. Therefore, all has been viewed as a business asset, and things like spirit and possibility are only meaningful if there is a financial return associated with that. This perception of life is largely physical-vital. That is, the prime orientation is one of aggressively imposing one's point of view and one's own interest on all of life. Life is only a field for appropriating or commandeering what is needed for the small self in its pursuit of selfish, myopic gain. Realistically speaking, the issue is, how much will this orientation change in the short term and this is the crucial question, since by many estimates the life of humanity can hardly sustain such continued shortsightedness. The implicit urge to move comfortably, along a slow path, is called out in Chapter 13, which addresses current practices of sustainability in stock exchanges. There appears to be an in-built bias to promote profit of stakeholders—the investor, the corporation, the stock exchange itself, the stock exchange investors. This is understandable but this means that more decisive action will need to be taken to promote humanity along a path of sustainability.

Climate change, for instance, has to be acted on within a finite, time-bound window, before a tipping point that yields disastrous returns is unleashed. The global financial environment has to be reconstructed urgently if humanity is to preserve its wonders of creation and proceed along a path of unending sustainability. There is no choice in these matters—failure to address these situations will cause the already forming forces of destruction to magnify and grow exponentially so that developed countries will topple, people will lose whatever freedom they have become used to, the bases of corporation and business activity will topple, not to mention the much longer-term damage of the base of wealth from the earth being pillaged and unable to return to a pristine state for at least a couple of millennium if not for longer. Of course, in one way of looking at it, perhaps humanity needs challenges and measures of this magnitude in order that the base consciousness at the root of the tremendously destructive world-fractal we see playing itself now may shift from its decidedly vital to a more mental state of being.

The mental here means that a truer force of inquiry, of curiosity, of questioning base assumptions has, come alive, and as a result, holism, sustainability, a larger basis of life is beginning to become the bases for even business standards of operation. SRI, principles of various sorts are meaningful attempts to make business operation more holistic. But the reality of these is that it is always difficult to make companies, and especially investors, in the heat of the moment, abide by these deeper standards. That primal instinct that belongs to the physical-vital consciousness is unfortunately so alive in the consciousness of humanity that all higher possibilities are often tossed aside, and whether the field be business, religion, or science, what matters most at the end of the day is whether the thwarted instrument is able to fulfill on its small, myopic, meaningless desires.

What Needs to Be Done Now

It is in light of this reality, of this real operating principle, that what is suggested now has to be put into action if we want to prolong order in the human race and develop along principles of wholeness and sustainability. This is, in fact, highly important since even abstracted out one level, to the level of regulation and policy, the same problem exists. In spite of best intention, of well-thought out principles, when push comes to shove, either the actors find loopholes or the regulator is unable really to regulate. If human consciousness is such that the investor and businessman and even the executor of regulation and policy cannot act with foresight as the whole of life were the field of operation, then the situation has to be forced. The setting of stock price has to be determined as though a whole lot more about the market were known. We have to approach the reality of an Efficient Market, even if it is artificial. In other words, it is not just simple demand and supply that will determine the price of stocks but a whole lot more that is being pointed to by the movements of SRI and sustainability principles and the Sustainability-based Indexes.

We have to embed in the act of buying and selling a broader intelligence that matters. Filters, heuristics, circuit-breakers that emulate the filters, heuristics captured by GRI, Sustainability Indexes, principles of investing have to be bought into the very act of trading. It is not enough anymore that they remain as filters that funnel money into stock markets from the outside. That is not good enough in these times when so much is at stake and when the act of trading has become such a way of life. If trading cannot normally consider the fullness of life, then more of the fullness of life has to be forced into the act of trading. There are a lot of current constraints of the type just discussed that this will overcome—in the short term. Further, the bases of organization will have more meaning since what is intended from the top-down will actually matter. If a government wants to govern, so that managing GHG emissions or water quality or working conditions in factories is critically important for the next three months, for instance, it does not have to do so by tax cuts and fiscal spending or other unpredictable incentives but embed that need into where it matters most—in the actual and instantaneous setting of stock price. If an oil rig leaks, then, it is pretty simple. The price of all oil stocks will be suppressed, reduced, until and unless there are a few measures that are taken and proved that illustrate beyond a doubt that the environment is being cleaned up, that affected ecosystem services are being restored, that social reconstruction is taking place, and that new technology that avoids such mishaps in the future is immediately being invested in. These filters are programmed into the way stocks are sold, and in fact, there is a moratorium on the sale of such stocks unless certain base conditions are immediately fulfilled. As another example, if there is a lot of unsubstantiated financial innovation taking place, so that derivatives and a whole host of other tranche-like products are unleashed by the financial sector, similarly a moratorium is placed on investment in companies engaged in such activities, unless it can be proved that these products are not potentially toxic and undermining of the true value that must be the bases of money creation. Further, the stock price is automatically depressed and gets undepressed in stages, based on sustainability-driven action that the company undertakes.

Obviously implementation of such an approach will require something different from current approaches to regulation. There needs to be an instantaneous aspect to this for it to work. This is where a few key technologies will play a major part. For one, sensors of various kinds will need to be placed in the environment. Such sensors will correlate sight, smell, touch, and sound to sustainable and unsustainable qualities in the environment instantaneously. If there are toxic substances being produced by a factory and leaking into the air or water or earth, nano-sensors placed in that environment will pick this up and report back through a global telecommunications network, possibly the Internet which is already ubiquitous. These reports will be fed instantaneously into filters in stock-trading algorithms in every stock market in the world. Not only will an offending company be immediately penalized but cautionary heuristics will kick in for every company in that class, and the company will have to prove through immediate action that the cautionary heuristics should be released.

Obviously the telecommunications/Internet security companies will play a pivotal role as well for the sensor-based information being relayed to stock markets around the world has to be extremely secure. Internet security services will therefore also need to be further developed and leveraged. Further, while sensor-based information will provide a lot of the hard evidence as to the environmentally based ill actions of companies, other stakeholder communities will need to also be tapped into around the world to provide a running commentary on action of companies. Internet-based social communities that monitor many actions of companies will report on these companies as well. This too may filter into setting of stock price, but obviously if so, it will have to be in another manner. Perhaps, it is so that if issues are called out by such a community that these need to be further investigated by deploying sensors to the region if the issue is environmentally based. If it is socially based, then perhaps there is communication with the company in question that needs to occur.

The funding of such activities will need to be paid by companies themselves. This will take place by taking a percentage of stock-based activity. So every player in a stock market is fully aware that a piece of every trade, whether buy or sell, will be used to create and use the apparatus aimed at securing the sustainable development of the world. Since it is arguably the companies and the investors that have played a key part in creating the frenzies in the first place, it is only just that they now compensate by putting into place such an apparatus that ensures that sustainability in action has become a prime operating principle in the scheme of things. This will of course also ensure that their interests in continuing with such activity do yield positive returns over the long term.

Further, such an edifice starting with the sensors, security, telecommunications, social network, moving onto the price adjustments, needs to be governed by a fully transparent body that is accountable to citizens of the world. Perhaps membership is on a rotating basis to ensure that all countries of the world are represented. Perhaps it is a combination of various stakeholders of life that come together to be the presiding governing body. Not just your usual run-of-the-mill business-types, though of course this type too should have representation on such a governing council, but people from different institutions and walks of life—artists, actors, craftsmen, nature-addicts, scholars, sportsmen, and so on. At any time all activity the council is presiding over should be fully viewable by anyone from anywhere in the world.

In a sense, this proposal seeks to integrate many of the growing concerns apparent in movements such as PRI, GRI, SRI, Sustainability Indexes, sustainability-minded shareholder resolutions, frameworks such as REACH, and leaderless movements such as pointed to by Blessed Unrest, so that given the clear and current biases in practical human consciousness, what these movements and developments are pointing to can be unquestionably integrated into the setting of stock price. In other words, given that we are not at the mental level and therefore definitely not in a reality of an Efficient Market where arguably price would automatically be the "true" price and therefore everything at least that all these movements are pointing to would be considered, we are forcing the integration so that the price approaches more closely the "true" price that the ideal of an EMH points to. This also counters the natural need to compromise sustainability by following instead the instinct to fulfill a small, selfish desire.

Conclusion

As the notion of fractal suggests, even this, while a huge step forward, will not be enough. If we want to allow truer sustainable development to take place, then the current world-fractal with its fixation of the physical-vital, will need to be changed at its root. This is what is being pointed to in Chapter 12. Developments at the level of companies will need to occur to stimulate such a change in consciousness to take place. Rather than allow unconscious movements of destruction, the phenomena of contrary-fractals, such development will need to occur consciously so that the world-fractal is consciously altered at its very root in the bargain. This will allow truer sustainability to come into being.

In such a development the focal point is quite clearly to what extent is the vital consciousness shifted to the mental consciousness. To what extent are the patterns of degeneration either as made obvious through movements such as fear, irritation, anger, prejudice, shortsightedness, complacency, vanity, amongst other similar movements, called out and unmade as the basis of day-to-day business operation. To the extent that such developments can be called out and rewarded, we will be beginning to change the world-fractal at its very roots.

Certainly as a start, a new section in the GRI, in the PRI, in many of the movements called out earlier will help. But there will also be limitations, and the question is, what will need to be done on this front, if anything is possible, to embed such developments into the setting of stock price? An approach is to have some kind of company-based community network that blogs about this. Or even, just as an industry with its eye on social and environmental accounting has popped up, perhaps in the short term, an industry of watchers that monitors and assess the subjective development of individuals. If there is truth to the fractal notion, and if the reality or landscape within determines the landscape without, then this may have to be set as a priority.

Perhaps it is not the result that is focused on here but what is genuinely being done with the process to make this shift happen? Are there sensors that can actually tell how much of one's time one is in peace and bliss versus fear and rage? This can probably be developed, but until that time, one cannot rely on such an approach. Further, the result of a shift in consciousness from the vital to the mental means that people will disengage with habitual patterns and ways of being and truly become more authentic. At its core, this authenticity means that different drivers outside of the set of common business drivers will come to animate action and thought of individuals. Perhaps such developments can be blogged about. Certainly, at the end of the day this will also be apparent in the action that a company may take. New models, new ways of thinking about problem and opportunity will surface.

References

Adam, David. 2006. "Royal Society Letter to Exxon." Available online at http://environment.guardian.co.uk/climatechange/story/0,,1876538,00.html (downloaded on 25.07.2010).

Adam, David. 2008. "Exxon to Cut Funding to Climate Change Denial Groups." Available online at http://www.guardian.co.uk/environment/2008/may/28/climatechange.fossilfuels (downloaded on 16.07.2010).

Anderson, Roger. 2007. "Demanding Perfection in Others." Available online at http://www.modernmagellans.com/2007/09/demanding_perfection_in_others.html (downloaded on 03.08.2011).

Arnott, Robert, Jason Hsu, and Phil Moore. 2005. "Fundamental Indexation." Available online at http://www.rallc.com/ideas/pdf/fundamentalIndexation.pdf (downloaded on 22.08.2010)

Associated Press. 2006. "Wal-Mart to Drop One-Size-Fits-All Approach." Available online at http://www.cnbc.com/id/14714027/Wal_Mart_to_drop_one_size_fits_all_approach (downloaded on 14.09.2010).

———. 2007. "Wall Street Slammed after China Stock Woes."Available online at http://www.foxnews.com/story/0,2933,254905,00.html (downloaded on 14.08.2010).

Authers, John. 2010. *The Fearful Rise of Markets*. New Jersey: FT Press.

Baker, Mallen. 2008. "Exxon Mobil and the Exxon Valdez." Available online at http://www.mallenbaker.net/csr/crisis03.html (downloaded on 04.07.2010).

Baker, Nina. 2008. *The Body Toxic*. New York: North Point Press.

Barbaro, Michael. 2007. "It's Not Only about Price at Wal-Mart." Available online at http://www.nytimes.com/2007/03/02/business/02walmart.html?pagewanted=print (downloaded on 14.09.10).

BBC News. 2001. "Nigerians Sue Pfizer over Test Deaths." Available online at http://news.bbc.co.uk/2/hi/business/1517171.stm (downloaded on 12.09.10).

Beltran, Luisa. 2002. "Wall Street Firms to Pay $1.4 Billion." Available online at http://www.marketwatch.com/story/wall-street-firms-to-pay-14-billion-in-probe (downloaded on 18.09.10).

Blackstone, E.H. 2005. "Could It Happen Again?: The Bjork–Shiley Convexo-Concave Heart Valve Story." Available online at http://circ.ahajournals.org/cgi/content/full/circulationaha;111/21/2717 (downloaded on 11.9.10).

Bronowski, Jacob. 1976. *The Ascent of Man*. New York: Little Brown & Company.

Campaign for Safe Cosmetics. 2010. Available online at http://www.safecosmetics.org/ (downloaded on 18.03.2010).

Carson, Rachel. 1962. *Silent Spring*. New York: Houghton Mifflin.

Center for Environmental Health Report. 2008. Available online at http://www.ceh.org/storage/documents/2008_program_update_digital.pdf (downloaded on 20.04. 2010).

Center of Public Integrity. 2001. "Top 100 PRPs Based on Number of Sites at Which They Are Involved." Available online at http://projects.publicintegrity.org/superfund/includes/Top100PRPs.pdf (downloaded on 09.03.2010).

Center of Responsible Business. 2010. "Studies of Socially Responsible Investing." Available online at http://www.sristudies.org/Key+Studies (downloaded on 02.10.2010).

Chan, June. 1998. "Plasma Insulin-like Growth Factor-I and Prostate Cancer Risk: A Prospective Study." Available online at http://www.sciencemag.org/content/279/5350/563.abstract (downloaded on 05.09.2010).

Daniel, Fran. 2010. "Head of Wal-Mart Tells WFU Audience of Plans for Growth over Next 20 Years." Available online at http://www2.journalnow.com/news/2010/sep/29/head-of-wal-mart-tells-wfu-audience-of-plans-for-g-ar-425152/

Day, Kathleen. 1998. "Citibank Called Lax on Salinas Money Trail." Available online at http://www.washingtonpost.com/wp-srv/inatl/longterm/mexico/stories/981204.htm (downloaded on 17.09.10).

De Vendômois, Joël Spiroux, François Roullier, Dominique Cellier1, Gilles-Eric Séralini. 2009. "A Comparison of the Effects of Three GM Corn Varieties on Mammalian Health." Available online at http://www.biolsci.org/v05p0706.htm (downloaded on 07.09.2010).

Democracy Now. 2003. "Monsanto Sues Milk Producer for Advertising It Sells Hormone-free Milk." Available online at http://www.democracynow.org/article.pl?sid=03/07/14/1437218 (downloaded on 10.9.10).

DJSI (Dow Jones Sustainability Indexes). 2010a. "Annual Review 2009." Available online at http://www.sustainability-index.com/djsi_pdf/publications/Presentations/SAM_Presentation_090903_Review09.pdf (downloaded 05.10.2010).

———. 2010b. "Monitoring." Available online at http://www.sustainability-index.com/07_htmle/assessment/monitoring.html (downloaded on 04.10.2010).

———. 2010 c. "Overview." Available online at http://www.sustainability-index.com/07_htmle/indexes/overview.html (downloaded on 04.10.2010).

Earth Charter Initiative. 2010. "Charter." Available online at http://www.earthcharterinaction.org/content/pages/Read-the-Charter.html (downloaded on 12.10.2010).

Edwards, Jim. 2010. "Blue Cross Names and Shames Pfizer Execs Linked to Massages-for-Prescriptions Push." Available online at http://industry.bnet.com/pharma/10008499/blue-cross-names-and-shames-pfizer-execs-linked-to-massages-for-prescriptions-push/?tag=shell;content (downloaded on 12.09.10).

Elliott, Ralph Nelson. 1938. *The Wave Principle*. Montreal: B.C.A. Distributors.

———. 1939. Various Articles. *Financial World*, New York, Various Issues.

———. 1946. *Nature's Laws: The Secret of the Universe*. Publisher s.n.

European Commission Environment. 2010. "Reach Overview." Available online at http://ec.europa.eu/environment/chemicals/reach/reach_intro.htm (downloaded on 07.10.2010).

EuroWeek. 2004. "Under Pressure, Citigroup Climbs down on Govie Trade." Available online at http://www.euroweek.com/Article.aspx?StoryID=436395&IssueID=11029 (downloaded on 19.09.10).

Ferguson, Niall. 2008. *The Ascent of Money*. New York: Penguin Books.

———. 2010. "Greek Crises Is Coming to America." Available online at http://www.ft.com/cms/s/0/f90bca10-1679-11df-bf44-00144feab49a.html (downloaded on 30.09.2010).

Foley & Lardner, LLP. 2003. "SEC and DOJ Enforcement Actions and Opinions." Available online at http://www.fcpaenforcement.com/documents/document_detail.asp?ID=1388&PAGE=2 (downloaded on 25.07.2010).

Forbes.com. 2011a. "Global 2000 Leading Companies." Available online at http://www.forbes.com/global2000/list (downloaded on 03.08.2011).

———. 2011b. "The Global 2000." Available online at http://www.forbes.com/lists/2010/18/global-2000-10_The-Global-2000_Rank.html (downloaded on 03.08.2011).

Gammon, Katherine. 2006. "The Father of Fractals Takes on the Stock Market." Available online at http://web.mit.edu/newsoffice/2006/fractals.html (downloaded on 26.05.2010).

Global Reporting Initiative (GRI). 2010a. "About GRI." Available online at http://www.globalreporting.org/AboutGRI (downloaded on 04.10.2010).

———. 2010b. "Fact and figures about GRI Reports." Available online at http://www.globalreporting.org/AboutGRI/FactSheet.htm (downloaded on 04.10.2010).

Greco, Thomas. 2009. *The End of Money and the Future of Civilization*. Vermont: Chelsea Green Publishing.

Greenhouse, Steven. 2004. "In-House Audit Says Wal-Mart Violated Labor Laws." Available online at http://www.nytimes.com/2004/01/13/us/in-house-audit-says-wal-mart-violated-labor-laws.html (downloaded on 16.09.2010).

Griffin, Drew and Andy Segal. 2002. "Feds Found Pfizer Too Big to nail." Available online at http://www.cnn.com/2010/HEALTH/04/02/pfizer.bextra/index.html (downloaded on 11.9.10).

Grocer, Stephen. 2009. "Wall Street Compensation–'No Clear Rhyme or Reason'." Available online at http://blogs.wsj.com/deals/2009/07/30/wall-street-compensation-no-clear-rhyme-or-reason/tab/print/ (downloaded on 20.09.10).

Grunwald, Michael. 2002. "Monsanto Held Liable for PCB Dumping." Available online at http://www.washingtonpost.com/ac2/wp-dyn/A54914-2002Feb22?language=printer (downloaded on 09.03.2010).

Harris, Gardiner. 2009. "Pfizer Pays $2.3 Billion to Settle Marketing Case." Available online at http://www.nytimes.com/2009/09/03/business/03health.html (downloaded on 12.09.10).

Hawken, Paul. 2007. *Blessed Unrest*. New York: Penguin Group.

Iati, Rob. 2009. "The Real Story of Trading Software Espionage." Available online at http://www.advancedtrading.com/algorithms/showArticle.jhtml?articleID=218401501 (downloaded on 10.04.2010).

Johnson, Carrie. 2005. "Citigroup to Settle With Enron Investors." http://www.washingtonpost.com/wp-dyn/content/article/2005/06/10/AR2005061000532.html (downloaded on 18.09.10).

KLD. 2011. "What's Happening at KLD." Available online at http://www.kld.com/newsletter/Newsline/0705Newsline/0705KLDResearch.html (downloaded on 11.7.2011).

Kredittilsynet (The Financial Supervisory Authority of Norway). 2007. "Forhåndsvarsel om tilbakekall av tillatelse." (in Norwegian) (PDF) Available online at http://pub.tv2.no/multimedia/na/archive/00527/Kredittilsynet_til__527202a.pdf (downloaded on 03.08.2011).

Landler, Mark. 2007. "U.S. Credit Crisis Adds to Gloom in Norway." Available online at http://www.nytimes.com/2007/12/02/world/europe/02norway.html (downloaded on 19.09.10).

Lehrer, Jim. 1998. "'Slick Deal?',NewsHour with Jim Lehrer." Available online at http://www.pbs.org/newshour/bb/business/july-dec98/oil_12-1.html (downloaded on 23.08.2010).

Little, Robert. 2002. "Even Renamed, Exxon Valdez Can't Outlive Stain on its Past." Available online at http://articles.baltimoresun.com/2002-10-15/business/0210150165_1_exxon-valdez-alaska-oil-spill-vessel (downloaded on 15.07.2010).

Lo, Andrew. 2004. "The Adaptive Markets Hypothesis: Market Efficiency from an Evolutionary Perspective," *The Journal of Portfolio Management*, 30th Anniversary Issue: 15–29.

———. 2005. "Reconciling Efficient Markets with Behavioral Finance: The Adaptive Markets Hypothesis," *Journal of Investment Consulting*. Available at SSRN: http://ssrn.com/abstract=728864.

Lovelock, James E. 1972. "Gaia as Seen through the Atmosphere." *Atmospheric Environment*, 6 (8): 579–80.

Malik, Pravir. 2009a. "Wal-Mart's Entry into India: A Time for Tests and New Measures." Available online at http://blog.aurosoorya.com/?p=140 (downloaded on 14.09.2010).

———. 2009b. *Connecting Inner Power with Global Change: The Fractal Ladder*. New Delhi: SAGE Publications.

———. 2010. "Unconsidered Bubble of Modern Day Life." Available online at http://blog.aurosoorya.com/?p=569 (downloaded on 10.12.2010).

Mandelbrot, B. 1963. "The Variation of Certain Speculative prices." Available online at www.e-m-h.org/Mand63.pdf (downloaded on 07.06.2010).

———. 2004. *Misbehavior of Markets*. New York: Basic Books.

Maslow, Abraham. 1966. "The Psychology of Science." Available online at http://www.scribd.com/doc/16370771/Abraham-Maslow-Psychology-of-Science-A-Reconnaissance (downloaded on 12.04.2010).

MEED. 2009. "Dubai Distances Itself from $63bn Debts." Available online at http://www.meed.com/sectors/economy/government/dubai-distances-itself-from-63bn-debts/3001679.article (downloaded on 29.09.2010).

Meek, Andy. 2006. "Down and Out in Covington - Farmer Struggles to Re-emerge after $3 million judgment, prison term in Monsanto case." Available online at http://www.memphisdailynews.com/editorial/Article.aspx?id=30496 (downloaded on 09.04.2010).

MEA (Millennium Ecosystem Assessment). 2005. *Ecosystems and Human Well-being: Synthesis*. Washington: Island Press.

———. 2006. "MA Conceptual Framework." Available online at http://www.maweb.org/documents/document.765.aspx.pdf (downloaded on 03.08.2011).

Monsanto. 2010. "Saved Seed and Farmer Lawsuits." Available online at http://www.monsanto.com/newsviews/Pages/saved-seed-farmer-lawsuits.aspx (downloaded on 09.03.2010).

Mufson, Steven. 2008. "Familiar Back and Forth with Oil Executives." Available online at http://www.washingtonpost.com/wp-dyn/content/article/2008/04/01/AR2008040100157.html?hpid=topnews (downloaded on 28.07.2010).

Mui, Ylan. 2008. "When Wal-Mart Moves in, Neighborhood Businesses Suffer. Right?" Available online at http://www.washingtonpost.com/wp-dyn/content/article/2008/06/22/AR2008062201717.html (downloaded on 14.09.2010).

Murray, Senan. 2007. "Anger at Deadly Nigerian Drug Trials." Available online at http://news.bbc.co.uk/2/hi/africa/6768799.stm (downloaded on 11.9.10).

O'Grady, Sean. 2008. "EU to Agree Code of Principles for Sovereign Wealth Funds." Available online at http://www.independent.co.uk/news/business/news/eu-to-agree-code-of-principles-for-sovereign-wealth-funds-787357.html (downloaded on 28.08.2010).

Olson, David. 2001. "Terrestrial Ecoregions of the World: A New Map of Life on Earth," *BioScience*, 51 (11): 933–38.

O'Reilly, Cary. 2008. "Exxon Mobil Must Face Lawsuit by Indonesian Villagers." Available online at http://www.bloomberg.com/apps/news?pid=newsarchive&sid=aRYhia8wUENs (downloaded on 15.07.2010).

Patel, R. 2007. "Food Glorious Food." Available online at http://www.abc.net.au/rn/bigideas/stories/2009/2534576.htm (downloaded on 15.09.2010).

———. 2008. *Stuffed and Starved: The Hidden Battle for the World Food System*. Brooklyn, NY: Melville House.

PERI (Political Economy Research Institute). 2010. "THE TOXIC 100: Top Corporate Air Polluters in the United State." Available online at http://www.peri.umass.edu/Toxic-100-Table.265.0.html (downloaded on 28.07.2010).

Perkins, John. 2006. *Confessions of an Economic Hit Man*. New York: Penguin Group.

Pollak, Michael. 2000. "Insulin-like Growth Factor Physiology and Cancer Risk." Available online at http://epirev.oxfordjournals.org/content/23/1/59.full.pdf (downloaded on 05.09.2010).

Pollan, Michael. 1998. "Playing God in the Garden." Available online at http://query.nytimes.com/gst/fullpage.html?res=9D03EFD8143DF936A15753C1A96E958260 (downloaded on 09.04.2010).

Research Affiliates. 2007. "Fundamental Index Newsletter." Available online at http://www.rallc.com/ideas/pdf/Fundamentals_200712.pdf (downloaded on 24.08.2010).

Responsible Research. 2010. "Sustainable Stock Exchanges." Available online at www.responsibleresearch.com/Responsible_Research___Sustainable_Stock_Exchanges_2010.pdf (downloaded on 20.10.2010).

Reuters. 2007. "Global Stock Values Top $50 trln: Industry Data." Available online at http://www.reuters.com/article/idUSL2144839620070321 (downloaded on 07.08.2010).

Roubini, N. and S. Mihm. 2010. *Crisis Economics*. New York: Penguin Press.

Sandhu, M.S. 2002. "Insulin, Insulin-like Growth Factor-I (IGF-I), IGF Binding Proteins, Their Biologic Interactions, and Colorectal Cancer." Available online at http://jnci.oxfordjournals.org/content/94/13/972.full (downloaded on 06.09.2010).

Seattle Times. 2007. "Exxon seeks Supreme Court review of oil-spill fine." Availbale online at http://seattletimes.nwsource.com/html/localnews/2003848272_webexxon22.html (downloaded on 15.07.2010).

Shinkle, Peter. 2003. "4-Patents: U.S. Farmer Who Lied in Dispute with Monsanto Will Go to Prison." Available online at http://www.gene.ch/genet/2003/May/msg00044.html (downloaded on 09.04.2010).

Siegel, Jeremy. 2006. "The Noisy Market Hypothesis." Available online at http://sec.online.wsj.com/article/SB115025119289879729.html (downloaded on 20.05.2010).

Sierra Club of/du Canada. 2010. "The World Trade Organization at Cancún—Agriculture and the Environment." Available online at http://www.sierraclub.ca/national/programs/sustainable-economy/trade-environment/wto-cancun-agriculture-env.html (downloaded on 09.04.2010).

SIF (Social Investment Forum). 2010a. "About Us." Available online at http://www.socialinvest.org/about/ (downloaded on 01.10.2010).

———. 2010b. "Shareholder Resolutions Advance Social, Environmental and Corporate Governance Issues." Available online at http://ussif.org/resources/factsheets_resources/2008_Advocacy_Success_handout3.pdf (downloaded on 01.10.2010).

———. 2010c. "Socially Responsible Investing Facts." Available online at http://ussif.org/resources/sriguide/srifacts.cfm (downloaded on 01.10.2010).

———. 2010d. "Socially Responsible Investing Facts." Available online at http://ussif.org/resources/performance.cfm (downloaded on 01.10.2010).

Soros, G. 2003. "Alchemy of Finance." Available online at http://www.freebookspot.cc/Comments.aspx?Element_ID=129635 (downloaded on 05.06.2010).

State of Alaska's Exxon Valdez Oil Spill Trustee. 2010. "FAQs about the Exxon Valdez Oil Spill." Available online at http://www.arlis.org/docs/vol2/a/EVOS_FAQs.pdf (downloaded on 10.07.2010).

Staton, Tracy. 2010. "BCBS Names Pfizer Managers in Kickback Suit." Available online at http://www.fiercepharma.com/story/bcbs-names-pfizer-managers-kickback-suit/2010-06-11?utm_medium=nl&utm_source=internal#ixzz0qZ8tboW4 (downloaded on 12.09.10).

Steinbrook, R. 2009. "Lobbying, Campaign Contributions, and Health Care Reform." Available online at http://healthpolicyandreform.nejm.org/?p=2358 (downloaded on 12.09.10).

Stempel, Jonathan. 2008. "Citigroup to Pay $18 mln over Credit Card Practice." Available online at http://www.reuters.com/article/rbssFinancialServicesAndRealEstateNews/idUSN2636973720080826 (downloaded on 20.09.10).

Stephens, Joe. 2006. "Panel Faults Pfizer in '96 Clinical Trial in Nigeria." Available online at http://www.washingtonpost.com/wp-dyn/content/article/2006/05/06/AR2006050601338.html (downloaded on 12.9.10).

Stone, Kenneth. 1997. "Impact of the Wal-Mart Phenomenon on Rural Communities." Available online at www.econ.iastate.edu/faculty/stone/vita-kes.pdf (downloaded on 14.09.2010).

The Australian. 2010. "Exxon Still Aids Climate Skeptics." Available online at http://www.theaustralian.com.au/news/world/exxon-still-aids-climate-sceptics/story-e6frg6so-1225894256861 (downloaded on 25.07.2010).

The Heat is Online. 2006. "CERES: ExxonMobil Shareholders Relying on Fumes." Available online at http://www.heatisonline.org/contentserver/objecthandlers/index.cfm?ID=5946&Method=Full&PageCall=&Title=CERES%3A%20ExxonMobil%20Shareholders%20Relying%20on%20Fumes (downloaded 28.07.2010).

Union of Concerned Scientists. 2007. "Scientists' Report Documents ExxonMobil's Tobacco-like Disinformation Campaign on Global Warming Science." Available online at http://www.ucsusa.org/news/press_release/ExxonMobil-GlobalWarming-tobacco.html (downloaded on 25.07.2010).

UNPRI (United Nations Principles of Responsible Investment). 2010. "About." Available online at http://www.unpri.org/about/ (downloaded on 06.10.2010).

Vidal, John. 1999. "World Braced for Terminator 2." Available online at http://www.guardian.co.uk/science/1999/oct/06/gm.food2 (downloaded on 09.05.2010).

Warwick, Hugh. 2000. "Syngenta - Switching off Farmers' Rights?" Available online at http://www.fao.org/righttofood/KC/downloads/vl/docs/AH428.pdf (downloaded on 09.06.2010).

Wasserman, Beach. 1934. "Some Neglected Monetary Theories of John Law," *American Economic Review*, 24 (4): 646–657.

Wernau, Julie. 2010. "Wal-Mart Impact: Pop Price War Warns of Wal-Mart Impact for Chicago." Available online at http://www.chicagotribune.com/business/ct-biz-0704-soda-wars-20100703,0,5230113.story (downloaded on 14.09.2010).

Wesley, John. 1872. "The Use of Money." Available online at http://new.gbgm-umc.org/umhistory/wesley/sermons/50/ (downloaded on 01.10.2010).

Wikipedia. 2010a. "1974 Stock Market Crash." Available online at http://en.wikipedia.org/wiki/1973%E2%80%931974_stock_market_crash (downloaded on 11.08.2010).

———. 2010b. "Algorithmic Trading." Available online at http://en.wikipedia.org/wiki/Algorithmic_trading (downloaded on 06.04.10).

———. 2010c. "Behavioral Finance." Available online at http://en.wikipedia.org/wiki/Behavioral_finance (downloaded on 14.04.2010).

———. 2010d. " Biomimicry." Available online at http://en.wikipedia.org/wiki/Biomimicry (downloaded on 13.10.2010).

———. 2010e. "Citigroup." Available online at http://en.wikipedia.org/wiki/Citigroup (downloaded on 16.09.2010).

———. 2010f. "Cradle to Cradle Design." Available online at http://en.wikipedia.org/wiki/Cradle_to_Cradle_Design (downloaded on 13.10.2010).

———. 2010g. "Crash of 1929." Available online at http://en.wikipedia.org/wiki/Crash_of_1929 (downloaded on 10.08.2010).

———. 2010h. "Criticism of Wal-Mart." Available online at http://en.wikipedia.org/wiki/Criticism_of_Wal-Mart (downloaded on 15.09.2010).

———. 2010i. "Dubai World." Available online at http://en.wikipedia.org/wiki/Dubai_World (downloaded on 26.08.2010).

———. 2010j. "Ecosystem Services." Available online at http://en.wikipedia.org/wiki/Ecosystem_services (downloaded on 10.10.2010).

———. 2010k. "Efficient Market Hypothesis." Available online at http://en.wikipedia.org/wiki/Efficient-market_hypothesis (downloaded on 05.04.10).

———. 2010l. "Elliott Wave Principle." Available online at http://en.wikipedia.org/wiki/Elliott_wave_principle (downloaded on 22.05.2010).

———. 2010m. "ExxonMobil Overview." Available online at http://en.wikipedia.org/wiki/Exxonmobil (downloaded on 01.07.2010).

———. 2010n. "Gramm-Leach-Bliley Act." Available online at http://en.wikipedia.org/wiki/Gramm-Leach-Bliley_Act (downloaded on 26.08.2010).

———. 2010o. "Modern Portfolio theory." Available online at http://en.wikipedia.org/wiki/Modern_portfolio_theory (downloaded on 05.04.10).

———. 2010p. "Overview of Monsanto." Available online at http://en.wikipedia.org/wiki/Monsanto (downloaded on 01.09.2010).

———. 2010q. "Pfizer." Available online at http://en.wikipedia.org/wiki/Pfizer (downloaded on 11.9.10).

———. 2010r. "Sarbanes Oxley Act." Available online at http://en.wikipedia.org/wiki/Sarbanes%E2%80%93Oxley_Act (downloaded on 26.08.2010).

———. 2010s. "Stock Market History." Available online at http://en.wikipedia.org/wiki/Stock_market#History (downloaded on 09.07.2010).

———. 2010t. "The Natural Step." Available online at http://en.wikipedia.org/wiki/The_Natural_Step (downloaded on 14.10.2010).

———. 2010u. "US Bear Market of 2007." Available online at http://en.wikipedia.org/wiki/United_States_bear_market_of_2007%E2%80%932009 (downloaded on 20.08.2010).

———. 2010v. "Wal-Mart." Available online at http://en.wikipedia.org/wiki/Walmart (downloaded on 14.09.2010).

World Federation of Exchanges. 2010. "The World Federation of Exchanges." Available online at http://www.world-exchanges.org/about-wfe (downloaded 07.07.10)

World Gold Council. 2010. "Gold Demand and Supply." Available online at http://www.gold.org/world_of_gold/story_of_gold/demand_and_supply/ (downloaded on 07.08.2010).

WSJ Market Data Center. "Historical Index Data - WSJ.com: All-Time Largest One Day Gains and Losses." Available online at http://online.wsj.com/mdc/public/page/2_3047-djia_alltime.html (downloaded on 04.09.10).

Yahoo! Finance. 2010. "Various Common Stock and Stock Market Trend Charts." Available online at http://finance.yahoo.com/ (downloaded 04.08.10).

Zimmerman, Ann and Kris Hudson. 2006. "Managing Wal-Mart." Available online at http://wsjclassroomedition.com/monday/mx_06apr17.pdf (downloaded on 13.09.2010).

About the Author

Pravir Malik is a change architect and strategic generalist who draws insight into potential futures through a study of global trends and patterns, systems theory, and human potential. He is the founder of Aurosoorya, a first-of-its-kind information technology services company focused on promoting Fractal Systems Architecture as a means to bring about deep organizational and systems change. He currently manages the design, development, and implementation of key performance management programs at the Stanford University Medical Center, California, USA.

Malik has also served as the Managing Director, Advisory Services for Business for Social Responsibility, a firm specializing in assisting corporations adopt more environmentally and socially responsible business practices. Prior to that, Malik worked as an Intent Architect assisting executives in the pharmaceutical, information technology, finance, and health care industries gain clarity and alignment around key directions and implementation of these at the corporate level. Malik was also a founding member of A.T. Kearney India and helped to bring about significant growth and brand recognition to it in the Indian market.

Malik has an MBA from J.L. Kellogg Graduate School of Management of the Northwestern University, Chicago, USA, with majors in Marketing, International Business, and Organizational Behavior; an MS in Computer Science from the University of Florida, Gainesville, USA, with a concentration in Artificial Intelligence; and a BSE in Computer Engineering from the Case Western Reserve University, Cleveland, USA.

He is the author of *The Flowering of Management* (1997), *India's Contribution to Management* (2000), and *Connecting Inner Power with Global Change: The Fractal Ladder* (2009).